GO FROM YOUR FATHER'S HOUSE

go from

A COLLEGE STUDENT'S

your father's house

NTRODUCTION TO THE CHRISTIAN FAITH

BY WAYNE A. MEEKS

ART BY MARTHA F. MEEKS

THE COVENANT LIFE CURRICULUM

PUBLISHED BY
THE CLC PRESS
RICHMOND, VIRGINIA

THE COVENANT LIFE CURRICULUM
the authorized curriculum
of the following denominations

Associate Reformed Presbyterian Church
Cumberland Presbyterian Church
Moravian Church in America
Presbyterian Church in the United States
Reformed Church in America

© Marshall C. Dendy   1964
Printed in the United States of America
Fourth Printing 1965
3251—KP—6508

preface

The Covenant Life Curriculum is offered to the churches as a new approach to Christian education. It has grown out of the work of a number of Christian scholars and teachers who were asked to take a fresh look at the task of building curriculum for Christian teaching and to suggest the pattern of a curriculum that would more adequately communicate the Christian faith in the life of the modern world.

The Covenant Life Curriculum starts with the fact of revelation. It is based on the conviction that God has made himself known to man in Jesus Christ. It has its roots in the Presbyterian and Reformed tradition with strong emphasis on the centrality of Jesus Christ as the source of the life of the church. It offers the Bible, the Church, and the Christian Life as three areas of study through which the living Lord may continue to confront men today.

The Covenant Life Curriculum is new in several important respects. It is new in its recognition of the total ongoing life and work of the church as the context in which Christian education takes place. It is new in its understanding of the crucial part that the adults of a congregation play in Christian teaching and in its appreciation of the essential nurture resulting from inclusion of children and youth in the total life and work of the congregation. It is new in its insistence on the necessity for careful systematic study of the Christian faith and of its relevance for today. It is new also in its recognition of the Christian home as having primary responsibility for the communication of the Christian faith and in its provision of a carefully planned teaching ministry for the home as an essential part of the total curriculum.

The Covenant Life Curriculum is designed with an understanding of the fact that an important part of curriculum-making takes place in the particular church. It furnishes materials for all age groups, guidance for the use of these materials, and suggestions as to the way in which each church can build its own program of Christian education.

The Covenant Life Curriculum is a challenge to the whole church to move forward in a teaching ministry that takes seriously the educational task of the church in our time. It is offered in the hope that God will bless it, and in the prayer that through it the faith of our fathers will come alive in the life of each succeeding generation.

contents

CONTENTS

GO FROM YOUR FATHER'S HOUSE

And the long street
rolls on around
like an enormous choochoo train
chugging around the world
with its bawling passengers
and babies and picnic baskets
and cats and dogs
and all of them wondering
just who is up
in the cab ahead
driving the train
if anybody
the train which runs around the world
like a world going round
all of them wondering
just what is up
if anything

from "The Long Street" by Lawrence Ferlinghetti[1]

By faith Abraham obeyed when he was called to go out
to a place which he was to receive as an inheritance;
and he went out, not knowing where he was to go.
By faith he sojourned in the land of promise,
as in a foreign land,
living in tents with Isaac and Jacob,
heirs with him of the same promise.
For he looked forward to the city which has foundations,
whose builder and maker is God.

The Letter to the Hebrews 11:8–10

introduction

This book is addressed to a person who is going to college for the first time. If you are such a person, it wants to enter into conversation with you. In our conversation, we shall have to take very seriously the fact that you "go" to college. The September of the freshman is a time of going away. It is a time of taking leave and breaking ties. It is therefore a time of joy and of sadness. Even if you do not physically move from your home, you will move emotionally and intellectually further from parental care and control.

If this fall is a time for breaking old ties, it is also a time for discovering new ones. It is therefore a time of expectancy and of fear.

Like many of the novelists and poets of our century, I am impressed with the importance of this "going" for the shape of your life. I am fascinated with the waves of movement and change which seem to characterize the modern world; movements of persons and nations, movements of mind and morals, a continual, flickering movement of our whole picture of what is real. In the course of our conversation, I hope to relate your going and the movement of modern life to an older movement, one which is, however, still going among us.

In the Bible, there are two great human types whose lives are characterized by going away. The first is Cain, whose refusal to be his brother's keeper leaves its mark in the restlessness that drives him out to wander the face of the earth. The second is Abraham, who is uprooted by the mysterious word that comes to him in the comfort of Ur and hurls him into the unknown. Cain is called a wanderer; Abraham we must name, not a wanderer, but a pilgrim.

On the surface, the wanderers and the pilgrims are not easy

to distinguish. Both are "on the road." Neither knows where he is going. But one is a rebel, the other, the "knight of faith." One looks back in anger, the other looks forward in hope. One bears always the blood of his brother, the other is the ancestor of him whose blood binds all brothers together. Sometimes the wanderer and the pilgrim exist within the same person—perhaps they always do—but they are always opposed.

As a freshman, you have begun your *Wanderjahre*—whether as a wanderer like Cain or a pilgrim like Abraham, at this point, no one knows, not your parents, and also not you yourself.

Often it seems that most of the older generation would be satisfied if you would just give up the whole *Wanderlust* and settle down. Even in your own generation the strongest pressures are exerted, not to move toward some new frontiers, but to settle into the shallow conformity of grouped, adjusted, and organized existence. You must resist such pressures at all costs. For a college student to settle down is a tragedy! Merely notice that it was Cain who, in the biblical parable, was the first settler. Cain built the city which became a wonderful refuge for people who did not want to be their brothers' keepers, but solved none of the problems that made them wanderers. It was precisely Abraham, the man of faith, who was not permitted to settle at all, but had to spend all his days as a "stranger and sojourner."

The decisive difference between wanderer and pilgrim can be stated very tritely: It is the difference between unfaith and faith. Unfortunately, however, the word "faith" is one of those coins of our language whose markings have been worn off by having been carried in too many indifferent pockets. It is the hopeful purpose of this book to help you engage in conversation with a great company of people who, like you, "went out, not knowing where they were to go." At some point in this conversation, perhaps years after you have forgotten this book, it may be that this word faith will again point to that which makes all the difference, and you will have become neither wanderer nor settler, but *pilgrim*.

PART ONE

big campus, little people

BIG CAMPUS, LITTLE PEOPLE

People on the road, whether wanderers or pilgrims, must be looking for something. What are you looking for, as you "go" to college? There are, of course, lots of possible answers: knowledge, skill, "kicks," *savoir faire,* something loosely called an education—how would you put it? But behind and within all the things you might name there are two goals that seem basic to any human life. The first is the search for one's self; the second is the quest for belonging.

In these weeks, months, and years of college, you are very likely getting to know yourself at a new level. You are having to ask new questions about why you do things and about what you want to do—and to be. There are new decisions to be made, and with them new opportunities for reflection and independent judgment. All this belongs to a deeper consciousness of yourself.

You are also getting to know a great many other people. You are living within new groups. In many cases, you are having to decide whether you want to belong to certain groups, organized or unorganized, or not. In other cases, your relation to other persons and groups, your belonging or not belonging, is much more ambiguous, not so much a matter of deciding as of wondering. But all in all it is clear that you are seeking substantial and creative ways of sharing your life with other persons.

In this first part of our conversation, we shall try to explore some

16

aspects of your quest of self and of community. Now obviously these two quests cannot be separated, but we may be able to think about them more clearly by looking first at some of the more private questions you may ask yourself alone, then at some of the questions raised by being part of a group. Along the way, we shall try to take a hard look at the fact that this double relationship has to be described so often as a problem. Why is it that our relationship with ourselves and with other persons so frequently takes a wry turn that is so different from what we had intended or deeply wanted? Why is it possible for one modern poet to say, "Hell is oneself, Hell is alone," another, "Hell is other people"?

Finally, we shall take a preliminary look at the claim by Christians that God has done something to alter our relationships, to create new persons and new community. That will get us on to the main subject of this whole book.

One warning: We may have to modify our original goals as we go further. We may discover that striving to lay hold on our mysterious selves is not the effective way to find them. We may see that real community is not given to those who try too hard to "belong." That's the thing about setting out on a road like ours: there may be something or someone ahead we had not expected.

✿　✿　✿

1

all by myself alone

The Changing Masks

In the course of your first weeks in college, you will meet hundreds of people. What happens when two persons meet? Suppose you and I had just been introduced. We would each immediately form a mental image of the other—a very vague image perhaps, or maybe a quite complete image—and then as we talked further and watched each other, we would either modify that image as necessary, or we would decide, "Yes, that is just the kind of person he is." Furthermore, we would be afraid of each other. I would be afraid that you might not like me, and you would be afraid that I would not like you. If I were a very important person to you—the rush chairman of the fraternity you would like to pledge, for example—then you would be more afraid than ever. You would be anxious for me to get the kind of picture of you that I would like and approve.

It is meetings like this that make the beginning of your college life both exciting and more or less frightening. You have arrived at a crucial stage in the journey of your life, a stage in which you will probably be very much preoccupied with yourself. In your preoccupation with yourself, however, you will be keenly aware of the importance of your encounters with those other people. Paradoxically, it is just because of those hundreds, perhaps thousands, of persons who jostle you in the little world of the campus that this may be one of the loneliest stages of your life. It is just you, you alone, who meet these strangers. It is only you, without the protection of traditions or family or previous acquaintance, whom they meet and, inevitably, judge. In the midst of the largest crowd one may feel most alone.

Because other persons' approval of us is so important, we all become actors. If you were to meet me on your campus, not only would you be more or less anxious for me to *see* you in a certain way, you would actually try to *be* at that moment the kind of person which you wanted me to see. If for any reason you wanted me to approve of you and like you, then you would probably, quite unconsciously, begin to act and talk like the kind of person you think I would like. On the other hand, since I am "a preacher," it is altogether possible you might choose to act a role you think would shock me. Obviously this also tells me something about the role you expect me to play. If I were not a minister but one of the actives in your fraternity, or one of the fellows in a bull session in the dormitory, then you might talk and act quite differently. That is the reason why some students are always embarrassed when I visit a fraternity house or dorm. They are caught with two contradictory and demanding audiences.

Except in a few cases, most of us do not consciously choose these roles we play. We simply slide into them, and only sometimes, if we are alert to ourselves, do we become conscious that we are acting. I have a friend who is a professor of speech. It was only after visiting him several times in his office that I became aware that, when talking with him, I was being very, very careful of my diction and pronunciation. One day, just after a conversation with my friend during which I had been rather satisfied with my precise enunciation and resonant pear-shaped tones, I happened to go directly to a service station to buy gasoline for my car. Talking with the attendant, I suddenly discovered, to my amusement, that I had slipped from my careful speech-department diction to the long-abandoned Alabama drawl of my childhood. Obviously, in both cases I was acting. I had taken on the mannerisms which I sensed would be most acceptable to the person I was with. Yet neither role had been put on consciously. Once I became conscious of my acting, then I was left with the puzzling question, Which speech pattern is really mine? Am I both the sophisticated orator and the Alabama country boy? Or am I neither?

The easy, automatic adoption of various roles is a social skill which is highly important to young Americans. Many of us begin our training for "fitting-in" in kindergarten and continue our pleasant but demanding process of adjusting to the life of the group through elementary school and especially in high school. Others of us encounter the need to be accepted as a complex demand first in the teen years. For many of us, one of the major reasons we looked forward to coming to college (and to leaving home) was the desire to learn how to get along with people.

The role which we play in this or that group is not always confined to superficial characteristics, like the clothes we wear or the way we speak, but involves our whole character, including the way we think, and especially the things and persons we like, the goals we choose, the actions which we regard as acceptable or unacceptable. The way in which groups of people our own age determine our character has become so striking that David Riesman, Nathan Glazer, and Reuel Denney, a group of sociologists, have written a book asserting that the typical middle-class, city-dwelling or city-oriented American is well on his way to becoming an "other-directed" person.[1] Other-direction is contrasted with our parents' generation, who were "inner-directed." That is one reason for your parents' frequent exasperation with your desire to "go along with the crowd." The inner-directed man knew who he was, what was right, and where he was going. He had a kind of gyroscope inside him that kept him on an even keel, no matter how stormy might be the winds from "the others." The gyroscope, of course, was just the image of his father, wound up by the discipline and training of his boyhood and pointed in the way he should go.

The other-directed person doesn't have a gyroscope. Instead, he has a much more sensitive and up-to-date mechanism: radar. This radar is tuned in, not on signals his parents gave in the past through example and training, but on the reverberations from people his own age. Beginning with the picture books that are read to him at age three, continuing through the carefully manipulated classroom democracy of the progressive schoolteachers, and climaxing in the social life of the college, the other-directed person is being almost continually trained in the technology of social radar. He learns to be alert to the faintest signals of approval and disapproval emanating from the various groups in which he moves. He learns to respond to these signals with instantaneous, scarcely perceptible changes in his bearing, speech, expression. The more well adjusted he becomes, the more complicated are the responses he is able to make.

The basic mechanism of the social radar, as Riesman indicates, is "a diffuse *anxiety*."[2] It begins as a fear that one will not be approved or liked, but soon becomes a very general kind of anxiety, which is felt not as a fear of anything in particular, but simply an anxiety about oneself, a general uneasiness. For the well-adjusted person, that is, for the well-trained receiver of social radar, this anxiety is no longer experienced as fear at all, but as a kind of exhilaration when he is involved in a group. He feels that he is "with it" or "in" or "swinging" or whatever the group's jargon may be for the insider this year. His anxiety has become like the stage fright of an experienced actor: just the tension that puts all of his reflexes and senses on edge, ready to respond in subtle and pervasive ways to his role and his audience.

When we have seen a great actor perform, completely identifying himself, as it seemed, with the character whom he was portraying, often we are prompted to ask after the final curtain, "I wonder what he is like in real life?" The same question can be asked of the other-directed person, just as we wondered what my real accent was like, and whether the real you was more like my imagined picture of you or your picture of yourself. Our life in relationship to other people and especially to people-in-groups is like that of the ancient Greek actor who dons now one mask, now another to portray different characters. Our word "person," in fact, comes from the Latin *persona,* which was the name of the actor's mask. We use the word with a very similar meaning when, after a party, we say, "Smith has a wonderful *personality*." But what is the face behind the different masks? That is one of the hardest of all questions for us to answer—if indeed it can be answered. But we have to ask it, because our acting never achieves its goal. We don our masks to secure approval. In this group and that one, before this person and another, we act our roles and receive their approval. But we are left at the end with the gnawing question, Who was it who was approved? Was it *I* who was approved, or *only the mask I was wearing at that particular time?* I have to go looking behind the masks, finally, because it is not enough to be liked. I also want to like myself, a thing which is very much harder, and that means that sooner or later I must make an effort to be honest with myself, even if not with the others.

Loneliness

"Why is it that you American students cannot stand to be alone?" The question was asked me several years ago by an exchange student from another country. Her observation was correct. We use every excuse to avoid being alone, even for a short while. We do not like to eat alone, or walk across the campus alone, or even to study alone. If there is, alas, no flesh and blood companion, then record player, radio, or TV has to serve as a substitute—again, even while we are studying. The more life crowds in on us, the more we are afraid to be alone. When examinations threaten, then we feel all at sea, and we decide to get together with three or four others in the course and go over our notes together. When there is a decision to be made, then we feel an overpowering desire for companionship, lest we should have to face that decision by ourselves.

The condition of togetherness, of course, is not unique to present-day Americans. In Denmark a hundred years ago, Kierkegaard already complained that ". . . people shudder at solitude to such a degree that they know no other use to put it to but . . . as a punishment for criminals."[3] But why is it, to persist in the question of my foreign friend, that we are driven so compulsively together?

As a matter of fact, it is not so much that we like to be together as that we are afraid to be alone. The same diffuse anxiety which served as our radar in the group now has no object to bounce off, so it turns in on ourselves. In the group, this anxiety, which stemmed, you remember, from our fear of not belonging, not being approved and liked, would have turned into either the exhilaration of conquest or into the concrete agony of rejection. But alone the anxiety feeds on itself. I am left to wonder if I am alone by chance, or by my own choosing, or because "nobody wants me." I may find myself remembering all my mistakes at the last party, or the silly grin and thick-tongued stuttering that was the only response I could make in the classroom discussion today. *Only if I have experienced acceptance by others can I stand being alone.*

Alone, I not only feel anxiety, I may feel empty. I am like an actor without an audience. I have learned to play many roles, but what role do I play when only I am watching? Trained to respond continually to my radar signals from the members of every group, I am left alone, with no signals coming in, although my social radar is still turned on. All I get is an internal hum and a lot of incomprehensible noise inside.

I am afraid to be alone, because I find that I am alone with myself, and I am a questionable, mysterious character to myself. All kinds of questions arise to plague me. Am I bright, or stupid? Am I sophisticated, or naïve? Do I expect too much of myself, or too little? The noise of togetherness drowns out the questions, but when I am alone, there is no keeping them quiet. There is no getting away from the question behind them all, Who am I? There is no way to maturity which does not somehow lead through this question. That is why you must learn to be sometimes alone.

Getting to Know Me

Once I ask the question, Who am I? I have let myself in for a difficult time. The best thing to do is to approach the question head-on, even though it will never be answered that way. By approaching it head-on, I mean to follow through on just the kind of self-examination which may begin when you find yourself alone. The starting point is just the attempt to be honest with yourself. What are the masks you catch yourself wearing? Why do you put on *these* masks? How do you act in this group or that group, and how differently in another? What are the things that make you do what you do?

Questions like these have to be asked, but they ought to be

asked with a certain reservation. Remember that no one ever succeeds in being entirely honest with himself. It may be that you will only succeed in explaining yourself according to some new, but still false, picture derived from your "armchair psychology." When you manage to strip away one of your masks, it is not your real face that appears behind it, but only another mask. " 'Think well, and you will see that there is nothing you can call 'I.' As you peel an onion, there is always another layer, but you never reach the kernel. So when you analyse the ego, it disappears completely.' "[4] Introspection is a very necessary activity for someone who is moving toward maturity. But it can easily become demonic and destructive activity. I may become so bogged down in peeling the onion of myself that I lose the living contact with other persons which nourishes that self. I can become like the characters in the "insane asylum" by which Henrik Ibsen parodied his society in *Peer Gynt*, ". . . themselves and nothing but themselves—sailing with outspread sails of self. Each shuts himself in a cask of self, the cask stopped with a bung of self and seasoned in a well of self."[5] Or I may make the terrible discovery that you never reach the kernel, and be left only with that smothering sense of emptiness of which many students have complained to me in the last few years. Introspection is necessary, but something more is also necessary.

All my life, my self has been taking shape. I have been becoming a person as I have encountered my world, and especially as I have encountered other persons in my world. As a very small child, already I began to reach out and grasp for contact with the world. The first thing I encountered was my mother. Yes, I encountered her first as a thing. She seemed to be part of my body. But the more I learned to control my own body, the less I was able to control my mother, and this was the source of my earliest frustrations. "I" had met "not–I." But as I became more conscious of what was going on in my world, I discovered that now I was in a new kind of relationship with my mother, a relationship very different from my relationship to my toes. The new relationship was love. First I had to distinguish between "I" and my mother; only then could I be related to her as one person to another. On changing levels, this process of separation and then relation has had to occur again and again through my life.[6]

Because of this "double movement," as Tournier calls it, of becoming who we are, both solitude and fellowship are essential to our full life. Either solitude or fellowship, without the other, quickly becomes demonic. The person lost in introspection ties himself in knots and begins to feed cancerously on his own soul. Togetherness involving individuals who are afraid of being alone and who cannot live with themselves becomes an oppressive nightmare, as we shall see in the next chapter. Only the man who is really a person, who is not trapped in anxiety about himself, can be personally involved in community. But only the man who has been personally involved in real community becomes a true person.

This paradox of our life can never be torn apart. To get ahead of our story a bit, it is just in the events in which God comes to man that the paradox is held together. In these events—the story of which will occupy most of this book—God comes to us as someone who is not-ourselves. He knows who we are, even though we do not know ourselves. But he comes to us to engage us in dialogue, in the speaking and hearing, the demanding and responding which produce both real individuality and real community. What the church calls grace is just this fact: that God knows all our masks and even the faceless face that escapes us behind them all, and nevertheless he claims us, loves us. Only the man who is loved can love; only the man who loves can be a person.

> For whoever determines to save his self will lose it; but whoever loses his self for me and the gospel will save it. For what good does it do a man to get the whole world and lose his self?
> For what can he pay to buy his *self?*
> (Mark 8:35–37, author's translation)

ANNETTE

by Joy Patterson

The dormitory was almost empty, and the only sounds she could hear were Mrs. Ashley's fat, housemotherly voice and the sharp clip of her own heels along the corridor.

"This will be your room, my dear. The trunk has already arrived. Your roommate will be checking in at almost any time," crooned the soft voice. "Make yourself comfortable, and if you have any questions, you know where to find me." Mrs. Ashley opened the door and stepped aside so that the slender, young blonde could enter.

"It's a very nice room, Mrs. Ashley, and I'm sure I'll like it. Thank you." Mrs. Ashley turned to go, then paused and glanced at a card she held.

"Annette Lucille Wenzler. And what are you called, dear? Ann, is it?"

"No!" she exclaimed, then more gently added, "No. Please call me Annette."

She closed the door quietly behind the housemother's retreating figure and turned to smile at her new residence. A long ray of autumn sunshine slanted across one of the unsheeted beds, and beckoned her to the open window. From it she could see an attractive part of the campus, sloping lawn and multicolored trees, with only a glimpse of the sturdy gray buildings. Her eyes danced with ecstasy as they slowly traveled every inch of the room, visualizing the banners, photographs, books, and stuffed animals that would soon label this room as the domicile of college women. Then she crossed to the smartly styled dresser and laughed at the image in the mirror.

"Tut, tut, Ann. If you're going to become Annette, I'd suggest you do something to that stringy hair, and try out some of that new makeup that's in your bag. Wouldn't it be a shame if your roommate walked in here and found plain old Ann? You might never make her recognize the real you, the Annette you."

As she rummaged in her suitcase for dresser accessories, the phrase "the Annette you" idled through her mind like a re-membered song. Everything was a song now. She was through being Ann. Ann, who had sat at home with a book on Friday nights, while all the other teen-agers were at the movies with dates. Ann, who hadn't even gone to the Senior prom. Ann, who had been oh, so madly in love with Jeff Williams, only to lose him before she had him, lose him to Miss South Central High, curvaceous Alice Daniels. She thought of Jeff with only a slight pang of regret. That was all in the foolish years of the past; it had happened to another girl in another part of the country. When she had said good-bye to her parents at the train station—listened gravely to her father's stern warning not to speak to the soldier who had just boarded the train, and to her mother's tear-ful pleas to have a good time but not neglect her studies—she had hidden the gaiety that bubbled within her. She had left Ann behind with them. And when the station platform was safely out of sight, she had slid into the seat beside the soldier and introduced herself boldly and joyfully as Annette.

The first few, crowded weeks of college slid by, and Ann never showed her unfortunate face. But Annette was everywhere, never alone, and always laughing. She managed her generous allowance in a way that would have made her father frown, had he known. Almost every Saturday morning she could be found downtown, shopping for sophisticated, somewhat daring outfits to replace the modest, more youthful clothing her mother had lovingly packed. Her hairstyles were always chic, sleek, and provocatively feminine. The carefully planned metamorphosis was easily achieved.

Once suitably costumed for her role as Annette, the lines came naturally. So did the sly winks at the cute boy in her math class, the raised eyebrow and jaunty tilt of the chin in response to flirtatious remarks murmured in her perfumed ear. Ann was carefully buried, with none of Annette's crowd suspecting that such a person had ever existed.

"Annette, why don't you arrange a blind date for me for Satur-day night?" her roommate blurted out one day. "Surely Ted has a friend that would like to double with the two of you." Patti had supposedly been studying history while Annette applied a brilliant new nail polish.

"But, Patti," Annette had countered, "hadn't you rather wait until someone asks you to the dance? I thought that you disapproved of blind dates."

"I'm desperate! Here it is Thursday afternoon, and no date yet! I simply can't miss this dance, too! Won't you try?"

"Sorry, Roomy, no can do. You wouldn't like any of Ted's friends, anyway. They aren't your type."

Or your speed, Annette added to herself. Patti was likable, a good roommate, and attractive in her own naïve way, but hardly the gal for any of Ted Collins' friends. The old Ann might have double-dated with Patti, but not Annette. Certainly not Annette!

Patti went to the dance after all, with a pleasant fellow named Tom, who had straight A's and freckles.

"Freckles!" yelled Annette, when she and Patti had joined the girls across the hall after the dance. She fell across the nearest bed, laughing.

"They're letting them in college young nowadays, aren't they?"

"Really, he . . . he wasn't so bad, Annette," spoke up Patti defensively. "In fact, we had a lot of fun."

"Sure, Roomy, sure," said Annette, sitting up and looking at her closely. "No hard feelings. Each to his own taste." She lit a cigarette.

"How did you and Ted make out?" asked Joyce, a plump, talkative girl with a zest for spicy stories. "Did you have a good time?"

"Oh, we did some fine 'making out,'" laughed Annette. "That guy knows how, all right. Mmmmm," she moaned, closing her eyes and swaying, "I think he invented the French kiss!" She opened her eyes to a slit and regarded the three girls that stared at her wonderingly.

"How far did he go?" whispered Joyce, eagerly. "Did you have to fight him?"

Annette stood up and stretched. "Nope. I never fight." Patti gasped, and Peggy, Joyce's roommate, smiled and shook her head.

"Don't jump to conclusions, girls," Annette grinned slyly. "I know how to handle guys *without* having to fight them." She moved gracefully toward the door, and tossed one parting remark over her shoulder. "That isn't to say I'm a prude. I'm just particular."

Later, when Annette was almost asleep, Patti's gentle voice penetrated the darkness.

"Annette? Say, you know when we were talking about . . . petting . . . and all, a little while ago? I don't mean to pry, but what did you mean, you're 'just particular'?"

"Exactly what I said," murmured Annette sleepily. "Some guys thrill me, others don't. Ted does, but not enough."

"And if he did thrill you . . . enough?" Her voice was troubled, like a child asking about death.

"What do you think?" She chuckled and turned over. "Like I said, I'm no prude."

"But, Annette, surely you don't think it's all right! You'll be married someday. Don't husbands expect their wives to be . . ."

"Lily-white? Not in this day and age, Roomy. Moral values change, just like everything else." Annette sat upright, at the same time shaking away an image of her father's disapproving countenance. "They vary from generation to generation, from nation to nation. Why, did you know that Eskimos lend their wives? Their custom is to show hospitality to their guests by offering their wives, and what right has any other race to condemn them for what they believe is right? Well, I believe in the modern code of love and sex. The words 'I do' and a ring don't make much difference. It's the way two people feel toward each other that counts!"

Annette waited for an indignant response, but there was none, and soon Patti's regular breathing indicated that she was asleep. But Annette's arguments had pulled awake her own heavily laden eyelids and churned her thoughts into action. She had surprised even herself tonight, with her vehement vote for pre-

marital sex and her earlier subtle implications of worldly knowledge. True, she was learning fast, but her experiences were
hardly as advanced as she had implied. The other girls believed
my every word, she thought in amazement. Except perhaps
Peggy, who seldom chimed in with questions and whose glances
were less envious than shrewd. Could she know about Ann? No,
of course not. All of these girls knew only Annette! . . . Poor
Patti! She should have changed her identity, too.

*   *   *

The days flashed by for Annette like gold nuggets swirled
down a sparkling stream, with silver nights that shone more
brightly with each succeeding party. Her occasional letters home
were those of a stranger, and she realized this with no regret.
She maintained a low C average, and was satisfied, for after all,
brains didn't easily harmonize with her new role. Her only fear
was vague and nameless, a fear perhaps of being discovered,
perhaps of reaching a turn in this strange but wondrous road
she traveled and of lacking the courage to pursue her course
any further.

She combatted this fear by remaining too busy to reflect upon
it. She managed never to be alone, and occupied her mind by
battling with Mrs. Ashley; treating herself to prolonged self-
beautification; deliberately arousing new envy among the girls;
and making it a weekly game to see how many new men she
could bewitch into asking her out. Then shortly before the start
of Christmas holidays, she arrived at the inevitable turn in the
road.

It was the night of the interfraternity Yule Ball, a traditionally
riotous affair held off campus in pseudosecrecy and attended
primarily by the most jolly and unreserved group of upperclass-
men. Annette was one of the few fortunate freshmen girls to be
invited, and the only one in her dorm. She had modeled a gown
purchased especially for the occasion, an off-the-shoulder red
chiffon, for Patti, Joyce, and Peggy, and had been pronounced
dazzling. The night of the dance she dabbed a few drops of
My Sin behind her ears and at her throat, and piled her sunny

curls high on her head in a sophisticated style that made her look, she decided, at least two years older. The scene was set for a dramatic third act.

Her date was a tall, red-haired football player who drove her to the dance in a white Austin-Healy convertible, and promptly began to get drunk. As his two hundred pounds became more and more of a dead weight on the dance floor, Annette began to dance more and more with other, more sober acquaintances. And when, at 10 P.M., the halfback's buddies carried him away to sleep it off, she was assured by sympathetic members of the stag line of her choice of escorts back to the dorm.

She was rather relieved to be rid of her date, for she had found that an overattentive date often spoiled her fun. And, too, there was a particular young man present that she was resolved to meet. He fascinated her by not asking her to dance, and he was obviously stag. He stood and watched her drift across the floor in the arms of a dozen different fellows, and when she caught his eye and smiled, he winked and returned the smile with a slow, disarming grin that for some unknown reason made her look away in confusion.

At last she persuaded a dancing partner to introduce her to the strange young man, whose name, she learned, was Bill Leslie. When they approached him, he didn't seem surprised, but merely regarded her with keen blue eyes that reminded her of Peggy. Odd, she reflected, Peggy's eyes are brown.

"Have some punch?" He was still gazing at her.

"Thank you," she replied, suddenly wishing she hadn't left the dance floor. He made her uncomfortable, and she didn't know why. She touched the folds of her crimson dress, and it rustled reassuringly.

"That's a very becoming dress," he said matter-of-factly. "Would you like to dance?"

He held her much too closely, but she resisted the urge to pull away. He does not frighten me, she told herself fiercely. No man frightens Annette. I can handle any person, any situation. I am no shy, awkward child.

As if he had sensed her uneasiness, he relaxed the arm around her waist and began to talk. They danced and talked together through the rest of the evening, and to her own surprise, she enjoyed being with him. The self-assured air which had bewildered her at first became attractive when she discovered one cause of his alienage: he was an older man. He had served four years in the army before beginning college, he said, and told her of his travels in glowing, colorful words. Yet she couldn't dispel the self-consciousness that gripped her when he glanced at her sideways, and called her "Baby" in a low voice that held subdued mirth.

Bill insisted on dancing the entire last number with Annette, to the frustration of several admiring males who tried to cut in. The moment the dance ended, Ted Collins sauntered up.

"The jalopy's outside, Annette. Ready to go?"

"Sorry, Collins," Bill put in. "This gal's doing me the honor tonight."

Before Annette could protest or assent, Ted had shrugged his shoulders, said "Yeah? Have fun, you two," and disappeared.

Alone in the car with Bill, Annette clasped her hands together in her lap to hide their trembling. As the car swung out of the parking lot and onto the highway, he suddenly threw his arm about her shoulder and pulled her closer to him. She sat up straight and reached for the knob of the radio.

"How about some music?" Relax, she told herself. Here's a special guy, and he likes you. Don't goof.

She found some rhythm and blues, and settled back against his arm, acutely aware of the hand on her arm that patted it in time to the music.

When they turned onto a narrow dirt road, she stiffened, then instantly chided herself.

"A new route to the campus?" Her voice was low, with studied nonchalance.

"The best," he replied. "And the longest." He glanced at her quickly. "You've got an hour before the deadline, Baby. Don't sweat it."

He pulled to the side of the road and switched the motor off.

"Lock your door," he said, and locked his. He knows all the

rules, she thought, grateful for an excuse to slide to the opposite side of the car. He quickly moved toward her, and before she could think of a witty remark, he kissed her. His kiss was as startling as his personality, holding none of the tentative inquisitiveness of the other first kisses she had known. When she pulled away, that odd look was again in his eyes.

"Look, Bill," she began, searching for the right words.

"What's the matter?" he asked quietly putting both arms around her. "Don't you like the way I kiss? I've never had any complaints before."

"It's just that . . . well, I hardly know you . . ."

"I'm trying to get acquainted, Baby. Now come here and stop being coy." He drew her to him, and kissed her so determinedly that she was unable to resist. His hand toyed with the soft sleeve of her dress, and her fears were confirmed. He meant business.

At last she broke completely away from him.

"Stop it, Bill, please. I don't know what you think I am, but I want to go back to the dorm right now."

He looked at her for a long moment, then laughed softly, and started the motor. He deposited her at the door with a simple, "Good night, Annette," and turned away.

The dorm halls were empty, and as she opened the door to her room, Patti's giggle from across the hall told that the three girls were waiting together to descend upon her with the usual questions. She thought of Peggy's eyes, and was glad they hadn't heard her come in; they no doubt expected her to be late enough to arouse Mrs. Ashley's battle cry.

She flicked on the lamp and tossed her shoes toward the closet, her purse toward the bed. She jerked off her earrings, and sitting down before the mirror, began idly to brush her hair. She remembered the way Bill had looked at her and laughed before starting the car. "I like him," she thought. "That's the darned part of it. I wanted him to kiss me, and then I pull the 'Don't Touch' routine. I meet a guy who does thrill me, and then I won't go along with him. What's wrong with you, Annette?" she asked the mirror image. The image blurred, and she realized there were tears in her eyes. She blinked, and saw a tired, thin face with smeared lipstick and limp blonde hair hanging loosely around slumped shoulders. "Ann!" she whispered in horror. No. She straightened, wiped off the lipstick with a tissue, and looked again. There. That was better. A little more like Annette. But still . . . something was missing. What? The tilted chin, the saucy smile? She was too tired to make the effort. The role wasn't natural anymore, it was artificial. Annette had missed her cue tonight, and the mask had slipped. "But who is to take Annette's place?" she asked the strange image. "Ann? No, Ann is gone forever. Who then?" she asked. "Who?"

2

almighty group

The Trouble with Shumacher

Shumacher's strange behavior first came to the attention of his friends when they happened to see him at three o'clock one morning, as they were carefully navigating their way back to the dormitory from a beer bust, arm in arm. Shumacher, however, was not arm in arm with anyone. He was walking straight across the Quadrangle, hands in pockets, scuffing his unpolished black loafers in the wet grass and whistling.

"Hey," said one of the group, "what's the matter with Foots?"

"He's cold sober," remarked a second. "He's slipped a marble."

"Hey, Foots!" yelled the third. "Where ya been?"

"Oh, goofing off in the physics lab," replied Shumacher. "I got behind in a couple of experiments, and Dr. Michelson said I could work some nights."

"You have just missed out, Foots!" said one of the comrades, throwing a patronizing arm over Shumacher's shoulder. "We have been having a ball!"

Shumacher accompanied the merry trio back to the dormitory, shushing them firmly to avoid the rage of the Resident Head as they stumbled up the stairs. No one said any more about Shumacher's peculiar visit.

In the following weeks, though, it came repeatedly to the attention of Shumacher's friends that all was not normal with him. True, he seemed happy enough. Often he went about whistling, and sometimes he would smile and chuckle quietly to himself, as if remembering a secret joke. But that was just the trouble. He seemed quite content to share his jokes and his thoughts only with himself. With friends, he was cordial, but somehow aloof, and he began to spend much time alone. His roommate noticed that the nocturnal visits to the physics labora-

35

tory became more frequent, and finally the president of Shumacher's fraternity was moved to speak to him about his problem.

"Look, Foots, ole fellow," he said. "I know you're taking some rough courses, but how about slacking up a little? We don't see much of you around the house anymore, and it looks bad to the pledges and the three guys we're rushing in open rush. Why don't you stick around after dinner an hour or so in the evening, chew the fat with the brothers, you know? Now don't misunderstand me. I'm not trying to tell you what to do, but some of the brothers have been talking. They think you're beginning to act like a grind, and it doesn't look good. I'm just telling you this for your own good, Foots. We like you, see, and if there's something wrong, we want you to tell us."

Shumacher assured him there was nothing wrong. "I've just been busy, that's all," he said. But he promised to spend more time around the house.

Nevertheless, Shumacher continued to spend much time alone, and his friends grew more and more disturbed. He in turn was annoyed by their solicitude, and began to lose some of his cheerfulness. A further effort by the fraternity president to encourage his fraternal gregariousness brought only a furious outburst from Shumacher.

"Why don't you go eat yourself a pledge manual?" Shumacher growled, and stormed out of the house, violating Rule Number 4 of the House Rules, "The Zeta Phi Chi is always a gentleman, and the screen door is to be closed quietly when leaving the House."

As Shumacher became grumpier in his less and less frequent encounters with fellow Zepps, his moodiness came to the attention even of Dr. Michelson, who prided himself in being more than ordinarily sensitive to the morale of his students. One afternoon while Shumacher was putting away the apparatus after Electricity and Magnetism Lab, Dr. Michelson put a fatherly hand on his shoulder. To Shumacher's surprise and delight, the professor invited him to go to the Sludge Shop for a cup of coffee.

Settling into a booth, Shumacher stared down at the muddy

liquid that swirled in little vortices and ripples around his spoon, waiting tensely for Dr. Michelson to begin the conversation. To his surprise, the professor did not want to talk about the experiments they had been doing, nor about the possibilities of a vocation in physics for Shumacher. Instead, he expressed concern that Shumacher was not quite himself lately.

"Of course, I have no complaint about your work in my courses," he reassured him. "You've showed steady improvement, and I think you have a real grasp of the basic theory. But frankly, I'm concerned about you, Shumacher. I find myself wondering if you have many friends, people with whom you can share the things that are on your mind."

Shumacher assured his professor that he had friends, at least, he thought he did, he supposed as many as most people. But the things that were on his mind didn't seem to interest them too much, which was all right, too, because they were probably none of their business.

The conversation with Dr. Michelson went on until groups of students began to drift in to buy sandwiches and bowls of chili for supper. As the two talked, or rather, as Dr. Michelson talked and Shumacher became more and more silent, Shumacher grew increasingly restless under the professor's steady, inquisitive gaze. He found his thoughts trailing off and he caught himself listening distractedly to the rising, incoherent chatter of hundreds of voices penetrated by the deep, booming base of the jukebox. With a start he realized that Dr. Michelson was looking at him intently, and knew that he had been asked a question.

"No, sir, I . . . I really don't know. I don't know what is wrong with me. But I appreciate your interest."

Dr. Michelson studied him a moment longer, then glanced at his round steel wristwatch and slid out of the booth. Then he paused, standing over Shumacher.

"Remember this, son. Even we scientists have to live with people. The days of the genius isolated in his laboratory are gone. Today's research is teamwork, and the man who gets ahead is often the man who is best able to work with his associates."

There was another silence, and then Michelson continued.

"There is a counseling service on campus, you know. Perhaps you might benefit from a chance to talk over with one of their staff the things that are bothering you."

Shumacher sat for a long time after Dr. Michelson had left, absently tracing with his finger the countless initials carved into the tabletop. He tried to sort out the contrary impressions and thoughts that flooded through his mind. He could not suppress a rising anger, a persistent feeling that somehow he had been betrayed. But how? Who had betrayed him? Why should he feel angry at Dr. Michelson, who obviously wanted to help him? At last he shook his head and stood up, brushing his face with his hand as if he had walked through a cobweb, and walked back to his room without eating.

Shumacher still felt a mixture of resentment and confusion as he sat in the counselor's office two weeks later. With some anger he reminded himself that he would never have come here except that Dr. Michelson himself had made an appointment for him. Not that there was anything here to justify his anger. The young man who sat on the other side of the sleek walnut desk regarded him quietly, with just a hint of a smile. Beside the desk was a large box from which sprang a mass of climbing green plants, their leaves glistening in the warm sun that bathed the room. Behind the counselor was a reproduction, tastefully framed, of a modern painting. It was this painting on which Shumacher had fixed his eyes during most of their conversation so far.

Now the conversation seemed stymied, and Shumacher had shifted his gaze to the mechanical pencil he was holding, which he methodically dismantled and reassembled. The counselor did not break the silence. He seemed determined that Shumacher should do all the talking, which was very disconcerting, since Shumacher could not think what he ought to be saying. At last he shoved the pencil back into his pocket and looked up into the calm blue eyes that had been watching him all the while.

"Look, Doctor," he said. "I'll tell you exactly what's eating me. I am sick and tired of people." He paused.

"You feel ill at ease with people," murmured the counselor.

"I didn't say I felt ill at ease. I said I'm sick and tired of them.

I'm not afraid of people. I like people fine—sometimes, in small quantities. I even like parties and I very much enjoy bull sessions. But I like to choose the times I'm with them. The thing that bugs me on this campus is that there is no time and no place where any person can ever be by himself. Everywhere, all the time, there are people, people, people, chattering, asking questions, interrupting, all demanding that I be enthusiastic about everything they want to do, all wanting me to be just like them. Now all I want is just to find some hours when I can be alone, away from this whole jabbering mob. Does that make me some kind of nut?"

"You feel that I misunderstood you," intoned the counselor quietly. "You feel hostility toward people in groups and you want to be alone."

Shumacher looked at him curiously. Again he was conscious of a rising anger, the feeling of being betrayed. His chest felt constricted, and he swallowed hard against a pressure in his throat.

On the steps of the counseling center, Shumacher stopped and looked across the Quadrangle. The yellow-green leaves of the newly foliate trees danced in a light breeze. The early afternoon sun was warm on his shoulders. On the sidewalk in front of the steps, a solid mass of students, four abreast, surged by, hurrying from one class to another. As Shumacher watched them pass, the focus of his eyes unconsciously changed, until he saw, not individuals, but a blurred mass of moving faces, arms, and feet. He blinked and began to swear quietly to himself. A girl swinging by turned to look at him, her eyebrows raised in question. Shumacher did not see her. Thrusting his hands into his pockets, he pushed through the crowd and began to walk across the grass of the Quadrangle. A thin powder of dust settled on his unpolished black loafers, and as he approached the Physics Building, he suddenly laughed out loud and began to whistle.

❋   ❋   ❋

The Age of Togetherness

Shumacher will have a difficult time ahead, for this is the Age of Togetherness. It is the aeon of the American Family, grouped in harmonious silence around the TV. It is the age of the Group, the Gang, and the Set, of the Bermuda shorts and the Ivy League collar. Never before have so many of us been so much alike from coast to coast. Sensitive observers of American life since the end of World War II have been raising cries of alarm about the overwhelming conformity which increasingly casts Americans in a single mold.[1] They point out that this new conformity penetrates more deeply than the likeness in manners and dress that has always amused foreign visitors in America, extending to thought, goals, values, taste, indeed, to the very image which each has of himself.

Togetherness is everywhere, but nowhere so happily ascendant as on the college campus. Students arrive at the college with many similarities—they are of the same age, most of them are from families of similar economic and social levels, they are passing through the same stage of adolescence—but once on the campus they are immediately caught in enormous, if benevolent and almost invisible, pressures to make them virtually identical. In an extensive study of student values published in 1957, Dr. Philip Jacob sums up this trend:

> American college students today tend to think alike, feel alike and believe alike. To an extraordinary degree, their values are the same wherever they may be studying and whatever the stage of their college careers. The great majority seem turned out of a common mold, so far as outlook on life and standards of conduct are concerned.[2]

In one Southern university, the student body cast votes each spring to elect the "Typical Ed" and "Typical Co-Ed." This rather surprising honor points to the new kind of leader who, as Riesman explains, emerges in the other-directed society. The "taste leader" does not lead his group from out front, but from the middle of the group. He is just like everybody else, only more so.

Not only are American students alike, they are daily becoming more alike than the day before. Dr. Jacob looked in vain for significant changes in values of students during their four-year stay in the university, but he did discover that they tended to become more similar:

> There is more homogeneity and greater consistency of values among students at the end of their four years than when they begin. Fewer seniors espouse beliefs which deviate from the going standards than do freshmen.
>
> The impact of the college experience is . . . to *socialize* the individual, to refine, polish, or "shape up" his values so that he can fit comfortably into the ranks of American college alumni.[3]

As the pattern of life in the university propels the student gently but firmly toward complete conformity, it is preparing him well for docile and secure life in the highly organized complex of his postgraduate existence. William H. Whyte points out that life in a large modern suburb closely approximates that of the college fraternity or sorority, and the concern of the personnel managers of large corporations aims at the same spirit of the "happy group." The college, then, serves as the final paint-and-polish stage on the assembly line which runs from kindergarten to suburb, turning out conveniently identical, or nearly identical, parts for the social machine.

Never Alone

Such a pervasive pressure toward conformity can only be explained by the presence of powerful forces not only in the society as a whole, but within each of us. What are some of these forces?

A visit to a children's book department can be very enlightening. Recently, for example, such a visit turned up on a single shelf half a dozen books with one heavily emphasized theme: The main character—a duck, a bunny, a doll, sometimes even a child!—is "all alone." Therefore he is also miserable. But somehow, altogether miraculously, a companion appears—an egg is found and hatches quite by itself, or the door opens, and there are the bears! Then the problem is solved. The bunny and the duck or the doll and the bears or the chimpanzee and the elephant are together. Frequently that is the end of the book. No need describing what they *do* together, even; enough that ultimate happiness has been reached and that, as one story puts it, "no one was ever alone again."

Being all alone is nothing new. A generation ago children read about the Ugly Duckling, who was alone, rejected, and persecuted because he was different. But the Ugly Duckling overcame all this and triumphed gloriously in the end by becoming a beautiful swan, far superior to the other ducks. What is new is that we feel solitude to be a great problem, and already, when our children are two years old, we are teaching them that no one must ever be alone. Furthermore, aloneness can be overcome quite simply, not by striving toward personal identity and fulfillment, as was the case of the swan, but simply by being together, ignoring even the differences between ducks and bunnies. If Shumacher would only spend more time around the house, making the effort to identify himself with his more "normal" brothers, then he would stop standing out so disgustingly by breaking the curve on examinations and otherwise behaving like a "grind." He would fit in, become well rounded, and be content with a gentleman's C like everyone else. Then he would never have to be alone again.

As the fable of the Ugly Duckling illustrates, being alone has not always seemed such an ultimate tragedy. The more or less official philosophy which is still expressed in newspaper editorials and political speeches exalts rugged individualism. But the sound has a hollow ring. The fact is that we are standing at the end of a long road of individualism, and perhaps it is just the excesses of the era of individualism which have helped produce the conformist reaction.

In philosophy, modern individualism began in the seventeenth century, and most of the clichés of the man on the street today had their start then. In economics, free enterprise was built on the idea that what was best for each individual was best for the nation. The "invisible hand" which moved the market to its proper level grew from "enlightened self-interest." Every man, we have firmly believed, held his destiny in his own hands. Every man could rise above his environment; if any man did not succeed, he had only himself to blame.

Today this ideal of the free individual is still a very strong item in our personal and national creed. One of the most successful mass-advertising campaigns in recent years was that of the cigarette designed for "the man who thinks for himself." The irony of this appeal, of course, lies in the fact that a man who really thinks for himself would not be influenced by the Madison Avenue gimmick. But the appeal was successful because even those of us who were most thoroughly dominated by unconscious and nonlogical influences of the herd continued to believe that we were individuals and desperately wanted to think that we thought for ourselves.

The fact is that we are today so emotionally isolated from one another that we can no longer endure in reality the kind of individualism we idealize in theory. It was fine and pleasant to talk about individualism when we were in small towns with stable neighborhoods, where we felt a deep solidarity with our neighbors and ties of memory with the past generations of our families. But today, most of us live in a city—probably a different city from the place of our birth. There, no one remembers our parents; no one is aware of our place in the community. We are on our own. Increasingly the dominant characteristic of a civilized people is the rapidity with which they move. Their mobility includes both their geographical movement and their movement up or down the social ladder. When persons have been uprooted from the ties of clan and community and plunged as isolated individuals into the anonymity of the city, into the routine replaceability of the factory system, into the gears of human organization, then the problem becomes loneliness. Countless and growing numbers of individuals throughout the world today feel this loneliness as an acute pain. In *Orpheus Descending,* Tennessee Williams has one of his characters say, "We're all of us sentenced to solitary confinement inside our own skins, for life!"[4]

The more the individualism we believed in has become a reality, the more we are afraid of it. The more we discover our loneliness, the more we are tempted to allow some kind of collective, some kind of totalitarian group, to swallow us.

Germany was one of the first nations to feel the extreme development of individualism. Between World War I and the depression, a large number of the German lower middle class—small businessmen, tradesmen, craft workers, farmers, unemployed ex-soldiers—felt themselves completely outside of society. They seemed to themselves to be victims of an economic fate that fell on them from forces they did not understand. The result was a festering sensation of terrible isolation. In the midst of their feeling of isolation and detachment from the world of other men, there arose a strange little fanatic who began to make grandiose speeches about "Das Volk," about the great, ancient Aryan solidarity, the magnificent superrace whose roots lay in the mythical past of Siegfried and the Nordic tribes. Here for these anonymous little people was something they could cling to, and which would cling to them. Here was solidarity and belonging with something great and mysterious. So they joined the Nazi Party.

A second example, far different in scope, may be seen in the plight of adolescents. When you become a teen-ager, something happens to the family. Suddenly it becomes very difficult to tell your parents about things; they seem not to understand you, and you have trouble understanding them. The more the solidarity of the teen-ager with his parents is broken, the more important is his solidarity with people his own age. Pretty soon many parents are driven, if they want to maintain contact with their children at all, to try to keep up with them by conforming themselves to the values of the group of teen-agers. If the family solidarity is totally dissolved, as often happens under the pressures of life in a slum, for example, then the solidarity of the teen-ager with his group may become so total that he belongs body and soul to the gang.

A third, again quite different, example of individualism in our time is the young management trainee, the junior executive, of a large corporation. During his early years with the company, he is moved from one place to another frequently, to make sure he will fit in anywhere. No sooner has he bought an $18,000 ranch style house in Park Forest than it is time for a transfer to Levittown, where he will invest for five years in a $22,000 ranch style house. He gravitates to the suburbs, where most other people are in similar situations. Because he is forever moving, there is no opportunity for deep relationships to develop. His only security, therefore, his only belonging is derived from feverish participation in the suburban groups. Of Park Forest, Illinois, for example, it is said, "Every minute from 7:00 A.M. to 10:00 P.M. some organization is meeting somewhere."[5] Where roots cannot go deep, isolation forces the roots to go horizontally, like those of a tree clinging precariously to a canyon wall. Again, however, as in the other two examples, there is the danger that the individual who has no other roots, no other source of inner security and meaning, will lose himself quite literally in the group.

From these three examples it will be seen that the collective, or totalitarian group, does not really provide the security it appears to promise. The individual is granted acceptance by the group only so long as he conforms. In fact, then, it is not *he* who is accepted, but only the group's standardized image of its members. Once inside the group, the sensitive individual is likely to find himself at least as lonely as before and more afraid than ever. The mechanism which enforces conformity, as we saw in the previous chapter, is precisely the diffuse anxiety which every collective encourages. For this reason Riesman very perceptively and accurately labeled the other-directed group *The Lonely Crowd*. The novel *Nineteen Eighty-Four* by George Orwell described the ultimate in collectives, a totalitarian communist state, in which "Big Brother" is always watching. The fearful emotion that grips the reader of this novel is just the horrible, hopeless loneliness of the main character, a man who belongs *totally*. This is the irony of our modern situation: Loneliness produces the collective; the collective in turn makes us feel more lonely than ever.

Togetherness on Campus

I do not mean to imply, of course, that you will find a Neo-Nazi Party, a Communist cell, or even a street gang in your university. But almost every college student experiences to some degree the uprootedness that compels men to grasp for fellowship, and every campus has groups which have the potential of gaining godlike predominance over individuals who join them.

The omnipresence of togetherness in the university is a direct reaction to the psychological isolation of late adolescence. One of the most important facts in your life right now is that you have left home. You have to a large extent detached yourself from the group to which you have been most intimately related until now, the group that sheltered you, guided you, implanted in you your earliest sense of value and meaning, disciplined you, and, in fact, loved you. Now you are no longer living in the midst of that group. True, you still have strong ties with your parents, both financial and emotional, but when you return on your first holiday, if you are at a distant school, both they and you will discover that you are partially strangers. Even if you continue to live in the house with your parents, the beginning of college intensifies the process of loosening ties with them. For many commuting students, the return home each afternoon becomes a crisis until they and their parents can both recognize that childhood bonds in the family can no longer be maintained. It is true, as Thomas Wolfe said, that *You Can't Go Home Again*.

Our campus togetherness, then, is nothing less than the search for new families, for new primary groups, as sociologists call them, into which we can transplant our severed roots. This search is reflected in statements made by some fraternity members about their house:

> The campus is so big, you can get lost in it. But in the house, you feel that they accept you. It's like a family. You really get to know people. Not so impersonal—like a family. You have a place where you feel at home and people you feel at home with.
>
> You feel you belong somewhere. You're not so alone any more.
>
> . . . a group of people you feel really close to.
>
> . . . people who really mean something to you.[6]

From these statements it is immediately obvious that fraternities and sororities are among the most important of the substitute
families which are sought by students. The fraternity or sorority
is in fact the very institutionalization of the desire to belong.
Everything possible is done by the organized house to promote
"belongingness." Members are selected with great care to insure
that they are as much alike as possible in background, relative
wealth, general religious affiliation, interests, and personality.
Then they are subjected to intensive training as pledges, including study of the traditions and history of the group, memorization
of names and home towns of all the brothers, and extensive practice in social skills. The size of the group encourages close relationships, and a round of life is developed within the house which
involves doing a great many things together. In many ways, then,
the fraternity or sorority serves as an ideal family substitute.
Within its structure, an individual may find security and acceptance, and genuine, lasting friendships flourish between members.

On the other hand, the structure of the fraternity or sorority
gives it enormous power over the life of the individual member.
The very same factors which give him a sense of security and belonging so long as he fits the prevailing pattern of his house may
become terribly threatening if he finds himself out of step with
the group mind. To most fraternity members, the fraternity
seems to have a personality of its own, over and above the individual members.[7] To the nonconformer, the group personality
can be overpowering. The control exercised by the group is most
obvious in such superficial matters as dress and speech—almost
every house develops certain phrases which constitute its own
jargon, a kind of code language known only to members of the
family. Control extends, however, to such areas as drinking,
choice of recreation, sexual morality, amount of time spent in
study, and attitude toward cheating. In sororities, control is especially rigid in dating practices. In many sororities it is a written or
unwritten rule that no girl will date an "independent." Often the
rule is extended to cover also members of certain fraternities regarded as lower in status.

It is not only fraternities and sororities which have the potential of dominating individual personalities, however. Any intimate group may develop the same functions. Some students have observed wryly that even religious groups sometimes are tempted to become "poor men's fraternities," transforming themselves into cliques that enforce a rigid conformity on their members. In one sense the pressures exerted by fraternities and sororities on their members are less insidious, because they are so obvious, than the pressures more subtly applied by an unorganized group. The same man who gains a reputation in his fraternity as a nonconformist may completely transform his personality to fit the image cherished by the intimate group of writers and cynics who hang out in the office of the humor magazine, or the pattern exhibited by the little society of philosophers, psychologists, or jazz addicts who meet daily for coffee in the Union Building. The visible restrictions he will fight to the death, but the subtle, inward pressures—which may be just as foreign and just as destructive to his real self—he accepts without even being aware of their existence.

A careful observation of the campus leads us to the conclusion that the other-direction seen by Riesman is here particularly active. We breathe the daily atmosphere of conformity. How can an individual be an individual in this atmosphere? Must he withdraw from all groups? As a matter of fact, it is not unusual to see an especially sensitive upperclassman who decides to "go inactive" in his fraternity and to resign from all the extracurricular activities with which he had busied himself and perhaps gained campus-wide fame. He chooses to endure the loneliness for the sake of escaping the pressures.

Withdrawal, however, is not a realistic solution. A person cannot be fully human without participating in human community. When we do attempt withdrawal, often our escape proves illusory. The nonconformity which we see on college campuses frequently is pathetic but at the same time comic, because it turns out to be only conformity turned wrong-side-out. The belligerent nonconformist is shaped by the very social forces he is fighting: He becomes their image in reverse. This bondage of the outsider was nowhere more clearly demonstrated than in the "beat generation" of the fifties. The "beats," whose originals began a protest against the mechanization, superficiality, and conformity of modern life, gravitated inevitably into groups which themselves came to demand the most exacting conformity in taste, dress, and (negative) morality of all who desired to be accepted as "hip." Neither a romantic yearning for the rugged individualism of former generations nor a cynical attack on "the squares" will cancel the unsolved problem: How can I really be myself and at the same time really have fellowship with other people?

To reiterate what was said in chapter 1, genuine human life is polar. It requires both solitude and community. Yet we have seen in these two chapters that this polarity of our life gets pulled apart. Solitude becomes lonely isolation in which we drown in ourselves; our attempts at community become demonic collectives that crush the possibility of true selfhood or honest confrontation with other persons. It is as if there were a flaw, a twist in our human nature which ironically distorts our every attempt to live.

The experiences of loneliness and of oppressive togetherness which overshadow the first months of your college career are not unique. They point to the profoundest questions of the human condition and cry out with a cry as old as man for life, real life, and for communion with others.

A Brief Quiz for No Grade!

Do you agree or disagree with each of the following statements? Why?

	AGREE	DISAGREE
1. Because other persons' approval of us is so important we all become actors.	( )	( )
2. Most American students cannot stand to be alone.	( )	( )
3. Only if I have experienced acceptance by others can I stand to be alone.	( )	( )

4. Only if I can stand being alone with myself can I participate in real community. ( )   ( )

5. If you're going to be a real person you have to be a nonconformist. ( )   ( )

6. Actually there's no such thing as a nonconformist. ( )   ( )

7. Loneliness produces the collective; the collective in turn makes us feel more lonely than ever. ( )   ( )

8. No group could ever control the way I think or feel or the people I associate with. ( )   ( )

9. Annette is finally on her way to becoming a real person at the end of the story. ( )   ( )

10. Shumacher will never find anyone he can really talk to. ( )   ( )

3

the people of god's secret

Life Says No

To all our attempts to live as independent individuals and to all our attempts to grasp the security and approval of human fellowship, life is always saying No. This No shatters our dreams and frustrates our longing for unity. Annette's brittle freedom breaks up on the rock of herself, when she discovers that she is not free at all, but held fast by something inside her which she does not understand. Shumacher's wish to be *both* really himself *and* well liked by the gang tears apart. He cannot have it both ways. These crises are very painful, but in them the possibility of genuine life opens up again. There awakens in Annette and Shumacher the gnawing sense that life ought to be different. What is the source of this sense of the dislocation of life? Why can we not succeed in being what we wish to be? Answers to questions like these can only be pointed to by parables. Let us consider two parables, one from family life and one from the Bible.

In some way, in every life, the limit symbolized by No must be learned. When a child begins to crawl, the lesson has to begin, not only to save the furniture, but also to save the child. The baby must discover that between him and Daddy's books, between him and Mother's china, between him and the electric heater, there is a moral barrier represented by the "No, no!" which is spoken against him.

A crucial day comes when the No is internalized. The child one day looks at the china lamp, looks then at the parent, and firmly tells *himself*, "No, no!" The parents congratulate themselves: they have succeeded. This is a significant moment. The baby has now become a moral being. In biblical language, he knows good and evil.

But this is also an ominous moment. For when the child has learned what No means, he can also use this No as a weapon against his parents. If he can say, "No, no," to himself when tempted to touch the lamp, he can also say "No, no," to his mother when she tells him it is time to go to bed. The more the child learns of good and evil, the more moral responsibility he is capable of, the more also he can turn this knowledge against his parents, against his brother or sister, against his playmate.

The knowledge of good and evil has a peculiar double edge to it. It is the basic equipment for responsible life, but it is also the implement of rebellion, a weapon to be used against other persons. This fact is exactly the theme of the story found in the third chapter of Genesis, a story which also contains the clue to the flaw or twist in our life that makes it go awry. Now read this short narrative (Gen. 3)—not as you would read the morning paper, but as you might savor a poem, letting the mood and rhythm of it speak to you.

*   *   *

Why is it that in this ancient story we are told about a tree whose fruit symbolizes the "knowledge of good and evil"? The chapter speaks of the grave changes that invade man's life when he eats this fruit. What are these changes? What does it mean that his "eyes were opened"? What manner of story is this? We begin to suspect that there is more here than an ancient folktale about why snakes have no legs and why men wear clothes. We begin to sense that this is not a story which happened "once upon a time" to a couple of early anthropoids someplace in Iran. No, this is a story of something which happened last evening in your dormitory and this morning during the quiz in English. This is the story of something which happened to the human race, and therefore to your life—and goes on happening, day after day. This is the story of your life and mine. The very name of the central character gives us the hint: *Adam*, the Hebrew word for mankind. This is the story of Everyman.

The story treats of rebellion. It is the story of man exceeding his limits, of man using his knowledge to destroy the possibility of paradise. It is the story of the command, "Thou shalt not . . . ," spoken by God to his creature, and the inevitable temptation, "Why not?"

What happens? The serpent tempts Eve in these words: "You will not die. For God knows that when you eat of it your eyes will be opened, and you will be like God, knowing good and evil." The most basic temptation of all—and the one which is always present because we are human beings—is the temptation to be God for ourselves. Because God, as Genesis 1:27 says, made us in his own image, made us to have dominion over all animals, we are able in a sense to stand outside many of the barriers and limits of the natural world. When we consider how much mankind knows, how much we have accomplished, it is easy to imagine that we are the center of the universe. We become irritable when anyone tells us we must not do something. God becomes a threat to us, because he reminds us of our limits. The self-assertion of Adam—of Everyman—is rebellion against the God who limits him.

What a burden we take upon ourselves when we attempt to become the center of the universe—the burden of proving to ourselves that we are perfect. To do that we must become judges for life. To defend my image of my own perfection, I must become the judge of my neighbor: if I am not absolutely good, at least I am better than Jones or Smith. When Adam is confronted by God with his disobedience, he turns upon his wife: "The woman whom thou gavest to be with me, she gave me the fruit." Eve, alas, has no one to blame but the snake, "The serpent beguiled me, and I ate."

Not only must I judge my neighbor, I must also judge myself. I can justify my rebellion against God only if I am self-sufficient, if I am perfect, so I paint a picture of myself as an angel. When I do not live up to this picture, then I condemn myself.

Obviously, if I could succeed in being honest with myself, I could never play this game. Either I would have to acknowledge my rebellion, or I would have to destroy myself. In practice I manage to live with my god-image by wearing masks, by pretending, even to myself, to be what I am not.

When the man and the woman had eaten the fruit, "the eyes of both were opened, and they knew that they were naked; and they sewed fig leaves together and made themselves aprons." Each has pretended to be God, but before the penetrating and jealous gaze of the other person, each stands naked. Before the eyes of the other he cannot pretend to be God. So the only thing to do is to hide from the other. How does this hiding poetically symbolize the beginning of that anxious role playing we discussed in chapter 1? From this moment on, man is a problem to himself. Man in rebellion cannot be simply and honestly himself, because too much is at stake. His own image of himself as God is at stake.

No wonder, then, the man and woman must hide finally from God also. Most of all from God, for to continue their make-believe, they must pretend that he does not exist. "And they heard the sound of the LORD God walking in the garden in the cool of the day, and the man and his wife hid themselves from the presence of the LORD God among the trees of the garden." How beautifully simple is the language with which the parable speaks of God. We know, of course, that we cannot hide from God behind some bushes! How can we hide from God? The simplest way is just to go away into our own affairs and pretend that he does not exist. Modern man has made the exhilarating discovery that the world goes on just about as well without God. As the mathematician Laplace said to Napoleon, "Sir, I did not need that hypothesis." Perhaps a characteristic fact of modern life is that most of us are *practicing* atheists, no matter how much we may assert our belief in God.

A less obvious, but perhaps more effective, hiding place from God is religion. Among primitive peoples, religion developed around rather naïve rituals which were designed to appease the gods and make them leave the tribe alone—by offering them sacrifices, for example, or by performing ecstatic dances for them. Our own rituals seem less naïve—or are they in fact more naïve? We assume that by sacrificing an hour a week of church, or perhaps by giving up a whole host of active hours in the church program, we can persuade God to leave our social life, our study habits, or our romantic life alone. Our worship services are designed to ease our tensions and help us to relax. Some prefer elaborate formality, so that the long-accustomed and beautiful routine will exorcise our guilt-feelings; others like a relaxed and homey service, which leaves us with a general glow of good fellowship when we are finished. But at all costs we want to avoid in church any sort of situation that would lead us to say with Adam, "I was afraid, because I was naked, and I hid myself."

God Comes Looking

So far the story has given us a vivid, if unflattering, picture of human life. Here we see our shame and our loneliness, our pride and our bitterness, graphically reflected. But there is more to the story. The last word is not man's action, but God's. Though man hides from God, yet "The LORD God called to the man, and said to him, 'Where are you?'" In the midst of a fallen and broken world, God still comes, God still speaks, God still confronts the rebel.

God confronts the rebel in judgment. Ironically, the man who has made of himself the judge, choosing to decide for himself and his neighbor what is good and evil, must recognize in God's coming the limit to his own capacity to judge. "Have you eaten of the tree of which I commanded you not to eat?" The ultimate judge remains God, not ourselves. No matter how thoroughly we have convinced ourselves that a certain course of action is good, because it seems good to us, sooner or later the consequences of the action will become obvious, and whether or not the action was good will be clear, even to us. How did Annette encounter judgment with Bill Leslie? Who was being judged and by whom? Judgment in that case meant that the logical consequences of the decision she had made were simply exposed and she saw them, saw the meaning of Annette for the first time.

The judgment of God confronts us with our limit as judges, and more than that, with our limit as living beings. "You are dust, and to dust you shall return." My attempt to make myself the center of my universe, or even of my group of friends, or even of my family, really makes sense only if I cannot die. It is not accidental that in our culture, in which we worship so unabashedly our own success, we have desperately tried to convince ourselves that death is not real. The mortician proudly displays the body of our dead friend, which he has made to look "just like he's asleep." When a relative, or even a pet, dies, we tell our children, "He's gone away." Even in the church, ignoring the plain teaching of the Bible, we have often encouraged this wish-thinking by such sentiments as "Death is only a graduation"; "The real life lies on the other side of the grave"; "Death is just another stage in life's progress." The Bible is much more realistic: "You are dust, and to dust you shall return." Though this is not the Bible's last word, death still is the last enemy, and every man must face him. Only when we have taken seriously this fact will we be prepared to listen soberly to the God who goes on walking in our spoiled garden and speaking to us above our rebellious shouts.

God, however, does not come only in judgment; he comes in love. Even when he confronts us with his judgment and with our death, he does so because he loves us. Only a thoughtless parent will permit his child to go on living forever in a dream world, even though reality may be very painful. But God also cares for us, in our fallen estate, with the mercy and tenderness of a father. How does the story express this? Look at verse 21. God has pity on our flimsy defenses, our fig-leaf aprons, and himself hides our nakedness. God accepts our shame, does not turn away from our broken lives.

The ideal world is shattered. Paradise is an impossible possibility. Before the garden stands a flaming sword and the cherubim—there is no way back to Utopia! Before God we must go on living, not in any ideal world, but in *this* world of separation and shame. The story leaves us with the uneasy feeling that there are no shortcuts back to Eden, but only a perilous journey forward through a shadowy history. The story is, by itself, unfinished, a kind of prologue to the history of God's acts among his pilgrim people.

This Twisted World

There follows in the succeeding chapters of Genesis an epic of broken community. The epic links together a number of separate sagas, of which only two can be mentioned here: the stories of Cain and Abel, in chapter 4, and of the Tower of Babel, in chapter 11. In each of these, man's rebellious willing to be God works itself out as a dark nemesis that warps and kills human life, culture, and relationships.

Cain and Abel, like Adam, are not merely individuals, but represent whole cultures. The story has to do, on one level, with the bitter enmity between sheepherders and homesteaders—a hostility celebrated in modern times by the TV western. The hatred between the settled, agricultural peoples and the nomadic shepherds is not seen in this saga as inevitable, the normal state of affairs. The depth of the biblical awareness of human life as unity and fellowship is seen in the very fact that these alienated peoples, the murderer and his victim, *are nevertheless brothers.* The way we have spoiled the life that God intended for us is revealed in Cain's question, "Am I my brother's keeper?"

The man who hates his brother is already a murderer (1 John 3:15), doomed to spend his days restless, wandering beyond the inaccessible paradise. The community which he builds for himself brings no genuine fellowship, for it will always be the refuge of those who do not want to bear responsibility for their brothers. With irony, the Bible tells us that Cain built the first city. The city is the place where the wanderer goes. It is also the place where we are free from our neighbors, free to shrug our shoulders at the cry of pain from the stranger: It is not our business. Am I my brother's keeper?

The Bible is likewise unimpressed with the advance of civilization and technology. Cain's "grandsons" are the inventors, the technicians, the agriculturalists, and the artists and musicians (Genesis 4:20–22). Cain will become the creator of all things. He will create a new system of values based on the things man makes. Is paradise closed? Then he will build a new paradise.

Only thus can he forget his encounter with the Creator of heaven and earth. Paul Claudel writes,

> The city is resplendent
> With a fabricated light.[1]

The more brilliant the lights of the city, the more dimly one is able to see the stars. The more wonderful the creation which technology lays before us, the more easily man can forget that Creator who comes and asks us about our brother's life. Charlie Brown stands through a whole comic strip gazing at a sky full of stars. Then in the last frame he says, "Let's go inside and watch television. I'm beginning to feel insignificant."

Man's struggle to make his life significant is also depicted in the Tower of Babel story, given in Genesis 11. Its theme is the collapse of the power to communicate. The men of Babylon built their tower because they were afraid, lest they "be scattered abroad." The plain of Shinar is broad and flat, with no natural barriers to invasion. The men of Babylon sensed the precarious- ness of their life, so they set out to erect an artificial mountain, to impress their enemies with their great strength, a temple, to make sure that the gods were on their side.

We, too, are threatened by our world. What are the towers we build? We plan for a vocation, a good life, home, family, security, success—but we are also aware of the draft and the bomb. So we erect our tower of shallowness. We refuse to discuss the possibilities. We will live for the day. We will get what we can; we will take the shortcuts. We will live for security, because we are vaguely aware that there is no security.

We are threatened by loneliness, by the fear that we shall not be accepted, that we shall not be liked, so we throw ourselves into the feverish pantomine of belonging. Threatened by forces we can never control, we seek refuge in towers of pretense, towers of our own making. Thus we seek to make "a name for ourselves." As a result even our language is poisoned.

Language is the vehicle of community. It is in speaking to each other and listening to each other that we become genuinely human. But language is also the vehicle of estrangement. With the same tongue you can say to your roommate, "God bless you," or "Go to hell!" The same jargon that gives the in-group a special sense of belonging, of participation in shared memories, shuts out the one who does not belong. The private joke draws the circle of exclusion.

In the parable of the Tower of Babel, it is God himself who "comes down" to scatter the builders and to "confuse their language." Such a picture of God offends us. We would never think of God as such a spoilsport, jealously invading our life to knock down our creations and break up our togetherness. But the Bible dares so to speak of God, because it knows that the destructive acts of God are also grace. He "comes down" to shatter our poor illusions of security and of fellowship, so that our empty hands may receive the life he himself is preparing.

The murder of the brother, the artificial paradise, the distortion of language—these are the aftermath of rebellion. There is always aftermath of rebellion, and the deepest remorse cannot wash it away. The consequences must run their course. But there is also a sequel to that other act, the seeking, caring act of God. God will not give up on mankind; the rebel cannot evade his love.

The Other Adam

If we can dare to speak as humanly of God as do the biblical writers, we can say that God's plans for mankind fell to pieces. But, unlike us when our world falls part, God did not despair. God has a secret. This secret of God is the new meaning, the new hope, the new possibility that gives to us rebels life, right in the middle of our constant blundering into death.

Here and there God's secret breaks into the light. Woven into the tangle of history, it begins to emerge in the form of a People. Quickly on the heels of the debacle of Babel, the biblical writer inserts the story of Abraham, who had to get out of that artificial paradise, because God said to him, "Come on, let's go." God said to him, "I have a secret, and I will show you."

> And I will make of you a great nation,
> and I will bless you, and make your name great,
> so that you will be a blessing.
> I will bless those who bless you, and him who curses
> you I will curse;
> and by you all the families of the earth shall be blessed.
> (Genesis 12:2–3, R.S.V. margin)

This People appears in time as a confederation of certain desert tribes who know that something extraordinary has happened to them. Suddenly they begin to be conscious that they are under a special obligation:

> You shall be my own possession among all peoples;
> for all the earth is mine,
> and you shall be to me a kingdom of priests and a holy nation.
> (Exodus 19:5b–6a)

The People of God's Secret grows, errs, fails, agonizes over the meaning of its existence. It is not an impressive people. It has no status, wealth, culture, or sophistication. All of these things it wants to have, and again and again it repeats just the sin of Adam, wanting to secure its existence from within itself, wanting to be as God. It tries to be like all the nations, but it cannot be. It is laden with the consciousness of a *mission:*

> I will give you as a light to the nations,
> that my salvation may reach to the end of the earth.
> (Isaiah 49:6b)

The People of the Secret did not understand itself. Above all, it could not understand why its life, if God had chosen it, was not a glorious, exalted life, instead of the lowly suffering life that kept on failing, trying, failing anew. The meaning of its existence did not fully appear until God's secret broke openly into its history in such startling form that even these People did not recognize what had happened. The parable of Adam and the secret of Abraham remain unfinished until Jesus Christ appears.

In Jesus both the judgment and the love of God are fulfilled. Man the rebel has become the judge, knowing good and evil, submitting himself, his neighbor, even God himself, to his judgment. But Jesus comes as one who does not judge at all, but submits *himself* to *our* judgment:

> For God did not send the Son into the world to judge the world, but for the world to be saved through him.
>
> (John 3:17, author's translation)

He comes bearing the message, "Judge not, that you be not judged." To the woman taken in adultery, he says, "Has no one condemned you? Neither do I condemn you. Go, and do not sin again." He comes not to judge, but to let us judge him. We who have made ourselves judges end by hanging God on a gallows. And here, of course, in our very act of judging we are condemned. Here our pride is unmasked, our angelic pretenses revealed. Here the final No of God to all our false striving, our pride, our will to power, our self-destructive togetherness, is openly announced. But in the fact that he absorbs our hostility, bears our judgment, here is also his Yes.

God's secret is that there is *another* Adam, *another* mankind, which he preserves alive in the midst of a deadly world, and finally reveals when the time is ripe. Jesus Christ is the new Adam, the new Everyman. This does not mean that he is only a symbol. It means that just this flesh and blood man who was hanged on the cross, who bled and hurt and choked with thirst in the hot sun, this Jesus carries the meaning, the hope, and the possibility of real human life for all men.

Now the secret is out. The new Everyman is alive in the world. He, the authentic God-man, has overcome the death that threatens us God-pretenders. And now he is running history. To most of the world, he is still a secret. Chance, fate, mechanical forces, indeed the very powers of evil seem to be running the world. But there are those who know the secret, and they see that already "the kingdom of the world has become the kingdom of our Lord and of his Christ, and he shall reign for ever and ever" (Rev. 11:15). The ones who know the secret are now a new community. They are the ones who have to live in the world with a special obligation and a special style of life. They are to live as the *sign* to the world that the new mankind is real, that genuine life and genuine community are here, open and available to the man who is given eyes to see them and faith to trust his life to them.

The life God gives to man is not a theoretical life. It is not only an ideal life, that men have to try to attain. It is not only a concept of life, for men to try to comprehend and follow. It is life. It is concrete, human life, breaking forth among the fishermen and prostitutes and tax collectors, clerks, officials, weavers, jailers, even among its enemies, here and now. We want to know, where do we find this life? The New Testament tells us, where Jesus Christ is, there is life. But, we say, where can I find Jesus Christ? I have never seen him. No, says the New Testament, you cannot see him, but he is here. We know he is here because we see his body. His *body*? Yes, for those people who have been seized by the secret are Christ's body.

The One and the Many

The body of Christ is not to be confused with togetherness. It does not emerge from the association of people who are alike, but from the fact that Jesus Christ makes peace between people who are enemies. From those who were alienated, strangers, separated from one another by walls of hostility, he makes one new man. The strangers become one household, one family. But they do not thereby cease to be different or to be individuals. On the contrary: it is in this family that for the first time a man discovers the freedom to be a true individual.

> For just as the body is one and has many members, and all the members of the body, though many, are one body, so it is with Christ. For by one Spirit we were all baptized into one body—Jews or Greeks, slaves or free—and all were made to drink of one Spirit.   (1 Corinthians 12:12–13)

Christ makes the many into one, but they go on being many. The church is not a club of people who wear a special kind of religious mask. It is just the alliance of those who know that they are sinners, and therefore can take their masks off. Every genuinely Christian act of worship begins with the confession of sins. The act of confession, if it is anything more than prattling words, ought immediately to wave a flag in our minds, reminding us that we do not have to pretend in *this* place to be good, bright, witty, up to date, sophisticated, or anything else. God knows better, and loves us nevertheless. Christian fellowship exists among persons who know better, but nevertheless love each other—not because they like each other, but because they cannot help it.

It is the "nevertheless" of God's love and of the love of the Christian for his brother that points to the miracle of the New Adam. God did not wait for me to be pious, moral, or sweet before he decided in my favor. I, the Old Adam, who have spent my whole life trying to justify my pretense to be God, am shattered and restored by this "nevertheless." Slowly and fearfully, I lower my guard, and with wonder I discover that the universe does not dissolve when I crawl down from my throne. Instead, I discern that there is a new dimension in the universe—invisible from the ingrown earth I had ruled—the dimension of love.

All our lives, as we saw in chapters one and two, we have been learning to hide our true selves by becoming actors. As quick-change artists, quickly shifting roles to suit each occasion, we could win approval by groups that were important to us. But the irony in our efforts was the fact that, even though we belonged, we remained strangers. It was not we, not our true selves, that were accepted by the others, but only the flexible masks we wore. Within this new community, the body of Christ, however, we are drawn into a dialogue that does not conceal us from our neighbor, but reveals us. Gradually, tentatively, we discover that it is possible to drop the pretense and begin to speak to another person about the things which are hidden in our hearts. And strangely, our Christian brother is not shocked by these words. He dares to listen, no, more than that, he tries to open himself to the meaning which lies behind the words, the meaning we cannot bring into words. Suddenly our life opens, the shell of our manifold defenses cracks, and for a brief, fragile moment, we and this other person really are sharing common life. There, in that moment, the New Adam is visible.

Because we are set free to reveal ourselves to each other instead of concealing ourselves, the body of Christ brings the acceptance and the unity with other persons which we have sought in vain through the cliques we have created. The metaphor of the body points to the fact of our unity. We are all organs in one body. If one of the organs of my body becomes infected, then my whole body will be sick. In the same way, in the body of Christ, "If one member suffers, all suffer together; if one member is honored, all rejoice together." Unlike Cain's city, this is the community in which we are each our brother's keepers.

The Church Is Sinful

But, you are saying, you have been in the church most of your life, and it is not like that. It is a club of religious people most of whom pretend to be better, kinder, and more harmonious than they are. The fact that we are more hesitant to show our true feelings in church meetings and discussions than anywhere else is a clear sign of how little we have had our eyes opened to the fellowship which Christ gives us. The church is sinful. But that fact should neither surprise us nor cause us to despair of finding the new mankind.

Christian fellowship is not an ideal that the church has to try to realize; it is a reality which God gives to the church, which it has to uncover. Paul does not tell us to become one body, he says, "We were all baptized into one body—Jews or Greeks, slaves or free." Baptism is a passive act; it is something done *to* us, not something we do. In talking about the other Sacrament, Paul writes, "Because there is one bread, we who are many are one body, for we all partake of the same bread." As we received our physical life at birth, without having any choice in the matter, so we also receive the new life-in-community. It is given to us as the life of Christ invades our existence in Baptism, the Lord's Supper, and the proclamation of the gospel.

The problem in the church is to uncover the fellowship which has been given us. This is a work of faith. Martin Luther reminds us that, in the Apostles' Creed, we say that we "*believe* in the holy catholic church." We believe in it, even though we do not see it—just as we believe in Jesus Christ, although we do not see him. But faith means more than just believing that the church is there—it means acting on the basis of that belief. The Christian fellowship is uncovered and experienced through the venture of faith. Concretely, when I dare to open myself to a person who, like me, has been baptized into the body of Christ, even though we do not know each other, even though we may not like each other, even though our opinions may differ radically—when I venture to expose my life to him in this way, then I discover that he and I *have* communion with one another. I am held within the Christian fellowship *even when I do not feel that I belong*. The life we share does not depend on the way I feel, but on the fact that Christ has reconciled me to my brother.

We should not be surprised to find that the church is sinful; we should also not be surprised to find real life and real community outside the church. Jesus Christ is also Lord over the world, and he is working out there as well. The church has no monopoly on the life which he brings; its mission is to be the sign, the light which shines into all the world, pointing to him who wants to restore genuine life to all men.

The church does not exist to glorify itself, but just to serve its Lord by serving the world. When it forgets that and tries to make the world serve it, then it falls into the worst of its sins, and God must come in judgment on his household, to break its pride and raise up new messengers. This judgment and renewal happens in every generation of the church's life. For the New Adam cannot be smothered. He will go on living, and he will go on giving life to all who hear his call.

PART TWO

landmarks of
pilgrims past

If I ask you who you are, you will probably respond by telling me your name. But even this name, which is yours alone, points beyond yourself, for it was given to you by your family. If I ask again, "Who are you; what is it that makes you *you?*" perhaps you will tell me about your family—where they came from, the images under which they see themselves, the things you have done together, the limits they have set you, the quarrels you have had, and so forth. Or perhaps you will go beyond your family to tell me about your wider environment, some of the things that stick in your memory as turning points in your life, some of the forces that have acted on you, some of the events that forced you to make decisions. To discover your identity means, in part, to discover your *history.* But your history, the history that makes you *you,* is not the same story that a historian might write about you. No, this history is discovered from within: it is your history. These events and forces of your past are still woven into your present, still shaping you. To discover who you are means to face these events openly and consciously *as they live in you now.*

Now this book is asking me as I write it and you as you read it, Who are you? Our answer may be, first off, "Christians." But the question persists: What does this mean? What is it that makes us Christians? Here again, we cannot answer the question in isolation, but we have to point to the family to which we belong. We have to trace the events that made this family and brought us within it. To be members of the People of God means to have a special history.

It is the special history of the People of God—in a very abbreviated, bird's-eye view—which we are now to examine. Perhaps it ought to be emphasized, however, that we are not getting ready to study history in the way in which a sophomore, for example, studies History 111 because it's required. Rather it is our purpose to recite the story of our life. The history of the People of God is your history, because these events, that happened "back then," are still alive, still shaping your present, still confronting you with who you are.

❀   ❀   ❀

4

birth of the priestly people

Where does the story of God's people begin? All through the Bible there are road signs and arrows pointing back to a beginning, to a birth of the people. If we follow these clues, we shall discover a central event that overwhelmingly shapes the consciousness of the biblical writers.

The First Letter of Peter is an appropriate place to look for clues, for that letter itself celebrates a beginning. *Read 1 Peter 2:4–10.* Probably this letter was intended as an exhortation to recently baptized Christians in the churches scattered through Asia Minor. If so, then the first readers were newly initiated into this new, "picked-out" race, this consecrated nation (1 Peter 2:9). Yet the history of the race into which they had been initiated is very old. The words are quoted from an ancient saying, addressed originally to Israel (compare Exodus 19:5–6). In the same way, the "once" when they were "no people" points not only to their own immediate past before their Baptism, but also to another "once" when Israel was "no people," and to "mighty deeds" of God through which they, like Israel before them, were "called . . . out of darkness into his marvelous light." This passage says quite clearly that the Christian community did not begin in the first century A.D., but is the continuation and rebirth of Israel. There is a sense in which every Christian is a Jew: the past of Israel is our past; the story of Israel is our story.

If we turn now from Baptism, the sacrament of initiation into the community of God, to Communion, the sacrament of sustenance and renewal of the community, we find again words which point back to the past, to Israel's beginning. *Read 1*

Corinthians 11:23–26. What do these words mean: "This cup is the new covenant in my blood" (v. 25)? This cup of wine we drink stands for something which is called a "covenant." But why a "*new* covenant"? And why is it said that this new covenant is "in Christ's blood"? Why are the sacrifice and covenant celebrated by eating and drinking? The answers to these puzzling questions become somewhat clearer when we follow the clue of the new covenant to look for the foundation of a former covenant. A further decisive clue appears when we recall that the Jewish festival out of which the Communion at least partially derives is the Passover, for the Passover clearly celebrates and preserves in living force one central event: the Exodus.

It is the Exodus that created Israel. This is the birth to which the psalmist points when he sings, "It is [God] that has made us, and we are his" (Ps. 100:3; that creation of the nation, not of individuals, is meant, is shown by the parallel line, "We are his people, and the sheep of his pasture"). This is the event which, beyond all others, gives to the people Israel a burning self-consciousness, the awareness of a unique being and mission.

What Happened?

What was this overwhelming holy event? What happened that so engraved itself on Israel's memory through all coming generations?

There are several ways of asking this question. Usually when we inquire "What happened?" we mean that we want just the facts about an occurrence, and as many of them as possible. When did the trip take place? Who was the Pharaoh who caused all the trouble? Why? Was it the Reed Sea which the Israelites crossed (as the Hebrew Bible says) or the Red Sea (as the Greek translation has it)? In either case, just what body of water was so designated? And what took place there—magic, miracle, or natural phenomenon?

We could spend a great deal of time with these questions.[1] Most of them prove difficult, if not impossible, for a modern historian to decide. Does that mean our question about what really happened has to go unanswered? But there is another way of asking this question. If your roommate comes in looking as if the moonlight had been particularly blinding tonight, and you ask him, "What happened to you?" you do not really expect a statistical report in reply. "At 8:14 P.M. I called for Ann Jones at Harris Hall. At 8:33 P.M. she came downstairs and we drove 2.6 miles to the Armory, where a dance was in progress. The dance lasted until 12:58 A.M." No, no, that is not what you asked. Perhaps, if he is going to answer you at all, "I fell in love," would come nearer telling you what really happened.

Now when we ask the Israelites themselves what happened at the Exodus, their reply sounds like a strange blend of the historian's bare facts and your roommate's new love. Listen: this is the way they used to answer the question during the harvest festival every year:

> 'A wandering Aramean was my father; and he went down into Egypt and sojourned there, few in number; and there he became a nation, great, mighty, and populous. And the Egyptians treated us harshly, and afflicted us, and laid upon us hard bondage. Then we cried to the LORD the God of our fathers, and the LORD heard our voice, and saw our affliction, our toil, and our oppression; and the LORD brought us out of Egypt with a mighty hand and an outstretched arm, with great terror, with signs and wonders; and he brought us into this place and gave us this land, a land flowing with milk and honey.'   (Deuteronomy 26:5–9)

What happened? "The LORD brought us out of Egypt." A modern historian, examining the event, might focus his attention on political developments within Egypt, shifts in the international balance of power, shifts in the economic and social atmosphere of the Middle East, all of which made possible the migration out of Egypt of some seminomadic tribes that had been conscripted for forced labor. Well and good. Israel knew about some of these factors—there are even hints of them in the confession we just quoted. But for them these facts did not explain the Exodus. Behind the social, political, and economic factors, but working in and through them, there was active one whom they call "the LORD."

God Has a Name

Who is this LORD? The "LORD" in our English translations stands for the mysterious Name of God known uniquely by Israel, spoken always with awe and deep reverence, often with fear, but spoken out of the sense that "This is *our* God; he has entered into relationship with us." The name in Hebrew is written YHWH and probably was pronounced "Yah-weh." No one is sure what it meant originally. What is certain is that in the Exodus event YHWH becomes for the Israelites the name of him who speaks to them and to whom they can reply. God has a name: they can call to him.

The close connection of the name Yahweh with the Exodus is shown by the story of Moses and his encounter with Yahweh in Exodus 3. What happens in this marvelous story? Moses is met by the flaming presence of God, who says, "I have seen the affliction of my people who are in Egypt, and have heard their cry because of their taskmasters; I know their sufferings, and I have come down to deliver them . . ." (Exod. 3:7–8). Here is the God with whom we have to do in the Bible—not an aloof, changeless being, no mere First Cause and Unmoved Mover to philosophize about, but a God who sees, hears, and knows the plight of suffering people, and who acts in the midst of history to save them. Of course it is much more uncomfortable to run into this kind of God than the ones we only have to think about. Naturally Moses wants to wriggle out of the assignment God has for him. Don't we all? Groping for a way out, he asks a significant question:

> If I come to the people of Israel and say to them, 'The God of your fathers has sent me to you,' and they ask me, 'What is his name?' what shall I say to them?

God's answer to the question sounds like a riddle: "I AM WHO I AM." Let's look at this answer more closely. Moses asks for God's name; God responds with a verb, *ehyeh*, "I shall be." But this verb "to be" in Hebrew designates a very concrete "being," so concrete that it is often translated "it came to pass," or "it happened." Hence perhaps we should understand what God says to Moses as "I shall be present just as I shall be present,"[2] or even "I shall cause to happen what I shall cause to happen."[3] The dialogue in Exodus 3 suggests that the mysterious name YHWH is to be understood as a form of this same verb, *yahweh,* "he shall be present," so that the name of God points to his faithful, but unpredictable, coming to meet his people in his world, in the events which he causes to happen.

A name gets charged with meaning through the experiences we have that are related to someone bearing that name. A name may be just a name, or it may mean far more to you than you can say. Martha is a common name; but for me it is not a common name, for it is the name of my wife, and to say this word conjures up all that we have been through together. The word YHWH got filled up with meaning through the Exodus—that is, it was filled by the event which Yahweh himself caused to happen. Indeed, the event becomes as it were *part of his name:* "I am Yahweh your God, *who brought you out of the land of Egypt, out of the house of bondage*" (Exod. 20:2; cf. 6:7; 13:9; 29:46; 32:8; Lev. 19:36; 22:33; etc.).

How about it? Does God have a name for you? It is comparatively easy for most of us to say, I believe in God. But what or whom do those letters *G-o-d* point to? Maybe it is significant how frequently the New Testament speaks of "God, who raised Christ Jesus from the dead." That is an exact parallel, you see, to "God, who brought you out of the land of Egypt." The God who has claimed us is not anonymous.

God of Our Fathers

A new event, a new name—but this was not a new God. He is also the "God of Abraham, the God of Isaac, and the God of Jacob." Once the Israelites have a chance to get their breath after the Exodus, they can look back to see that through a long history Yahweh was preparing the foundations for this event which so suddenly erupted into their existence. True, they are something brand-new now: before they were not a nation, now they are. Yet some of them preserve the memory of a family history, beginning with Father Abraham, and this family history becomes, after the Exodus, also the history of the new nation— even of the strangers and newcomers who at various times are drawn into the life of Israel. Yes, it even becomes *our* history, for everyone who belongs by faith to Jesus Christ is one of the children of Abraham (Rom. 4:16; 9:6ff., etc.). We, too, can recite with the Jewish family, "*We* were Pharaoh's bondmen in Egypt: and the LORD our God brought *us* out therefrom with a mighty hand and an outstretched arm."

In the story of Abraham's call, Genesis 12, it is graphically shown that the God of Abraham is the same Yahweh, the same "I shall be present," who plucks Israel out of Egypt. The first word Yahweh speaks to Abraham is "Go!" Here is the same unsettling, uncontrollable God who later will not let Israel vegetate over the "fleshpots of Egypt." God comes to Abraham with a promise: he will lead him on the way he is to go, and he will make of him a great nation which will be the means of blessing for all the world. That is all Abraham gets: just a promise, "I will show you," no road map.

What a peremptory, upsetting, overpowering way God has with his people! But we shall completely misunderstand these stories from the Bible unless we see that God upsets people because he loves them. He will not let Abraham sit still in Haran, because he loves Abraham—and because he loves the world and wants to use Abraham and Abraham's descendents to show the world its real life. That is why Abraham has to leave everything and go—just go, wherever God will lead him.

The last chapters of Genesis are filled with the stories of Abraham's family. Like Abraham himself, these people are always on the move. At first glance, their wanderings seem quite aimless, the kind of to-and-fro you would expect of desert tribes that move from pasture to pasture, now and then spending a while in some civilized area, but never really settling down. At first glance, yes, but there is more to be seen here. These people are not wanderers but pilgrims, whether they know it or not. As we follow their story, we keep running into landmarks which are set up to guide their wanderings—the places where God has come to meet them: Mamre (Gen. 18:1–15; cf. 17:1–21), the birth of Isaac (21:1–2), the offering of Isaac (22), Beth-el (28:10–22), Mahanaim (32:1–2), Peniel (32:22–32), the descent to Egypt (46:1–5), and many others. These people are pilgrims because God is leading them toward something. He is moving them toward the Exodus, the new nation, the covenant, and all that lies beyond that: the salvation of the world.

A People for God

Coming back to the Exodus now from the other direction, out of the age of the Fathers, we see that what is brand-new, emerging out of the event, is a nation. Where before there were these persons, who seem bigger than life, with their families and their immense destinies; now there is a people. Stop and read Exodus 19 and 24, chapters that tell the story of the foundation of the people. The chapters in between (20—23) give its constitution. (As it stands here, much of the material in this constitution, the second portion of which, 20:23—23:19, is called the "Covenant Code," reflects later times. Perhaps we could call it the "amended constitution.")

In chapter 19, we see the Israelites three months out of Egypt. After these months of hard going in the wilderness, they have come to a towering landmark: the awe-inspiring mountain, sometimes called Horeb, sometimes Sinai, where Yahweh has come to meet them. At this point these migrants are not yet a people, nor are they very likely candidates to become one. The three months' forced journey has dampened whatever enthusiasm first prompted them to join Moses in his desperate venture, and they have shown little regard for his leadership. Again and again they have displayed their divisions, their lack of discipline, their disorganization, and their cowardice. They stand before the holy mountain, not as a united people with a national self-consciousness, but as a motley collection of mutually suspicious tribes. Nothing holds them together except their common memory of Egyptian oppression and their common experience of the "wonder" by which they have been set free. We could almost say that these people have been dragged here against their will (Exod. 14:12), that they are not a nation and do not want to be a nation.

But they are not the principal actors in Exodus 19. Who is the subject of the dramatic sentences in verses 4 and 5? "What *I did* . . . how *I bore you* . . ." This is the secret of that dreary march through the wilderness. Before this moment, they were not a people; from this moment on, no matter if new groups join them or new divisions erupt in their midst, they will always perceive themselves as a peculiar people. The difference is the Lord's doing. The Exodus, which first they greeted as a miracle beyond comprehension and then, in the wilderness, as terrifying confusion and hardship, now eyes of faith perceive to be a mighty outpouring of God's free grace. Even the terrors of the wilderness are now revealed to be God's carrying them, as an eagle was thought to carry its young, on lofty wings to bring them to himself.

To the act of grace they must now respond. "Now, therefore, if you will obey my voice and keep my covenant, you shall be my own possession among all peoples . . ." (19:5). The life of God's people will be a life lived in dialogue, in hearing God's word and making answer to it. God has spoken—he is always the one who initiates the life-conversation—and his speaking was the very historical event which set Israel free from Egypt. The liberation not only speaks to them; it also creates the possibility of their answering, for now they are a free independent community, able to take upon themselves an obligation. Just as God's speaking to them, his call, was not merely verbal but a historical act, so their reply has to be not just talk, but life. Henceforth, if they will accept God's offer, theirs is to be a life in *covenant*. A covenant is not the same thing as a contract, for in the case of this covenant, the two partners are clearly not on the same level. Instead, a free and absolutely sovereign king *gives* the covenant to his vassal. At Sinai, Yahweh offers to bind himself to Israel if they will keep his covenant. For his part, he will be their God, he will lead them, as he led Abraham, Isaac, and Jacob through the unknown, and he will bear them as he has borne them in the Exodus. Their part is to be his people, to follow him wherever he may lead, and to obey him unconditionally.

The structure for keeping the covenant is the Law. The Law does not define all possible obligations, but only points to the absolute claim laid on all life by the God who created the people. Obeying the laws can never be a way of laying claim on God, of earning his pleasure—though later generations were so to misunderstand the Law. God's grace comes *first*, then he gives the Law, just as in a family parents must first give love and unqualified acceptance to their children and only then, on the foundation of this grace, can they realistically require obedience and discipline. Moreover, these laws were not intended just to make communal life more livable, but to provide the guideposts for Israel to grow into the kind of community God could use for his mission to the world. Indeed the Jews refer to the Law as *Torah*, which means "teaching," "guidance."

The Law ("all the words of Yahweh," Exod. 24:3) is announced to the assembled people, and they respond, "All the words which Yahweh has spoken we will do." Now they are ready for the solemn ratification of the covenant itself, which is described in Exodus 24:4-11. There are five steps mentioned: (1) building an altar and setting up memorial pillars as a visible reminder of the unification of the tribes, (2) offering of sacrifices, (3) the reading of the "book of the covenant," and the people's response, (4) sprinkling of the blood of the sacrificed animals on the altar and on the people, and (5) a ceremonial meal.

The last two steps are especially puzzling to our modern minds. First of all, in order to understand the meaning of the blood of the covenant, we must remember that for ancient peoples, blood was regarded as the very essence of life. When an animal was sacrificed, the blood was carefully retained to be the vehicle of union between God and man. When Moses offers half of the blood to God and sprinkles the other half on the people, then symbolically God and the people come to participate in a common life. In similar fashion, the ceremonial meal of the representatives of Israel in the presence of God is a further expression of the fellowship into which God has now entered with them.

On this basis can you see why the central act of Christian worship is a ceremonial eating and drinking? Who is present with us at our meal, and what event of the past does it bring alive into our present? Do you see why, in the Words of the Institution, we are told, "This cup is the New Covenant in [Christ's] blood"?

The covenant is established. The dialogue is begun. From this moment on, Israel knows itself to be a people—a people under orders. Now it is ready to set out on the long journey which leads into its unknown future. Its leader on the journey will be the one who is present to them *as he will be present*, who speaks to them his free word, who causes always the unexpected, the new thing, to happen. But wherever he leads, light on their way will shine from this holy event when he first created and claimed them, and those whom he appoints to be their guides will ever and again point back to this constituting moment as the source for understanding every new situation.

5

the flame of holy love

There in the wilderness, with the wonder of their miraculous escape still burning in their memory, the Israelites could readily cling to Yahweh as the Leader-God, who had burst suddenly into their existence and now moved ever before them, proceeding always into the unknown, preparing again and again to amaze them with some event utterly new, and holding before them his constant promise of a land that would be their own. But when that promise was fulfilled, what then? With the Jordan crossed, the decisive battles won, the hill-country taken, and Palestine stretched before them with its walled cities, its ancient vineyards and olive groves and grain fields—what would Yahweh's leading mean here? Could the God of the desert and the road be also the God of the vineyard and grain field? Could he who had led them successfully in battle "with a strong hand and an outstretched arm" win for them also the struggle with the unknown mysteries of the soil and seed? Conquest of Palestine and beginning of settlement there marks the end of the first stage of Israel's apprenticeship as the People of Yahweh. Now there began another great test, more dangerous than the sojourn in the wilderness, a test of their faithfulness and their capacity to perceive the nature of the God who had called them to be his own.

Sheepherders to Homesteaders

As any fan of Western motion pictures knows, transforming sheepherders into homesteaders would be a complex and frustrating task in any age. For some of these homesteaders then to take the further enormous step to become city-dwellers, tradesmen, manufacturers, and merchants involves changes in ways of living, thinking, and acting that are almost revolutionary. Anyone who has looked with care at the rapid changes taking place in the southern United States, not to mention the far more explosive changes in the so-called "underdeveloped lands" will be aware of the human dislocations and tensions that result in these circumstances. In the period of Israel's history which we are now considering—a broad sweep in time from the eleventh century B.C. until the sixth—both these extraordinary transitions occurred in the life of the Twelve Tribes. Through the biblical narratives, we get accurate glimpses of the far-reaching social, economic, and political crises which confronted the nation. But the biblical writers—and in particular the strange group of men with whom we are now most concerned, the prophets—saw in these human crises a deeper crisis of faith. In each social change, each shift of economic power, each political challenge, their ears heard the question, What will be Israel's relation to their God, Yahweh, who had brought them into being at the Exodus?

Looking back from a later vantage point to the first stage of the long struggle, the book of Judges puts the faith-question in a nutshell. The successful campaign to win strategic dominion over the land of Palestine has just been described, and the death of Joshua, Israel's leader in that struggle, has been recorded:

> And all that generation also were gathered to their fathers; and there arose another generation after them, who did not know Yahweh or the work which he had done for Israel. And the people of Israel did what was evil in the sight of Yahweh and served the Baals; and they forsook Yahweh, the God of their fathers, who had brought them out of the land of Egypt; they went after other gods, from among the gods of the peoples who were round about them, and bowed down to them; and they provoked Yahweh to anger. They forsook Yahweh, and served the Baals and the Ashtaroth.
> (Judges 2:10–13)

With the hindsight of the writer of Judges or with the insight of the prophets before him, it was apparent that "serving" the

"Baals and the Ashtaroth" meant "forsaking Yahweh." If we consider the situation into which the Israelites were suddenly thrust when they settled in the Land of Promise, we will see how very strong the temptation was to give up their faith. A seminomadic people for generations, the Israelites had met Yahweh at the mountain in the wilderness. As the "God of their Fathers," he seemed somehow tied to their fathers' way of life. They knew the ways of sheep and goats, the technique of camping, breaking camp, moving on with their flocks to new pasture. They had long ago learned the tricks of the desert. But now these rough, cunning, independent people had entered a very different world. That one could bury a dead kernel in the soil and then from that spot see a living plant emerge to grow and bear grain was to their eyes a frightening mystery. The pruning of the white-green shoots from the gnarled olive trees was a strange process. The vines bore fruit whose juice when fermented attained magical powers, singing in the blood and putting a strange new spirit in a man's heart.

Moreover, while on the surface the life of the farmer seemed far more settled and secure than that of a homeless herdsman, they soon saw that farming was precarious in a different way. One season the fields would flourish and bumper crops would be stored away, with great celebration, for the winter, but another time the same fields might wither and turn brown before the harvest, or unseasonable rains, hail, or wind might make havoc of the neat hillside patches. Who could predict the result of his planting? How could one secure his life against the whims of nature? The peoples round about them, the Canaanites who still lived among them (Judges 2:21–23, cf. 3:1–6), had an answer, an answer as natural and convincing to them as crop rotation and artificial fertilizers are to our farmers. But this was the twelfth century B.C.; for the Canaanites not science, but religion was the answer to the problem of agriculture. Precisely those deities whose names appear so often—and with such disfavor—in the biblical narratives, those Ba'alim and Ashtaroth, were the ones with whom one had to deal if he wanted successful crops.

Orgies and Agriculture

The Canaanite gods were violent, passionate figures whose actions mythically reflected the violent changes of nature and especially the cycle of the seasons. The head god was El (*"the god"*), whose wife was Ashirat (in the Bible she appears as Asherah). This pair was not so important in the popular religion, however. The main actors were Ba'al and Anath. Ba'al was the Sky-god, the Storm-god, the Rider-of-Clouds, in short, the god of the powerful, life-giving fluids and forces. Anath was goddess of earth, the mother of all living things. Their annual mating was the focal point of Canaanite religion.

The mysterious cycle of seasons—from the death of vegetation in winter to the burial of new seed, the descent of rain, and the springing forth of newborn vegetation and at last the harvest and the repeated death of all—is "explained" in a great myth of Ba'al and Anath. Ba'al is overcome by Mot, "Death," god of the underworld (the fields languish and die). Anath mourns for Ba'al and goes into the underworld to search for him. She kills Mot in a terrible battle, grinds him to flour, and scatters his pulverized corpse on the earth (the fields are planted with new grain). Ba'al is revived by this sympathetic magic, and he and Anath are reunited. Their union produces as "offspring" all the fruit of the earth (the fields sprout, bloom, and bear again).[1]

In every plot of ground the Hebrews undertook to till, they met the Ba'al. Ba'al was not one god, but many. Each tract of land had its own Ba'al and Anath, its Lord and Lady. Deep beneath the soil they struggled and loved—otherwise no crops could be expected. But how could anyone predict, or better, control, the strange love affair of those gods? Here the primitive concept of sympathetic magic comes to the aid of the farmer. If a primitive man wanted rain he might, for example, climb into a tree and pour water downward, by this dramatic action hoping to demonstrate to the gods just what was wanted, and in fact magically to influence them to do it. If you reflect on the fact that what was desired in the Canaanite view of agriculture was the sexual union of Ba'al and Anath, then you will understand the disgust with which Israel's prophets regarded this religion. The religious rites of Baalism were in fact performed by prostitutes (known as "the holy ones") both male and female. The "worship" was an orgy.

Baalism came to the Israelites as an overpowering but subtle temptation. They did not see Ba'al as a rival god to Yahweh, but simply as operating a different department. Yahweh was unquestionably the God of war and of history; he was their leader—if they were going somewhere. But what did the God of the road have to do with agriculture?

A King like All the Nations

The tension between Israel's pilgrim faith in Yahweh and the magic of culture reached a new intensity when Israel became a monarchy, roughly two centuries after entering Canaan. The covenant had made the Hebrew tribes into a confederation of worship. They were held together solely by their common reliance upon Yahweh and their responsibility to him, not by any sort of political organization. Yahweh himself was regarded as the only king the confederation had or needed. In times of particular stress, Yahweh's "stormy spirit" would rush upon some individual, who then became the Great King's deputy for the rest of his life, to judge Israel, that is, to vindicate the cause of justice, both by conducting guerrilla warfare against oppressors and by acting as a magistrate to settle internal disputes. When the judge died, the central government died with him, and the suggestion that his son should succeed him, thus beginning a royal dynasty, was rejected as a sign of unbelief (Judges 8:23).

Modern warfare changed all that. When Israel's enemies introduced new superweapons, such as camels and iron-plated war chariots, it was evident that they had adopted a policy of "overkill." If Israel was going to survive, it needed a government able to mobilize all the resources of the tribes and to keep them at a high level of preparedness. The answer seemed to be a king.

Apparently not everyone in Israel agreed with this solution. According to one view expressed in First Samuel, the anointing of the first king, even though it was performed as a sacred setting-apart of a man chosen by Yahweh himself, was a compromise of true faith. Samuel accompanied the anointing of Saul with a solemn warning that the people did not know what they were getting themselves into (1 Sam. 8:10–18, compare 12:6–25).

Saul still resembled the spirit-led judges more than an Oriental king. It remained for David, by exercising fantastic military and political shrewdness, to bind the northern and southern tribes together under his sole power, and for Solomon his son to construct a little empire from Dan to Beersheba, complete with the trappings of an Eastern court and harem. Solomon achieved his success only at the cost of alienating many of his people by his attempt to change the whole pattern of their life, even to the point of using Israelites in forced labor battalions. When he died a revolution took place, and the kingdom was split into a northern part, henceforth known as Israel, with its capital in the new city of Samaria, and a southern part, known by the name of its major tribe as Judah, with Jerusalem as capital. The kings of Judah and Israel, as the editors of the books of Kings never tire of reminding us, fulfilled the worst predictions of those who had feared a kingdom.

The faithful adherents to the covenant saw in the kingdom principally two temptations. First was the tendency to make religion serve royal and national interests. This purpose was implicit in the erection of Solomon's Temple, as one building in the king's great palace-complex. Again it is seen in the appointment of priests by the kings and, in later periods, in the bands of hired prophets kept at the king's beck and call, to prophesy only the things he wanted to hear (1 Kings 22). The second temptation was that of syncretism ("mixing"), that is, that the Yahweh faith would be adulterated with practices and deities from other religions, especially Baalism. Before, Baalism had been practiced as a kind of magical cult, more or less private, while all public worship had been directed to Yahweh. But with the involved international politics of the new kingdom, Baals and other gods came to be officially imported, especially in connection with private chapels for the foreign wives in the kings' harems (1 Kings 11), and also in relation to certain treaties with foreign powers (2 Kings 16:10–16).

Besides these specifically religious challenges to the faith of the fathers, were the more general attractions of advanced culture and technology in themselves—something like the process which we in our time usually call "secularism." In the desert, these vulnerable bands of ex-slaves were utterly dependent upon Yahweh their God. But as years passed and their situation in Palestine became more settled and comfortable, the illusion of their independent security grew. Had they not by their own hands and hard work built the prosperity they enjoyed? Surely God helped those who helped themselves.

Not only was their relation to God endangered by the very success of their economy, but the same was true of their relation to each other. There in the desert, every man *had* to be his brother's keeper, or all would be lost. The sense that all were equally dependent upon the blessing of Yahweh for everything they possessed led to a vigorous practical democracy, at least within each tribe, and class distinctions were few. The nomad usually became distinguished by heroic action on behalf of the whole people, not by amassing a fortune for himself. In the settled land, however, values became different. Prosperity brought with it stratification of the society, setting landowners against peasants and leading to the exploitation of the poor by the rich. As we shall see, these developments, too, amounted to a falling away from the Yahweh faith, indeed a violation of the covenant which Yahweh had given them.

God's Angry Men

The enormous changes in Israel's life which we have just surveyed seriously endangered the covenant relationship. Could the memory of the God who was utterly free, who could not be "used" by men, remain central to their faith? Would the love of this God, his free act claiming them for his own by liberating them from oppression, stand up against the new religiosity of Canaan? Would the sense of mission implied by being "Yahweh's people," the kingdom of priests for the world, remain a living force in the face of temptations to fight the world for a place in the sun?

There were no easy answers to these questions, just as there are no easy answers to the church's questions today, as we live through rapidly changing times. *Can the church still be the church when it is no longer a struggling minority, but a wealthy majority? Can it become responsibly involved in the life of the communities around it without becoming just another social group? Can it find ways to speak understandably to people in new situations with new problems, without losing sight of what God did once for all?*

First of all, the memory of the great events by which God created his people had to be kept alive. It was this memory that had made Israel Israel. The fact that the traditions of those events, long kept alive by word of mouth, were gathered and written down in the form that we now read them in our Bibles is itself a sign of the struggle that was going on. For example, the stories which we read in chapters 3 and 4 in this book served once as powerful sermons calling Israel to return to its real foundation. They helped shape the nation's worship, legal procedures, and daily life.

But just keeping the memory alive was not enough. That can always take the form of mere romanticism, which imagines that all the troubles are caused by the newfangled ideas of the present and wants to flee away into the good old days of the past. There were people like that in Israel, of course. One group, the Rechabites, were determined to stay nomads. The old-time religion was good enough for them: they went on living in tents, herding sheep, as if nothing had changed since those years in the desert (Jeremiah 35:1–11). Maybe their protest stirred the conscience of some Israelites, just as the Mennonites, the Amish, and other groups have occasionally stung Protestant consciences by their attempts to live a simple life close to the primitive Christianity they see in the New Testament. But the Rechabites left no word behind for us; they were remembered only because the prophets wrote about them.

Men had to be found who would embody the tensions of the

times by holding firmly to the faith of the past without running from the life of the present. Out of the old words someone had to hear a new word for the new age. These men were found—or created. They were the prophets, and there was nothing like them in all the ancient world. Born out of the nature of the covenant itself, they were raised up as utterly free men, without any visible power, by the God who used them as his spokesmen.[2]

Look at these men: Here is Nathan, who stands before his king and with utmost clarity denounces the monarch's adultery and murder with the decisive words, "You are the man!" (2 Sam. 12.) Here is Elijah, standing alone against the power of King Ahab and his foreign queen Jezebel, who was trying to enforce Baalism as the only legal religion in Israel. Challenging Ba'al on his own ground—control of rain and drought (1 Kings 17:1; 18:44ff.) and the forces of the sky (18:20–40)—Elijah showed that Yahweh was Lord, not just of the old desert life, but also of the new culture.[3]

Good Times and Safe Religion

A century after the time of Elijah, the new culture of Israel and Judah had reached still greater heights, and the prophets confronted yet more serious challenges. Their responses to these challenges have given us the great prophetic books of the Old Testament, which consist of oracles spoken during the eighth, seventh, and sixth centuries, later written down, principally by disciples of the prophets, and carefully preserved.

The eighth century opened an era of peace and prosperity in both the Northern and Southern Kingdoms which was never equaled before or after.[4] The combination of weak enemies abroad and strong kings at home produced a comfortable security. Both Joash and his son Jeroboam II in the north and in the south the Uzziah whose death is recalled in Isaiah's temple vision (Isa. 6) were able military leaders and competent domestic organizers. Under their protection and leadership, not only did agriculture flourish, but Israelites entered a new field, trade. For the first time business became a major occupation, and a money economy catapulted Israel and Judah into a great boom. Now it suddenly became possible for an individual in this hard-bitten country to become rich, and this opportunity called forth a merchant class of people determined to climb to the top—no matter how many others they might have to trample on the way.

As we have observed in modern times, the transition from agricultural to commercial economy brings with it the growth of cities, and that was true of the kingdoms of Israel. All the prophecies of this century were spoken in towns, and especially in the capital cities, Samaria and Jerusalem. There we hear of the enormous expansion of private building. No longer are houses of adobe sufficient for the merchants and landowners: now it must be houses of hewn stone, decorated with ivory (undoubtedly split-level with stereophonic psalteries), and many seekers of status have both winter houses and summer houses. Speculators in real estate lie awake nights devising schemes for accumulating more land. For the wealthy, there is newfound leisure—time for dinner parties, jam sessions, and drinking bouts (Amos 6:4–6). The wives of the wealthy spend their time grooming themselves, inventing new hairdos and experimenting with the latest cosmetics, practicing the coquettish walk and posture (you can picture them standing before their mirrors with the latest issue of *Vogue* in hand) which is considered fashionable (Isaiah 3:16, 18). But all of this costs money, so they are continually driving their husbands to get more and more, however they can (Amos 4:1).

If urbanization and commercial ventures bring unheard-of wealth to the lucky, the strong, and the unscrupulous, they bring unheard-of poverty to others, the exploited. Many of the poor are tricked out of their land and reduced to the virtual slavery of sharecroppers (Micah 2:2, 8–9). Canny traders entice them into debt, just to seize their collateral, until their very clothes are taken off their backs (Amos 2:8). Some of the most vehement protests of the great prophets are directed against this kind of exploitation. No wonder they are attacked as meddlers in social and political issues. Very often they must have heard the warning, "Do not preach . . . one should not preach of such things" (Micah 2:6).

In all the preoccupation of Israel's newly rich class with profit, building, and pleasure, however, it cannot be said that they neglect religion. On the contrary, the age of prosperity brings with it a widespread religious revival. The Temple and all the local shrines are so filled with worshipers that they "trample the courts." "Come to Bethel!" they shout gaily to each other. "Go to church on Sunday!" Laymen take a great interest in the affairs of the church, meticulously bringing their sacrifices every morning and their tithes every three days—never mind how they got the money—even bringing extra and unusually liberal offerings—carefully publicized, of course (Amos 4:4–5).

But is this the religion of the covenant? To be sure, Yahweh is being worshiped—of course, these are Yahweh's people, are they not? Yahweh is the one who protects them, wards off their enemies. That is why it is important to be regular in the religious duties. On the other hand, there are some other aspects of life where the old-fashioned covenant laws seem out of date. What if a man takes extra precautions by visiting the Ba'al shrine on occasion—one cannot afford to take chances in things like crop insurance and making certain he will have plenty of sons—what of that? Surely Yahweh and his priests can afford to be broad-minded; they get their due. And the Ba'al ritual is very sincere, indeed very moving. After all, it is not *what* you believe so much as *that* you believe . . .

An Overwhelming Message

What does God say to his people when they have turned his covenant with them into either a worthless document or a blank check? When religion becomes a mask for injustice, grease on the skids of personal ambition and undisciplined self-indulgence, what is the word from the covenant? It is time we listened to one of those spokesmen whom God raised up.

Come and stand before Hosea the son of Beeri, prophet of Israel, and listen with your soul to the cry that is wrenched from the depths of his agonized existence, yet springs from his lips with clarity, power, and strange beauty. I suggest that you *read the book of Hosea all the way through at one sitting*. When you

have finished, then *study the first three chapters more carefully.*
To sharpen your perception, a few preliminary questions may
help. Look for references to the developments we have mentioned
in religion and society. Also look for references to the Exodus and
the covenant. What symbolic figures does Hosea use to describe
the covenant relationship between Yahweh and his people?
Which of these forms the basic parable? How is this parable
related to Hosea's own life? What are the two opposite themes of
Hosea's message to Israel?

*   *   *

Now that you have read Hosea, you can begin to see what
the peculiar assignment of the prophet is, and just what kind of
words these are. Above all, the prophet is a *messenger.* His job is
simply to deliver the word he has been given. That is why we
hear over and over again in all the prophetic books, "Thus says
the Lord." That is the regular formula used when somebody
sends word by a runner to someone else, for example, "And
Jacob sent messengers before him to Esau . . . instructing them,
'Thus you shall say to my lord Esau: Thus says your servant
Jacob . . .'" (Genesis 32:3f.). The message the prophet has to
tell is not his own; the "I" who speaks throughout chapter 2 of
Hosea is not Hosea but Yahweh.

Do you see how this "word of the Lord" brings the Exodus
and the covenant vividly into the present horizon of the people?
Yahweh was the God who *spoke* to his people in the Exodus and
at Sinai. The covenant was sealed by those people who could
respond, "All that the Lord has spoken, we will do" (Exod. 19:8).
But the God who spoke in the Exodus is still speaking in the
prophetic word. To have Yahweh's covenant means not to rest
secure on a settled constitution, but to have one's ears open and
one's heart ready for the ever *new* speaking of God.

Hosea is a messenger—but not just a Western Union boy
who can slide his sealed announcement under the door. The
word from Yahweh is something that seizes and flows through
the messenger's whole self. That is why, alongside the "I" of
Yahweh,

Ephraim is stricken,
  their root is dried up,
  they shall bear no fruit.
Even though they bring forth,
  I will slay their beloved children.
                              (Hosea 9:16)

we hear also the "I" of Hosea speaking:

My God will cast them off,
  because they have not hearkened to him;
  they shall be wanderers among the nations.
                              (9:17)

We find Hosea even telling us something about his own life in
chapter 3; and in chapter 1, one of his disciples, talking about
Hosea now in the third person, tells us more. All of this belongs
somehow to the message. It is not Hosea's words alone, but his
whole life that has been commandeered by God. Commandeered,
yet not in such a way that Hosea becomes a mere tool in God's
hands, for we hear him struggling with the message, agonizing
with it as it seeks to take shape in his own acting and speaking.

The way God's word takes over the messenger's life shows up
clearly in the *acted parables* with which the prophets frequently
address the people. For example, Jeremiah makes a yoke, and,
wearing it on his neck, walks through the streets of Jerusalem to
say, "Bring your necks under the yoke of the king of Babylon
. . ." (Jer. 27:1–15), and Isaiah before him had walked the same
streets "naked and barefoot for three years as a sign and a
portent against Egypt and Ethiopia" (Isa. 20:3). There is an
acted parable in Hosea, too. In fact, it stands at the center of his
message: the parable is nothing less than his whole married life.

A Wife of Harlotry

The first word Yahweh speaks to Hosea attacks him like a
hammer: "Go, take to yourself a wife of harlotry and have
children of harlotry." Do you hear the voice of that same commanding God who spoke to Abraham, the same "Go!" that tears

him up from the roots of all that is normal and pleasant and secure, and hurls him into the unknown? "So he went." This echo we have also heard before; for thus, unquestioning, Abraham also went, alone, unseeing, mapless, but trusting. Can you keep reading past that call and that response? Can you stand up to the words which may come through such a man?

The suggestion that God commanded one of his prophets to marry a prostitute has caused the readers of this passage all kinds of trouble. Many commentators have insisted that the marriage is only an allegory. But the plain sense of the text and the sober, realistic language (1:3; 2:2) count against that interpretation. Again, some have argued that it was only later, looking back over a tragic marriage, that Hosea perceived that somehow this was God's will. Yet 1:2 says, "When the LORD *first* spoke through Hosea . . ." For this writer, it seems better not to try to take the sharp edges off the command, but to try to understand what word of God was being announced in this extreme way.[5]

As scholars have learned more about the customs of those times, the probable meaning of the "wife of harlotry" has become clearer. In the ancient Near East it was very common for young women about to be married to go first to a shrine—in Palestine it would be a shrine dedicated to Ba'al or Ashtarte—and there to sacrifice her virginity to the deity by serving as a prostitute for a time. In return she expected assurance of fertility in marriage. It is likely that Gomer was such a girl, "one of those marriageable young women who had undergone the bridal initiation rite, customary in Israel for some time, that is, a typical 'modern' Israelite girl, easily recognizable by the cult-symbol she wore."[6] In this case it becomes clear that the important thing about this marriage is not that Hosea marries a woman who is immoral. The point is that this sexual religion, now taken for granted, is only one concrete instance of the way the entire nation "commits great harlotry by forsaking the LORD" (Hosea 1:2). God has directed Hosea to embody in his own marriage the relationship which now exists between God and Israel.

Yahweh is married to Israel! Here Hosea takes up the Baalists' own language and turns it against them. If they imagine that their prosperity depends upon the on-again, off-again mating of Ba'al and Anath, the Sky and the Earth, then their religion has fallen to the level of prostitution. The "spirit of whoredom" pervades their moral life (4:14), their meaningless religiosity (4:4–9), their business dealings (12:7), their political scheming and *coups d'etat* (7:6–7; 8:4; compare 2 Kings 15:8–18), their international "silly-dove" diplomacy (Hosea 7:11; 8:7–10). Yet the truth is that Yahweh wooed and claimed Israel in the Exodus and the wilderness, binding her to him with the marriage vows of the covenant. Israel's infidelity to the covenant is nothing less than a flouting of the marital bond.

What does the covenant now mean for Israel? It means that God must "cast them off" (9:17). They have broken the covenant; it is null and void. The word of God is that Israel is divorced: "she is not my wife, and I am not her husband" (2:2). Hosea's children, with the bizarre names he is ordered to give them, become signs of this utter rejection: "Jezreel" for the bloody deeds of Jehu in the valley of Jezreel, which will be avenged by the destruction of Jehu's dynasty; "Not Pitied" and "Not my People" for the severing of Yahweh's relation to Israel. The covenant had been summed up in the solemn words, "I will take you for my people, and I will be your God" (Exod. 6:7). With equal solemnity the prophetic message cancels those words: "You are not my people and I am not your God" (Hosea 1:9).

Is the rejection permanent? Is this a final divorce? Everything in the situation of Israel leads Hosea to believe so. Despite all that Yahweh has done with Israel, their perversion is hopeless. "Their deeds do not permit them to return to their God" (5:4). Instead of the Spirit of God, they are controlled by the spirit of harlotry. They may seem to repent in time of trouble, but their repentance is flippant, like the reported quip of the German poet Heinrich Heine on his deathbed, "God will pardon me; that is his business." That mood of penitence passes like the mist and dew on a hot morning, turning into routine and entirely superficial religion (5:15—6:6). Therefore they must be utterly destroyed. Thus Hosea speaks like a bailiff in God's courtroom, announcing the legal sentence of doom.

The Incredible Lover

All logic, all passion, all realism compels Hosea to accept this heavy sentence as the last word. But something will not let him rest with the verdict of divorce and death, and this growing, unreasonable conviction at last bursts into his consciousness as a new word from the Lord:

> And the LORD said to me, "Go again, love a woman who is beloved of a paramour and is an adulteress; even as the LORD loves the people of Israel, though they turn to other gods and love cakes of raisins."   (Hosea 3:1)

Again that hammer-word, "Go!" and again he goes. He goes in love, driven by love far beyond all law and reason. Again, it is God's word that he acts out in a living parable. Gomer, we now discover, has become the property, the concubine, of another man. How this happened, we are not told. Apparently that is not important. What we are told is that God commands him to *love* this woman—and he does. He goes and buys her back from the slavery to which she has sold herself (3:2). Now legally this is impossible, as Deuteronomy 24:1–4 makes perfectly clear. A woman, once divorced and married to another man, could never return to the first husband. And for an adulteress the law provided the death penalty. But God's command here cuts right across the law. Hosea is to *love* Gomer, and even God's law must not stand in the way of God's love.

Is not the fantastic love which drives Hosea the very love with which Yahweh loves his people? The very sternness of his rejection, his refusal to pretend that sin is not sin, is but the reverse side of his love. If Israel is "cast off," then that casting off will be transformed into another sojourn in the wilderness, a New Exodus (2:14–20) from which will come a renewed and lasting covenant.

Such love is not easy to believe. Throughout the later oracles that fill the remainder of the book, we can see Hosea still hurled back and forth between the two poles of God's "fierce anger" and his tender wooing. When we consider the historical events that

followed, we have to ask the question anew, was there hope for
Israel in Yahweh's purpose? For not many years after Hosea's
last prophecy, the Northern Kingdom was utterly crushed by
the might of Assyria, its leading citizens killed or carried into
exile, never to be heard of again, its land resettled with foreigners. A little more than a century later a similar fate would
befall Judah at the hand of Babylonia. Humanly speaking, all
was lost, all hope now gone. But Hosea was not humanly
speaking. The word of hope he could not help speaking came
from beyond all human hopes:

> How can I give you up, O Ephraim!
>   How can I hand you over, O Israel!
> How can I make you like Admah!
>   How can I treat you like Zeboiim!
> My heart recoils within me,
>   my compassion grows warm and tender.
> I will not execute my fierce anger,
>   I will not again destroy Ephraim;
> for I am God and not man,
>   the Holy One in your midst,
>   and I will not come to destroy.   (Hosea 11:8–9)

Through his own tragic life, love drives Hosea to grasp this
"impossible possibility" as the meaning of what God is doing in
the world. Thus he points far beyond his own age, to the time
when "God shows his love for us in that while we were yet
sinners Christ died for us" (Rom. 5:8).

The prophets of Israel stand always on the razor edge between
the old and the new. Facing new currents of life that threaten
the meaning of Israel's covenant existence, they begin by demanding that Israel "Stand by the roads, and look, and ask
for the ancient paths" (Jer. 6:16). The Exodus, the wilderness
wandering, and the covenant at Sinai comprise a once-for-all
event, the one that creates Israel. But it must not become just
something that happened once, while everyday life goes on,
getting what is to be gotten, paying respects to whatever gods
might claim attention.

In the same way our covenant life as Christians begins with certain facts about Jesus. But if the Crucifixion and Resurrection become mere happenings "once upon a time," if they cease to be living and present events, shaping our lives now, then God has to take his church into the wilderness again, to purge and renew her love. That is the trip Hosea takes us on, leading us into new and unexpected places, teaching us to listen again for that word that speaks like fire, which says, "Go!" and we must go.

6

behold my servant

When the Northern Kingdom fell in 721 B.C., after a painful three-year siege, one pole of Hosea's paradox had been fulfilled. The doom had fallen; Yahweh's decree of divorce from the harlot-people was pronounced with the awful finality of death and deportation. The future of this people had been blotted out; every political reality decreed that they would never return. No room was left for hope in the day of their destruction.

Yet hope refused to die. The other pole of Hosea's paradox persisted in the consciousness of at least some of the Israelites who survived the end of their nation. How do we know this? It is apparent in the fact that their books were preserved. In the chaos of Samaria's last days, someone—we shall never know who—gathered up the book of Hosea's prophecies, together with the other great books and traditions which had grown up in the Northern Kingdom, and fled with them to the south. How this was done, we do not know. We do know that they were brought, for their richness is now part of our Bible, and we know that their preservation meant that someone hoped. Someone believed that Yahweh would still—beyond the disaster—create a future for Israel in his own way and his own time. For that future, the story of Yahweh's actions in Israel's history had to be kept alive.

Could Judah be the bearer of that future? That depended upon the Southern Kingdom's learning the lesson preached to the Northern Kingdom by Amos and Hosea, a lesson driven emphatically home by that nation's destruction.

There were some in Judah who had learned that lesson. Through the next century and a half, as Judah swayed between enjoyment of good times at home and desperate anxiety about the international situation, a series of great prophets raised their voices in warning. Among them were Isaiah, Micah, and Jeremiah, whose words have been preserved in part. The final verdict of the prophets was that Judah had gone the way of Israel. Jeremiah, recalling Hosea's living parable, summed up the perversity of his people this way:

> The LORD said to me in the days of King Josiah: "Have you seen what she did, that faithless one, Israel, how she went up on every high hill and under every green tree, and there played the harlot? And I thought, 'After she has done all this she will return to me'; but she did not return, and her false sister Judah saw it. She saw that for all the adulteries of that faithless one, Israel, I had sent her away with a decree of divorce; yet her false sister Judah did not hear, but she too went and played the harlot. Because harlotry was so light to her, she polluted the land, committing adultery with stone and tree. Yet for all this her false sister Judah did not return to me with her whole heart, but in pretense, says the LORD." (Jeremiah 3:6–10)

A miraculous escape from siege in the time of Isaiah (701 B.C.) had convinced many Jerusalemites that, no matter what God had done to Israel, he would protect Judah. Words of the prophets like those just quoted from Jeremiah did not shake that simpleminded faith, but history did. God's decree of divorce had to fall on both halves of the people.

The verdict was executed by Babylonia, Assyria's conqueror and successor as the world power. In 597 B.C. Judah was invaded and several thousand of the leading citizens deported to Babylonia. Judah became a satellite of Babylonia, with a puppet king on its throne. Soon even the puppet Zedekiah was enticed into a conspiracy against Babylonia, and a tragically impotent rebellion was attempted. Nebuchadnezzar, the Babylonian king, marched his troops back into Judah and laid siege to Jerusalem. As the professional prophets parroted the former words of Isaiah, that Yahweh would protect his holy city, Jeremiah prowled the city, announcing that Yahweh would destroy it. Only those who submitted to God's judgment by surrendering to Babylonia would save their lives (2 Kings 24 and 25).

The Day of His Fierce Anger

When the end came (587 B.C.) it was not only the walls of Jerusalem which were broken down: the logic of life, the whole web of reason that gave meaning to events and assigned purpose to the march of Israel's history, shattered on that day. The bewildering confusion of the dying city, now swarming with foreign troops and soon to be filled with rubble and flame, was not more terrifying than the chaos which filled the minds and emotions of the defeated people. The terror of that hour still cries out in the poetry of the exile that followed:

> How the gold has grown dim,
>   how the pure gold is changed!
> The holy stones lie scattered
>   at the head of every street.
> The precious sons of Zion,
>   worth their weight in fine gold,
> how they are reckoned as earthen pots,
>   the work of a potter's hands!
> Even the jackals give the breast
>   and suckle their young,
> but the daughter of my people has become cruel,
>   like the ostriches in the wilderness.
> The tongue of the nursling cleaves
>   to the roof of its mouth for thirst;
> the children beg for food,
>   but no one gives to them.
> Those who feasted on dainties
>   perish in the streets;
> those who were brought up in purple
>   lie on ash heaps.
> For the chastisement of the daughter
>   of my people has been greater
>   than the punishment of Sodom,
> which was overthrown in a moment,
>   no hand being laid on it.

Her princes were purer than snow,
   whiter than milk;
their bodies were more ruddy than coral,
   the beauty of their form was like sapphire.
Now their visage is blacker than soot,
   they are not recognized in the streets;
their skin has shriveled upon their bones,
   it has become as dry as wood.
Happier were the victims of the sword
   than the victims of hunger,
who pined away, stricken
   by want of the fruits of the field.
The hands of compassionate women
   have boiled their own children;
they became their food
   in the destruction of the daughter of my people.

                                (Lamentations 4:1–10)

Again the Babylonians carried out their policy of deporting all persons thought capable of leading a rebellion. Through yawning gaps in the blasted wall they were led out, picking their way over rubble and corpses. The long line of silent captives, men, women, and children stumbling under heavy bundles, creaking wagons carrying plunder and women with nursing infants, wound slowly down from the dead city, through the narrow, rough valleys, while above on the hills neighboring tribes gathered to mock and taunt these Jews and their God.

The whole seven-hundred-mile march led downward, not only emotionally, but physically. When the Jews arrived at the Euphrates, they had left behind them the mountains of their homeland—their stronghold, the symbol of their life and strength, and above all the reminder of their God, Yahweh of Sinai. Before them lay the uninterrupted plain of Mesopotamia.[1]

But the towers of Babylon loomed above that plain like a man-made mountain. Before the Jews' awed eyes rose palaces, terraces, majestically landscaped canals and rivers, the fabulous hanging gardens. In comparison with this wealth, the

Jerusalem they had lost must have seemed like a backwoods county seat. And the God of Jerusalem—who was he, beside the mighty gods of Babylon?

When your world has fallen in upon you, what do you do? Disaster always brings the temptation to believe that when your world collapsed, the whole world, even God's world, died with it. History and life take on the shape of a steamroller, crushing all that is human in its path. Can one pray to the God who now appears as a steamroller, or can one only curse at him? And if, in the back of your mind, there lingers the gnawing knowledge that you are guilty somehow, that the rubble that fell on you had been set in motion by your own sin, does that ease the pain? Or does it rather inject a poison of morbidity into the wounds? Surely Judah was tempted to curse its fate, its God, and its captors:

> O daughter of Babylon, you devastator!
> Happy shall he be who requites you
> with what you have done to us!
> Happy shall he be who takes your little ones
> and dashes them against the rock!   (Psalm 137:8–9)

Again, you may face disaster with a strong mind and learn to accept the logic that the steamroller apparently expresses: that there is no logic. The relentless meaning of existence, you may conclude, is that there is no meaning. All those ideas of purpose, of destiny, yes, of God and his supposed loving intention for your life, all are grandiose fantasies. Shall you forget about this God, then, who has let you be crushed? Shall you lower your flags and just get on with the business of just getting on, soothe the pain by the opiate of routine? There is a good life to be had today, after all, if you do not permit yourself to think about tomorrow—or yesterday. The booming economy of Babylon supported that kind of thinking. There was employment for a few thousand foreigners, and room for advancement, even room at the top for a few.

Of course some of the Jews succumbed to these temptations. Maybe most of them did, more or less; can you blame them?

But beneath the memory of the burning homes, beneath the pain, beneath the stunned, broken logic of their minds, there was another memory that pricked the hearts of some of them, maybe most of them. Was there not another word, another meaning? Had not God himself, beneath it all and in it all, said something?

After some thirty-five years of exile, the Persian king Cyrus launched a series of successful campaigns and began to threaten the Babylonian Empire. Doubtless the immediate reaction of the Jews was fear. What new dangers lay ahead for them? Was the ominous approach of this Cyrus only the prelude to renewed chaos, in which even the relative security of their gentlemen's captivity would be snatched away?

Behold, a New Thing

In the midst of such questioning, among the exiles there began to be whispered, then perhaps circulated in pamphlets, and at last triumphantly sung, the words of a new prophet. We do not know his name. Apparently he belonged to the circle of Isaiah, for much of his language is similar, and his oracles were bound together with those of the earlier prophet, forming chapters 40—55 of our book Isaiah.[2] The important thing is that he was given a new word from God for these still disoriented Israelites.

Over against the confusion and disillusionment brought by the exile, and the new fears aroused by the approach of Cyrus, the first task of the Exile Prophet was to help his people make sense of history. How could they understand what had happened to them?

Two lines of thought were open to the Israelite. On the one hand, he could abandon the conception of Yahweh as world-ruler and admit that historical events were beyond his control. Either he could accept the assumption with which his enemies had often taunted him, that the Babylonians won because their gods were stronger than Yahweh, or perhaps he might even stretch to a point of view scarcely imagined in his age, that no God at all, but only blind chance or fate, controlled history. It is also conceivable that he might have encountered enough of Persian religious ideas in Babylon to see history as a battlefield on which matched forces of good and evil endlessly struggle: a world not ruled by God, but divided between God and Satan. No prophet of Israel, however, could ever embrace a view that denied Yahweh's rule in history, for to do so would demolish the foundation of Israel's life, the Exodus-event itself. If Yahweh was still Yahweh, he was still *he who would be present in the events he caused to happen.*

The second possibility was to affirm boldly and consistently that Yahweh causes *all* events to happen, evil as well as good. To accept this premise, one would then have to proclaim that Yahweh himself had brought the disaster upon his people—that he had made himself their enemy, who attacked and destroyed those whom he loved (Lam. 2:4–5). This is clearly the position which the Exile Prophet takes, and he pursues its logic relentlessly and with precision. With greater clarity than any writer before him, he declares that there can be only one God, and takes upon himself the burden of living with all the difficult consequences that follow from that affirmation:

> I am Yahweh, and there is no other,
>> besides me there is no God;
>> I gird you, though you do not know me,
> that men may know, from the rising of the sun
>> and from the west, that there is none besides me;
>> I am Yahweh, and there is no other.
> I form light and create darkness,
>> I make weal and create woe,
>> I am Yahweh, who do all these things (Isaiah 45:5–7).

Now the prophet sets out to demonstrate to Israel that their confusion and faithlessness have sprung from their inability or unwillingness to think so boldly as this of God. Their vision of God has been too small, too provincial, too timid; hence they have lacked the intellectual courage and emotional stability to accept their past or face their future.

Therefore the oracles begin with "Four Herald Voices," as George Adam Smith calls them, which summon the thoughts of

the hearer to sweep from heaven to earth, from Babylon to Jerusalem, from the valleys of Judah to the farthest star of the universe. Let's listen to these voices now. Stop here to read chapter
40, which forms a kind of overture for the entire book. See if you
can distinguish the four "voices" and the themes they introduce.

❃ ❃ ❃

Do you hear the echoes of Hosea's tragic love in the first
voice? Listen; this is spoken to the rejected "Not my People":
"Comfort, comfort *my people,* says *your God.*" The adoptive
words, the word of covenant (Exodus 6:7; contrast Hosea 1:9),
the marriage vow is spoken again. Yahweh has spoken to Jerusalem in the terrible thunder of conquest, destruction, and death;
now he speaks again with the "still, small voice." "Speak tenderly
to Jerusalem"; literally, "speak to the heart of Jerusalem." This
is the language of courtship. (Compare Judges 19:3 and especially Hosea 2:14.) Like the faithful Hosea returning at last to a
Gomer enslaved by her own sin, Yahweh woos again his adul-
terous, separated people, with the declaration, "You are forgiven." There is no pretense that the sin was not real, but only
acceptance of the penitent people. In fact, the Lord will gra-
ciously count their punishment as double any requirement, so
that the episode may be closed and the conscience freed for new
life.

The second voice cries: "In the wilderness prepare the way of
Yahweh." What is this wilderness? Again, we remember Hosea
2:14. As in that passage, Israel is challenged to remember her
beginning, the event that gave her birth. As in the Exodus a
path miraculously appeared through the sea, and Yahweh led
them through the trackless wilderness, now a broad highway is
being prepared from Babylon back to Jerusalem. Can they think
of all kinds of dangers and obstacles preventing a return home? Is
the approaching Cyrus a threat as well as a promise? Yet their
Lord rules over even mountain and valley, and nothing shall
hinder his purpose. Again he will be present to them as their
Leader, going before them on the road, as of old he appeared in
the pillar of fire. Thus, in the events which are about to happen,

the "glory," the awe-inspiring presence of Yahweh will appear again (v.5).

The third voice calls the prophet to his vocation. But he hesitates. Does he dare to proclaim good news so unequivocally, in the midst of the still uncertain affairs of Babylonia? Have not the fortunes of Israel and its stamina until now been as ephemeral as the beauty of wild flowers?

> The grass withers, the flower fades,
>   when the breath of Yahweh blows upon it;
>   surely the people is grass.

Yes, but the future does not rest on the doubtful stability of human leaders and human institutions, but on that word that calls the events of history into happening. "The word of our God will stand for ever."

The fourth voice, addressed to the whole people, is like a trumpet blast.

> Get you up to a high mountain,
>   O Zion, herald of good tidings;
> lift up your voice with strength,
>   O Jerusalem, herald of good tidings,
>   lift it up, fear not;
> say to the cities of Judah,
>   "Behold your God!"

Personified, the city and the holy hill stand for the whole people in exile. The exiles are now made the bearers of the good news: to the shattered cities of Judah, peopled by the demoralized peasants left behind by the exile, new life is now proclaimed. Where before terrified people, with superstitious awe, dared not even mention the name of Yahweh (Amos 6:10), now his name will echo with great joy. Did he seem weak before Nebuchadnezzar's armies? He comes now with might, as the Warrior God who fought with Moses, Joshua, and David; nothing can stand before him. Yet he comes with tenderness, leading this scattered and broken flock back to their homeland (vv. 10–11).

"Behold your God!" These words carry not only a promise, but also a dare. The prophet accuses his people of having lived as practical atheists, of having made Yahweh into a domestic idol, since they wanted to bottle him up in their ideas of what he was like. When he did not perform according to their pat formulas—the evil Manasseh lived to a ripe age, while the good Josiah died in his prime; pagan Babylonia conquered the world, while the Chosen People languished as deportees—then they jumped to the conclusion that Yahweh had left the scene altogether.

> Why do you say, O Jacob,
>   and speak, O Israel,
> "My way is hid from Yahweh,
>   and my right is disregarded by my God"?
> Have you not known? Have you not heard?
>   Yahweh is the everlasting God,
>   the Creator of the ends of the earth.
> He does not faint or grow weary,
>   his understanding is unsearchable.   (vv. 27–28)

What if it is not God who has failed, but their ideas of him? What if Yahweh is greater than they had ever imagined, so that these strange events, to them so evil and utterly without sense, hold in the secrets of the Almighty's purpose a meaning that their small minds could not fathom? What if God has not finished with them, does not intend to let them quietly dissolve into the peoples of Mesopotamia, but still has something he is going to do with Israel?

The rest of "Second Isaiah," as the anonymous prophet is called for convenience's sake, is like a symphonic movement elaborated from the themes announced in chapter 40. Majestically it unfolds the dare which is hurled at Israel: "Behold your God." Step by step they are challenged to stretch their minds to conceive what it will mean to say that "Yahweh alone is God; besides him there is no other." This argument leads up to the triumphant announcement of a New Exodus and restoration to the Promised Land. It will be helpful at this point if you will pause to *read through chapters 41—55* in their entirety, to hear the "symphony" for yourself. Mark the places where each theme of chapter 40 returns, and notice how each one grows and develops. We often speak rather glibly about "salvation." *What is the concrete event of salvation to which Second Isaiah points? What are the different changes it will make in the way life is lived and the way it is understood?*

❋   ❋   ❋

In the beginning of his songs the unknown prophet reminds us that, though human strength is like fading grass, "the word of our God will stand for ever." The group of poems we are considering comes to a close on the same note:

> For as the rain and the snow come down from heaven,
>   and return not thither but water the earth,
> making it bring forth and sprout,
>   giving seed to the sower and bread to the eater,
> so shall my word be that goes forth from my mouth;
>   it shall not return to me empty,
> but it shall accomplish that which I purpose,
>   and prosper in the thing for which I sent it.
>   (Isaiah 55:10–11)

For people who have lost their future, that word is a powerful comfort. But there is more than comfort here, for this is the same word we have met before, the word that unsettles those to whom it speaks, calling them and sending them. If some of the exiles are still complacently carrying on business as usual, so busy with making money that they have forgotten the higher vocation to which God had called them, then they have to hear that their real life is something their money cannot buy (55:1–3). Their real life is a life covenanted to God, but that covenant does not mean mere comfort. It means obedience. God is forgiving and recreating Israel because he is still going to use this nation as his "kingdom of priests," his missionary people to carry his secret to the whole world. That was the meaning of the first covenant (Exodus 19:6), and that is the meaning of the new covenant which this New Exodus from Babylon will establish (Isaiah 55:5).

But He Was Wounded for Our Transgressions

What kind of life is required to carry God's word to the world? To answer this question, Second Isaiah holds up before us a mysterious figure, the Servant of Yahweh. The Servant embodies in his life the mission God intends for his world, and as he embodies it, his life is shaped by suffering.

Behind this figure stands probably the prophet's own experience of the suffering brought by war and exile. Like that other great anonymous poet of Israel, the author of the epic of Job, Second Isaiah knows that among those who bore the punishment are also the innocent. Children, for example, have been born here in exile, and they have inherited the burden of their fathers' guilt: "Our fathers sinned, and are no more; and we bear their iniquities" (Lam. 5:7). Those who remained true to the covenant faith suffered as severely as the most hardened sinner. Jeremiah had laid open this problem (Jer. 12), which he felt acutely to be the problem of his own existence, and no sensitive mind which had heard Jeremiah's questions (as the Exile Prophet undoubtedly had) could ever ignore them. Jeremiah did more than raise the question, however, he incarnated it. Who had suffered more than Jeremiah, both before and after the fall of Jerusalem—Jeremiah, God's own man, who had seen far too clearly for his own comfort just what was happening and had borne the burden of that awful knowledge and of his people's obstinate hostility and blindness to the point of despair (see Jer. 14:17–22; 16:1–9; 18:19–23; 20:7–18; 23:9)?

Perhaps it was in contemplation of Jeremiah's burden, surely it was also in bearing such a burden himself (for one does not write words like these songs unless he has suffered), that the Exile Prophet began to conceive the image of the Servant. Like the babes born in exile, the Servant is innocent, but unlike them he does not unconsciously fall victim to the juggernaut of evil thundering down on him out of the past, and the net of evil thrown over him from his involvement in the whole society. Instead, like Jeremiah, he stands with eyes wide open, to receive the burden onto his own shoulders. Yet, unlike Jeremiah, the

Servant does not curse the burden and rail against the God who lays it upon him, but bows his back to it without complaining, affirms the meaningfulness of the evil whose meaning he cannot begin to understand, and bears it willingly, quietly, indeed with an irrational hope and an unbelievable but palpable joy.

At this point go back and *read the four poems that describe the Servant, the so-called "Servant songs" of Second Isaiah.* They are found in *Isaiah 42:1–4; 49:1–6 (1–13?); 50:4–9; and 52: 13—53:12.*

* * *

Who is the Servant? This is a question that has divided scholars for generations. If you read the songs carefully, you found a valuable clue in the second one: "And he said to me, 'You are my servant, Israel, in whom I will be glorified' " (49:3). Is the Servant then the whole nation of Israel? Notice how many times in the other oracles of the Exile Prophet God calls Israel "my servant" (41:8,9; 43:10; 44:1,2,21; 45:4). Israel is his "chosen one" (42:1), in whom his soul delights. It was Israel's priestly mission to be a "light to the Gentiles" (49:6, K.J.V.). If Israel is the Servant, then the astonished words of chapter 53 are those of the kings (52:15), who are startled by the restoration of the shattered Israel. These kings, who before had poked cruel fun at the defeated Jews, now "shut their mouths," for they see that the Jews suffered not for their own sins only, but for the sins of all these nations. By rights they should all have been marching in those lines of chained captives, instead of jeering from the hills, but all has been borne by Israel.

It is tempting, then, to say that Israel *is* the Servant—but the image does not quite fit. The very song which furnished us our clue goes on to say, the Lord "formed me from the womb to be his servant, *to bring Jacob back to him, and that Israel might be gathered to him . . .*" (49:5). The Servant has a mission *to Israel;* to Israel he is given as "a covenant" (49:8). Furthermore, the Servant is innocent, but the prophet never deludes himself about the guilt of Israel. The image of the Servant, who

> . . . will not cry or lift up his voice,
>   or make it heard in the street;
> a bruised reed he will not break,
>   and a dimly burning wick he will not quench (42:2–3);

who "was oppressed, and . . . afflicted, yet he opened not his mouth; like a lamb that is led to the slaughter, and like a sheep that before its shearers is dumb . . ." (53:7), is not the Israel we saw go into exile, cursing its neighbors, wailing to God, gnashing its teeth for vengeance against its conquerors! No, the Servant is not identical with Israel.

Could the Servant be an individual—perhaps Jeremiah? There is much, as we have already noted, that reminds us of Jeremiah, but again Jeremiah did not go "like a lamb to the slaughter." Is the Servant possibly the Exile Prophet himself? There is much that sounds like him, especially in the two songs which are written in first person (49:1–6 and 50:4–9). Both of these speak so intensely of personal mission and personal suffering that we can scarcely deny that the prophet's deepest self-understanding is poured out in them. But could he conceivably have written the first and especially the last song about himself? Could he think that "many nations" would look at a Jewish prophet and confess, "he was wounded for our transgressions, he was bruised for our iniquities; upon him was the chastisement that made us whole, and with his stripes we are healed" (53:5)?

Do you see now the mistake we made? Who is the Servant is the wrong question. To ask that is like asking the painter of an abstract painting, "What is that?" or after hearing a Mozart concerto to inquire, "What did that mean?" The Servant songs must be heard *as songs*, as poetry. The Servant is not anyone whom the prophet sees before him whole. Rather he is an image which has forced itself into the prophetic consciousness as the prophet struggles with the fact that punishment is mixed with martyrdom. Is the Servant Israel? Yes, he is the Israel that ought to be, that God desires and finally, in a way yet hidden, will create. Is the Servant Jeremiah? Yes, for in Jeremiah the Servant's mission was being performed, and the Servant partially, but imperfectly, present. Is the Exile Prophet the Servant? Yes, for the image of the Servant is the form into which his life is poured; yet he sees a far greater mission for the Servant than that which is given to himself. The image itself pushes on beyond them all into the future; the prophetic imagination "sees" a person who, self-consciously but without self-pity, embraces the web of evil that falls upon him, bearing it to the death, with love, for those who cannot bear it for themselves.

The prophet can only hold up the image for Israel to see, saying, "Look, here is your real life. This is the meaning." Whether the re-created Israel will take the image for its own, he cannot know. He knows only that the Servant stands for the purpose which Yahweh is working out, has been working out since the beginning, and that the Servant must at last appear in his wholeness. Was the prophet right? Will his image take flesh, the Servant live in Israel? That question must wait for a later chapter.

7

hope beyond hope

Before the eyes of the displaced persons in Babylon, the unknown disciple of Isaiah painted two magnificent images of Israel's life. The first showed a rejuvenated people, restored to their homeland by a historical event so startling that it amounted to a New Exodus. Jerusalem, lying long crushed and silent, would be roused like a drugged sleeper, shake off her despair, and, putting on her festive clothes, would dance and sing in the new day. All the scattered people of Yahweh would come trekking home, their paths miraculously prepared by God himself. Not only Israel, but all the nations of the world would see this event of redemption and be amazed. Israel would become a light to all the nations, and soon there would be lines of pilgrims, even kings of the earth, marching to Jerusalem to pay homage to Yahweh, Lord of all the earth. The second image showed a Servant—whether this Servant be Israel awakened to its real life, or the true Remnant, or one representative Man who acts out the role of the whole people—who finds the meaning of his life not just in the miraculous restoration to come, but already in the suffering that went before. In bearing this suffering, consciously and willingly, Israel would discover the heart of God's love for the world, indeed would suffer with God for his creatures.

In the years, even in the centuries which followed the prophet's proclamation, however, these images were far from being realized. Only slowly and with great toil did Jerusalem struggle to life again, and that life never came close to her former glory. Far from becoming the center of worldwide fame, she was doomed to be the capital of an insignificant nation; except for one brief flash of liberty she would always be a captive province of some great empire, scarcely heeded in the world of nations until again she would be crushed to ruins. And that other image, that of the Suffering Servant, was too demanding, too profound for the little country that emerged from exile. The image was not lost, but it was set aside, buried beneath the consciousness of the people, until a man would come to take it for his own.

Building the Walls of Judaism

Cyrus, emperor of Persia, lived up to the expectations of the Exile Prophet. In keeping with his enlightened colonial policy, he decreed in 538 B.C. that the Jews were free to return to their homeland and rebuild their Temple. Even the loot, including the sacred furnishings of the Temple, which Nebuchadnezzar had carted away to his treasury, were to be returned.[1] Not all the Jews in Babylonia responded, but there were enough who were stirred by the reminder of God's ancient covenant and the new promises now opening up to them that a renewed community life could take shape in Judah.

The leading figures in the new community were the priests, who increasingly became the political heads of the country, and the scribes. The scribes were men learned in the Law, whose intention was to shape the whole of Jewish life in accordance with the Torah. It was their leadership, more than anything else, which made the Jews the People of the Book.

The Time of Trouble

Under the easygoing rule of the Persians, the little priest-ruled country of Judah was able to continue its life untroubled. Soon, however, this calm was to be upset by the most remarkable conqueror of all time. At the age of twenty Alexander of Macedon began the fantastic series of conquests which were to make him, in the space of twelve years, ruler of virtually the entire known world. In 331 he overcame Darius III of Persia, and thus, in the twinkling of an eye, Judah came under the dominion of a new empire. Before he turned thirty-three, Alexander was dead and his astonishing empire divided among his four generals. Seleucus gained control of Syria and Mesopotamia, and Ptolemy ruled Egypt. Before long, Judah was caught up in the deadly seesaw struggle for supremacy between their successors, finally won by the Seleucids in 200 B.C.

From the Seleucid Dynasty there "came forth," as the first book of Maccabees puts it, a "sinful root, Antiochus Epiphanes." His father Antiochus III left not only dominion over Palestine, Syria, and Mesopotamia, but also an enormous national debt incurred in unsuccessful wars against Rome. When Antiochus Epiphanes succeeded to the throne, after a sordid series of intrigues and murders, he was faced with the necessity of consolidating and financing this disjointed empire. The condition of the treasury, added to the character of Antiochus, opened the way for politics by bribe and graft as well as for military expeditions to plunder such treasure hoards as the Temple of Jerusalem.

Antiochus was driven not only by practical considerations, but also by a great zeal to convert the culture of his scattered empire to the Greek way of life. How successful the aim of the Hellenizers was may be observed still today from the statues, copied after Greek originals, in Roman museums, and the ruins of Greek-style architecture throughout the Mediterranean world.

The zeal for things Greek included not only the arts, but also religion. Because of a real or fancied resemblance to common statues of Zeus, Antiochus called himself "Zeus Manifest, Bearer of Victory."[2] His common title Epiphanes ("the Manifest") is a shortened form of this claim. Besides such devotion to the Greek gods, the king saw a very important political advantage if all his subject peoples could all be melted together into the same Greek-Oriental mixture of customs, speech, and religion. A common culture would help hold the empire together, eliminating pockets of nationalism by wiping out the distinguishing characteristics of national groups. In particular, Antiochus tried to establish Greek cities throughout his empire. Established from the ground up as military colonies or remodeled out of older cities, these towns received constitutions patterned on Greek standards, granted directly from the king. The elite citizen corps of these cities received important privileges, including a measure of self-government and freedom from most taxes, and were therefore bound closely to the king.

There were people in Judah who welcomed Antiochus and his Hellenization. Shortly after he took the throne, one of them, a man named Jason, offered the new king a bribe of four hundred and forty talents of silver, which was accepted, for the office of High Priest. Also in the bargain was permission for Jason to build in Jerusalem a Greek gymnasium, ordinarily the center of civic life in a Greek city. Quite likely this meant that Jerusalem was actually reconstituted in the Greek mold, as "Antioch-at-Jerusalem."[3] Of course only a select aristocracy could be its citizens, so the other Jews were now disenfranchised. Jason was soon succeeded by Menelaus, who offered a larger bribe and then, when Jason tried to recover his office by force, called Antiochus' army to his aid.

Both Jason and Menelaus represent an extreme form of the pro-Greek party that existed in Jerusalem. It was especially strong in the Jewish aristocracy and among the priests. Out of the priestly group grew the later Sadducees, who were theologically conservative (in New Testament times we find them refusing to accept the relatively new doctrine of resurrection) but willing to accommodate themselves to the Greek patterns of life. Doubtless most of the Hellenizers believed that some such accommodation was necessary to avoid antagonizing the king, if Judah was to survive at all.

The vicious struggle between Jason and Menelaus for the high priesthood contributed nothing to the survival of Judah, however, but rather incited Antiochus Epiphanes to his first bloody invasion of Jerusalem. The king, who had just been forced to back down from an attack on Egypt because of the intervention of Rome, vented his frustration in a melee of destruction in the holy city. Even the Temple was not spared his plundering.[4] The following year, 168 B.C., he sent "a chief collector of tribute," with a large army which broke down the walls of Jerusalem and laid the city in ruins, massacring countless persons and seizing others as slaves.[5] Determined at this point to wipe out this troublesome sect altogether, "that all should be one people, and that each should give up his customs" (1 Maccabees 1:41–42), Antiochus issued a decree making illegal the practices of the Jewish religion. The burnt offerings and all sacrifices in the Temple were forbidden; all books of the Law were confiscated, and anyone found possessing a book of the Law would be executed; any woman who permitted her children to be circumcised would be executed and her baby hanged from her neck.[6] In December 167 B.C., a "desolating sacrilege," probably an idol of Zeus—perhaps it bore the image of Antiochus—was set up on the very altar of Yahweh within the Temple. All the surrounding towns were forced to erect altars to Zeus and the Jews were commanded to sacrifice on them. On every hand, the Jews were being pushed to fearful decisions.

Visions in the Night

> "Without warning he shall destroy many; and he shall even rise up against the Prince of princes; but, by no human hand, he shall be broken."   (Daniel 8:25)

At the opposite extreme from the Hellenizers and Sadducees, there were other Jews who rejected every possibility of compromise with the Greek culture. Following the line laid down by Nehemiah and Ezra, these groups saw that the very identity of Israel, the Chosen People of God, was at stake. If the Hellenizers were allowed to have their way, then soon the Jews would dissolve into the masses of the Seleucid empire, and the purposes of God for the world would be swallowed up in the lowest-common-denominator religion emerging out of the great mixing.

These extreme repressive measures of Antiochus naturally confirmed the worst fears of the opposition groups, and they began to consolidate into a rigorously dedicated party. At first they called themselves the *Hasidim,* which means "those who love God." The name is derived from the word which refers in the Old Testament to the mutual covenant relationship between Yahweh and his people, usually translated in the Revised Standard Version as "steadfast love." "Steadfast love" for the Hasidim meant the absolute, unyielding obedience to God's laws and, as a result, rigorous separation from every contaminating influence of paganism.

First Maccabees has this note about them:

> But many in Israel stood firm and were resolved in their
> hearts not to eat unclean food. They chose to die rather
> than to be defiled by food or to profane the holy covenant;
> and they did die. (1 Maccabees 1:62–63)

They withdrew from the less rigid Jews and formed their own
synagogue. Out of this company grew the most enduring sect
of Judaism, known as the "Pharisees" from an Aramaic word
meaning "the separated ones." Another later offshoot of these
Hasidim were the Essenes, who have made headlines even in
recent years, eighteen hundred years after the last Essene died,
when their long-buried library was discovered near the Dead Sea.

Among the opposition groups who were "zealous for the law,"
there was a division with regard to the best methods of resisting
the assaults of Antiochus and his soldiers. One group, including
some of the Hasidim, decided to take up arms and wage a holy
war against the king's troops and especially against the Jewish
Hellenizers, whom they regarded as traitors. These fighters, the
Maccabees, who were the spiritual ancestors of the "Zealots" we
hear about in the New Testament, produced one of the most
dramatic episodes in Israel's history, and we must discuss them
briefly in a moment. Most of the Hasidim, however, apparently
came to mistrust the methods of the underground fighters, and
adopted a pattern of passive resistance. They felt that no human
hand could save them from the overwhelming threat of Antiochus' power. Yet, if they were diligent to keep the Law and
waited patiently on Yahweh, he would redeem them, for he
was "strong to save."

Trapped in a present which promised only chaos and suffering,
the Hasidim, if they were to hope at all, were forced to turn to
the future. In the prophets they found passages which spoke of a
golden age to come, and now, with the present age utterly black,
these passages captured their fancy:

> It shall come to pass in the latter days
>   that the mountain of the house of Yahweh
>   shall be established as the highest of the mountains,
>   and shall be raised above the hills;

and all the nations shall flow to it,
   and many peoples shall come, and say:
"Come, let us go up to the mountain of Yahweh,
   to the house of the God of Jacob;
that he may teach us his ways
   and that we may walk in his paths."
For out of Zion shall go forth the law,
   and the word of Yahweh from Jerusalem.
He shall judge between the nations,
   and shall decide for many peoples;
and they shall beat their swords into plowshares,
   and their spears into pruning hooks;
nation shall not lift up sword against nation,
   neither shall they learn war any more.   (Isaiah 2:2–4)

These words still have the power to bring a lump to our throats when we consider our world; how much more poignantly they must have gripped the Hasidim suffering under a reign of terror. Gradually they became convinced that the world had become as bad as it could get, so bad that soon God himself would intervene. They concluded that Antiochus and his terrorists were not instruments in the hand of God—as Isaiah, for example, might have interpreted them—but actually enemies of God himself, representatives of all the evil forces of the universe rising up in one last outburst before God would quell them and bring his Kingdom of peace. Many of the Hasidim thus came to feel that they were living in "the time of the end." The true Jew, therefore, had only to stand firm, holding to his faith despite the worst terrors, for a little while until the end would come.

It was to encourage the weak but faithful Jews that a strange new kind of literature began to be written in some circles of the Hasidim. This new literature is called "apocalyptic," from the Greek word for "revelation," "unveiling." It is the future that is "unveiled," so that the faithful reader can see, through the visions of the writer, the miraculous things God is about to do and thus be encouraged to live steadfastly in the present evil time.

To us, the apocalypse itself seems "veiled," for it speaks in bizarre figures and symbols. These serve, on the one hand, as a kind of code, as meaningless to an officer of Antiochus' occupation force as they are to most of us, but to a Jew familiar with the things happening around him and with the traditions of Israel, they were quite clear. "None of the wicked shall understand," the angel promises Daniel in his last vision, "but those who are wise shall understand" (Dan. 12:10). Further to confuse "the wicked," the apocalypses are written under the names of great heroes of the past, as if I, wanting to warn present-day Americans against some goings-on I do not admire, were to publish them in the form of a "farewell address of George Washington."

On the other hand, the mystifying symbols served to remind the reader that the future is in *God's* hands, not theirs. There still remains a mystery about the future, even for the faithful. He knows *that* God will bring good to his people, but not *how* he will do it.

The book of Daniel is the earliest apocalypse extant, and the only one that found its way into the Old Testament.[7] It was written, scholars now generally agree, around 165 B.C.; that is, after Antiochus Epiphanes had begun his pogroms, although it disguises itself as a collection of stories (chs. 1–6) and some "prophecies" from the Babylonian and Persian ages. Take time out now to read the book, and you will quickly get a taste of apocalyptic's weird form. But if you will imagine, as you read, that you are sitting in some rocky cave in the valley of the Dead Sea, pausing between lines to scan the horizon for a sign of Antiochus' murderous troops, then perhaps you will also get a taste of the hope this book brought to its first readers and feel your backbone stiffen with the will to resist to the end. (If the combined pressures of a term paper due this week and a heavy date tonight do not permit such a long escape from your own oppressed situation, then a careful reading of chapters 7, 8, and 12 will be adequate for our discussion.)

❀　❀　❀

The vision of Daniel in chapter 7 begins with four uncanny beasts which arise, one after the other, out of the sea. The sea, for the Jews as for most of the Eastern peoples, was a symbol for evil and chaos (cf. Gen. 1:2; Isa. 51:9–10; Rev. 21:1). These monstrous beasts, who from their origins are marked with evil, are not specimens you will find in any zoo. The first three combine the attributes of many animals; the fourth is so horrible he cannot even be compared with any existing animal (v. 7). Obviously the beasts are symbols, but of what? For this much of the code the reader is fortunately given a key in verse 17, where an angel explains to Daniel that "These four great beasts are four kings who shall arise out of the earth." Perhaps they are better understood as four kingdoms represented by their rulers, as verse 23 suggests.

With a little knowledge of history, it is not hard to crack the code. The first beast must represent Nebuchadnezzar and the Babylonian kingdom, like the lion equipped with overwhelming strength to crush its opponents, and like the eagle or vulture soaring over the world in search of prey. In time, however, its wings are plucked off, for the successors of Nebuchadnezzar were not even able to hold on to the conquests he had made. The second beast, a bear, must represent the kingdom of the Medes, which "Daniel" thinks had a separate existence from the Persian kingdom. The winged leopard represents Cyrus and the Persian empire he established. The four heads of this strange cat presumably look in all directions, indicating the extent of this empire.[8]

The last, indescribable beast has to represent Alexander the Great, for to what could one compare this fantastic young conqueror? Clearly this beast is the one in which the author is really interested; the others serve only to build up suspense, and to bridge the gap between the time of Belshazzar and that of Antiochus. The fourth beast has "ten horns," apparently representing ten successors of Alexander on the throne of Antioch,[9] since the other three divisions of his empire are not suggested in this vision. But these ten kings are not important to the author either. He focuses on another "little horn" that springs up. This upstart horn has "eyes like the eyes of a man, and a mouth speaking great [i.e., presumptuous] things." Not only does he make war on the saints of God, seeking to "change the times and the law," he is rash enough even to challenge the Most High and to speak blasphemously against him. By now it is perfectly obvious that the little horn with the big mouth is none other than Antiochus Epiphanes.

If this were all of the vision, then the author would have said nothing that was not already only too well known, and the writing would have served only to provide a chuckle over his success in lampooning the terrible king. His purpose, however, is more serious than that, and there is another part of the vision. Beyond the kings which have come and gone in the past centuries, also beyond the present reign of Antiochus, which everyone can see all too plainly, Daniel sees something else. There is another throne, another king, another kingdom which are not visible. Like Isaiah in the year of Uzziah's death, Daniel is granted a vision of God himself, the "Ancient of Days," seated in his throne and surrounded by his angelic servants. This great King has come to sit in judgment, to try the case of the earthly king and the peoples he has subjected (v. 10b). Even as the "little horn," oblivious to the vast courtroom which stretches invisibly around him, continues his mad orations (v. 11), the sentence of the Court is delivered. Its execution is swift; "the beast" is killed and its body burned.

In the place of this beastly kingdom, now there appears another figure, this time not the figure of a beast, but a human figure. He does not arise from the evil sea, but comes "with the clouds of heaven."

> And he came to the Ancient of Days
>   and was presented before him.
> And to him was given dominion
>   and glory and kingdom,
> that all peoples, nations, and languages
>   should serve him;
> his dominion is an everlasting dominion,
>   which shall not pass away,
> and his kingdom one
>   that shall not be destroyed.   (vv. 13–14)

As the beasts represented conquering kings and their dynasties and kingdoms, the manlike figure is the symbol, as the angel explains to Daniel (v. 18), of "the saints of the Most High," or, in other words, of the true remnant of Israel. These shall be given "an everlasting kingdom."

The message of the first vision is now quite clear. Though Antiochus seems free to carry out his destructive plans unhindered, behind the scenes God is watching. The very successes of Antiochus' evil designs are merely adding up his sum of guilt before God's judgment seat. Soon God will deliver his judgment, and this tyrant will be shattered. In the place of his depraved kingdom will come the Kingdom of God, in which those Jews who were faithful to the end will reign forever.

The second vision, in chapter 8, is a variation on the same themes, as are the succeeding chapters. With more and more precision of detail, Antiochus and his deeds are identified, and the promise of salvation is elaborated. In chapter 8, the beasts are replaced by other animals. Nebuchadnezzar is left behind, and the Median-Persian empire is represented by a ram with two horns instead of by two beasts. Alexander's empire is depicted in more detail as a great billy goat, having at first only one "conspicuous horn," Alexander the Great. When this horn is broken, that is, when Alexander dies, it is replaced by "four conspicuous horns toward the four winds of heaven," representing the four generals of Alexander and the divided empire. Antiochus' presumption against the Most High is also more precisely described, with focus on his desecration of the Temple. Again, the speedy intervention of God is promised, and even the period of time until the Temple is to be purified is suggested. If the twenty-three hundred evenings and mornings (v. 14) are to be taken as eleven hundred and fifty days (reference is to the evening and morning sacrifices),[10] then the time corresponds with the three and one-half years of chapter 7:25. As a matter of fact, the Temple was spoiled on the 15th of Chislev, 167 B.C., and rededicated on the 25th of the same month, 164 B.C. A final notable point is made in verse 25, where it is emphatically promised that "by no human hand, he shall be broken." Very likely this is a subtle protest against the activities of the Maccabean resistance movement.

The vision found in chapter 12 reiterates the point that not human, but divine powers will bring God's Kingdom. It also introduces a new and very important thought. In the individualism which had developed in the Hellenistic Age, a question arose among the orthodox Jews which apparently had not received much attention before. Even though justice would be pronounced on Antiochus and the Kingdom of God at last established, what about those unfortunate Hasidim who had died in the cause, never tasting the joys of that Kingdom? And what of the evil-workers who had died peacefully in their sleep during this time, without receiving their share of that awful judgment? Daniel 12 suggests an answer by the first clear statement in the Old Testament of the idea of resurrection of the dead. Of course, this is not yet a general resurrection—it is supposed only that "many" of those who died during this age will "awake," "some to everlasting life and some to shame and everlasting contempt." Further, notice that there is no notion of a heavenly paradise included in this resurrection; the Kingdom is an earthly one. Nevertheless, the question has been raised, and an answer attempted. This as yet unclear hope is added to the reassurance of the apocalypse for those who are sore distressed.

The Hammer of the Lord

"Let every one who is zealous for the law and supports the covenant come out with me!"

(The summons of Mattathias, 1 Maccabees 2:27)

If some of the strict Jews were content to "go their way to the end," zealous only to "purify themselves, and make themselves white, and be refined," and meanwhile waiting patiently for the sudden intervention of God to end the struggle, there were others less patient. Resistance of the strict Hasidim was not to the taste of the sons of Mattathias of Modein and the fighters who gathered around them. When a group of the orthodox were massacred by Syrian troops as they sat in the caves where they had taken refuge, unresisting because it was the Sabbath, the followers of Mattathias decided that there were some limits to piety. "Let us fight against every man who comes to attack us on the sabbath day," they determined.

One can scarcely find a modern war novel more thrilling than the first book of Maccabees, which relates the astonishing story of the revolt against Antiochus. The central characters were a remarkable family, Mattathias and his five sons. Their battle with the oppressor began when one of the king's officers came to Modein to persuade Mattathias, as a leading citizen, to set a good example by offering the first sacrifice on the new local altar to Zeus. Not only did the old man refuse, he was so enraged by the suggestion that he killed a Jew who did make a sacrifice and then turned to assassinate the Syrian officer himself. Gathering his sons and all who were "zealous for the law," Mattathias then fled to the hills. When he died later the same year (166 B.C.), Mattathias passed his leadership to his oldest son Judas, who gained the nickname "the Hammer" (Maccabaeus), by which the whole family came to be known. Judas organized the growing band of rebels into tough fighting units and soon proved himself to be an instinctive master of guerrilla tactics. A series of lightning commando raids demoralized the Syrian occupation forces and terrorized the Jews who had collaborated with the enemy. By 164, despite the reinforcement of the Syrian garrisons, Judas recaptured Jerusalem and purified the Sanctuary. By 163 he had so soundly defeated the occupation forces and extended his control through Judah that Antiochus brought the full power of his main armies to bear on this unbelievable rebel. Antiochus' death in that year prevented the carrying out of this threat, and subsequent struggles over the succession to his throne forced the Syrians to sign a treaty with Judas, granting full rights to autonomous national life and worship. Despite new invasions by the Syrians in the following years, Judas and, after his death in battle, first Jonathan and then Simon were able to preserve Judah's freedom. These absurd rebels had won!

The skepticism of Daniel's author was nevertheless justified. While the Maccabees succeeded in casting off the Seleucid yoke and establishing, in 134, an independent kingdom, that kingdom

did not in the least resemble the Kingdom of God. The Hasmonaean dynasty of kings (Hasmonaeus was the family name of
Mattathias), begun by Simon's son John Hyrcanus, was not
characterized by peace and righteousness, but from the beginning
it was marred by murder, intrigue, and blackmail. Neither was it
"an everlasting kingdom," for in 63 B.C. Jerusalem was captured
by the Roman legions under Pompey and Judah became again,
this time until the end of its existence, a satellite country. The
Hasmonaean house crumbled and was replaced by the puppet
king, Herod, who was not even a Jew, but a Idumaean
(Edomite).

The Messiah

"Behold, O Lord, and raise up unto them their king, the
son of David, at the time in which Thou seest, O God . . ."
(Psalms of Solomon 17:21)[11]

The hopes aroused both by apocalypses like Daniel and by the
military successes of the Maccabees were shattered by the
Roman conquest. Yet the Jewish reaction to this double disappointment was not despair, but an altered form for their hopes.
Apocalypses, as we have seen, continued to be written, and
even the possibility of new military action was never discounted
altogether. In this respect the confidence in the Kingdom of God
expressed by Daniel remained alive, despite the failure of that
book's prophecies to materialize in the expected form.

In the years of Roman domination, both the hope of the
apocalypticists and the hope for political liberation by the
Zealots came to center around the expectation of an individual
leader, the Messiah. The word "Messiah," which was translated
into Greek by "Christos," literally means "anointed." In the Old
Testament many persons figure as "God's anointed," prophets,
priests, kings, even Cyrus (Isa. 45:1). After the end of David's
kingdom, the hope had begun to dawn in Judah for a future king
who would be an idealized version of David. Such a hope is seen
in the "wonder-child" of Isaiah 9:2–7 and in the "shoot of Jesse"
in Isaiah 11:1ff. During the Exile, this hope was postponed to a

distant future, but still a New David was expected, one who would reign over a reunited and purified people for ever (Ezek. 37:21–28).

The expectation of a New David was not the only form that the hope for future redemption took for the Jews in those trying years. Again and again some shift in their political situation, some new threat or awakening hope, would send them back to their Bibles, searching anxiously for some clue to the meaning of their future. The combination of various scriptural texts with the varying interpretations called forth by changing events produced a variety of images of the way God would act in the "last days." Some circles, like the Essenes by the Dead Sea, expected a Messiah of Aaron, a great High Priest, who would preside over the worship of the New Israel when the present age ended.[12] Others, reading Daniel 7:13f. as a reference to an individual rather than to the purified Israel, looked for a "Son of Man," apparently regarded as a heavenly, angelic figure. This Son of Man remains the most mysterious of the figures in the Jewish hope. Again, some looked for a "prophet like Moses" (Deut. 18:15) who would teach Israel a new and perfect Law and would lead them through a New Exodus. The figures of the Old Testament who had been miraculously transported to heaven, Enoch (Gen. 5:24) and Elijah (2 Kings 2) and, according to later legends, also Moses and Baruch, Jeremiah's scribe, were sometimes expected to return again at the end of time as God's forerunners. And there were many other variations. Sometimes no Messiah at all was expected, but God himself, it was believed, would directly and personally intervene and begin to reign as King of the world. Frequently several of the redeemer-figures were expected to come together. For example, the Dead Sea sect seems to have awaited the coming of the Prophet as well as the Messianic Priest and the Messianic Prince.

The wide variety of the imagery with which the Jews expressed their hope for the end-time only serves to underline the intensity of that hope and its basic agreement. Fundamental elements were common to all the pictures: *First, restoration.* Israel would be restored, and with it the whole world. This meant that the great saving acts of God in Israel's remembered past would be re-created in the last days. Creation would be made new, purged of evil and perfected in peace and joy; the Exodus would be fulfilled by a new and final liberation; the new covenant would be written on the hearts of the people. *Second, judgment.* All men must stand before God to have their lives weighed by his perfect righteousness. Primarily, however, this judgment was seen as the condemnation of the pagan nations and the vindication of God's own people Israel. *Third, the reign of God.* God, together with his people, would rule the world for ever.

It is a powerful picture. Can we not still share the longing of these people? What can we make of a life that again and again crushes our plans and hopes, in which every attempted logic of history is always smashing on some absurd turn of events, in which goodness and gentleness are rewarded by mockery and abuse while brute power and cunning win all? Will a good God let this go on? Will there not come a time when he will set everything right?

But there is one figure conspicuously absent from the picture. Where is the Servant of the Lord, who suffers abuse quietly, who offers up his life, so that the many may live?

Again the Covenant People had come to the end of an era, and again they emerged from its crises with a chastened and renewed hope. Again, that hope was mistaken—but nevertheless, though in a way they could not foresee, it was to be fulfilled.

8

the time fulfilled

About ninety-two years after Pompey's conquest of Palestine, that is, by our calendar, around A.D. 29, something happened in Jerusalem. On one Friday that year there was a public execution, performed in the customary fashion by the Roman authorities, of three Jews. Two of them were common criminals, convicted of robbery. That caused no stir; we do not even know their names. The third case was a bit unusual. The placard on his cross, which was supposed to give the charge on which he had been convicted, said only, "The King of the Jews." Apparently then he was executed for alleged sedition, a troublemaker accused of plotting an insurrection against the Roman occupation forces. Executions on this charge were also not infrequent in those unstable times. Remembering the giddy days of the Maccabean victories, there were always hundreds of Jews grinding their teeth impatiently under the Roman yoke and ready at a moment's notice to snatch up their hidden arms and follow the Messiah when he came. There was no lack of people in those days who did come claiming to be the Messiah, though their revolutions were short-lived. We even know the names of two of these—Theudas and Judas the Galilean—though not much else. Of all these, that other man is the one who was remembered. His name, a very common one, was Jeshua—the same name as Hosea and Joshua, and in Greek written Jesus. Why was he remembered?

If we could climb into a time machine and rocket back to first-century Palestine, we would quickly discover why Jesus was not forgotten. The reason lay with a little group of people who, after his death, went around talking about him constantly. The things they said about him caused a great upheaval in the Jewish community. The tenor of their proclamation alarmed and irritated the Jewish authorities, who doubtless were afraid that widespread talk of a Messiah could only bring trouble with the Romans. Yet no threat seemed sufficient to stop these stubborn people from their public harangues. When one of their number, who was a Greek-speaking Jew, not a native Palestinian, undertook to lecture the Sanhedrin on Israel's history and their sins, after the manner of the ancient prophets, it was too much for them. The council members stoned him to death for blasphemy, and all the Greek-speaking members of the new sect were hounded out of the city or imprisoned (Acts 6—8). Yet their very expulsion from Jerusalem only served to spread the infection. Soon little groups of the "Followers of the Way" were springing up all over Palestine and Syria, and indeed in every crossroads city of the empire. In one of the Syrian cities, Antioch, the sect began to be called "Christians," evidently because, even to outsiders, it was obvious that their life revolved around one "Jesus, who is called the Christ."

And all this began with a handful of men in Palestine? Let's look at that group again—there must have been something remarkable about them. But what? A short time before, most of them had been uneducated workers, hardly noted for their piety and certainly not for their bravery. As for powers of oratory, they stood out mostly for their uncouth Galilean accents—to the Jerusalemites, just "country hicks." They were not very likely prospects for starting a new religion. The only thing out of the ordinary about them, as the Sanhedrin noted (Acts 4:13), was that they had been associated with this Jesus who had been crucified. They had assembled around him, in fact, like disciples of a rabbi, and had followed him around the country, listening to his teachings and observing his actions. But when he had been arrested, they had taken to their heels in terror, completely demoralized. How are we going to explain the fact that here they are now, not scattered cowering in their rooms, but publicly preaching, making all Judah and finally the whole empire listen to their words? What happened to bring such a startling transformation? Perhaps we should listen to their own explanation.

The News

We do not have a time machine, of course. We have only the New Testament. That is where we find the early Christians' "own explanation" for the remarkable transformation of the first disciples. What was the central thing that set the Christian movement moving? What did the earliest Christians sing about? What kind of creeds did they recite when they were baptized? What was it they preached in their sermons?

Perhaps the best starting point is to ask what the early Christians preached about, for the first thing we found them doing was preaching. Maybe you find this disappointing, for most of us do not like to be "preached at." When someone "preaches at us," that probably means he is telling us what we ought to do, maybe urging on us a particular set of ideas, or at most teaching us some things we should know. But the preaching we encounter in the New Testament contains basically not an argument, but an announcement. Something has happened! The word which is translated "preacher" in the New Testament really means "herald," "town crier." The herald was five-minute news break, sound truck, TV commentator, and local gossip columnist all rolled into one. He is still the main means for spreading the news in parts of the East. This was the way the first Christians thought of themselves. They were the ones with the news.

What was the news? Let's see if we can hear some of its echoes. In the book of Acts there are recorded a number of sermons, the news as it was announced by such preachers as Peter, Stephen, and Paul. To be sure these sermons are not verbatim accounts, and in their present form they all reflect the high literary style of Luke. However, they still retain the basic message of the earliest Christian groups. Even earlier are the letters of Paul. There are places in those letters where Paul has quoted from the preaching which was already "standard" by the time he was converted within a decade after Jesus' crucifixion, as well as some of the creeds that were recited and hymns that were sung in the churches he knew. With effort and imagination, then, you can put yourself back into the first century to listen to those Christian criers of the greatest news yet.

As samples of the Acts sermons, look at Acts 2:14–36, 38–39; 3:12–26; 4:8–12; and 10:34–43. A few of the important summaries quoted by Paul are Romans 1:3–4; 3:24–25; 4:24–25; 10:9; First Corinthians 15:3–7; Philippians 2:5–11 (a hymn). It will be helpful if you will underline the main points in the Acts sermons as you read, and then prepare a sample outline of one of them. What things do you find common to *all* the sermons? Now compare the brief formulas quoted by Paul. What points do these have in common with the preaching recorded in Acts? On the basis of these comparisons, see if you can put in your own words the central message of the earliest Christians.[1]

* * *

Here is a one-sentence summary of the news; see how it compares with your discoveries: The news is: The world has been transformed by the double event of Jesus' being killed and being raised from the dead.

Jesus' death and resurrection were really just one happening, as the heralds saw it. Now they emphasize one side and then the other, but both belong together.

It was the Resurrection that made the difference in the disciples themselves. That is the only real explanation for their astounding transformation from cowards to martyrs. The Sanhedrin and the Roman officers cannot frighten them, just because they know that the Sanhedrin and the officers are not actually in control. They have already used all their power to destroy Jesus—but he is alive! They know that he is alive, because they have seen him. They offer no proof, no argument, no explanation. They just say, "We are eyewitnesses." "We cannot but speak of what we have seen and heard." It is important to remember that when the New Testament talks about "witnessing" the word means just what it does in a courtroom: to tell what one has seen and heard. These witnesses offer testimony to just one thing: they have seen Jesus, *alive* again. Their unshakable faith that Jesus has been raised is the one basis for the power that has seized them.

But the death of Jesus is also part of the news. No longer the destruction of hope, now it is the center of history. The death is important, not just because Jesus had to die before he could be raised, but because the death itself means something. The power of the Resurrection opened their eyes to see what the death meant. It meant that the hope of Israel, in the moment of its fulfillment, was turned wrong-side-out. They had hoped for the Messiah to come, the anointed King, who would drive out the enemies of the nation and of God, rule them with a rod of iron, and introduce the golden age of peace. But that was not the way God had come to his people. He had come in this man who suffered, who received the curses and beatings and spitting with silence, who carried his own death-cross to the place of his execution, and there without protest gave up his life.

The Resurrection opened the eyes of the disciples and quickened their memory. Had they not heard, somewhere before, of one who "gave my back to the smiters, and my cheeks to those who pulled out the beard; [who] hid not my face from shame and spitting"? In the Prophets was it not written:

> He was oppressed, and he was afflicted,
>   yet he opened not his mouth;
> like a lamb that is led to the slaughter,
>   and like a sheep that before its shearers is dumb,
>   so he opened not his mouth.
> By oppression and judgment he was taken away;
>   and as for his generation, who considered
> that he was cut off out of the land of the living,
>   stricken for the transgression of my people?
> And they made his grave with the wicked
>   and with a rich man in his death,
> although he had done no violence,
>   and there was no deceit in his mouth.   (Isaiah 53:7–9)

This was what the death of Jesus meant: the mysterious image of the unknown Servant, the real Israel that never was, taking upon himself the suffering and guilt of the whole world, this image had now come to life before the disciples' eyes.

Their master's death and resurrection, these witnesses were now bold to say, were *the* events which made a New Israel. It was nothing less than a New Exodus. This is made quite clear in the worship of the new community, which centered around a meal they shared. The Christian "breaking of bread" reminds us clearly of the Passover, which was the "dramatized memory," as we saw in chapter 4, of the Exodus out of Egypt. In the Passover, the Jew celebrates that which made him who he is, the event which gave birth to his people. In the same way the new Jew, the Christian, as often as he "eat(s) this bread and drink(s) this cup . . . proclaim(s) the Lord's death until he comes" (1 Cor. 11:26). On the night when he was betrayed, Jesus had said, as he passed the after-supper cup of wine to his Disciples, "This is my blood of the covenant" (Mark 14:24). The first Exodus had founded a covenant between God and the people he had made. The death of Jesus was the foundation of a new covenant, the basis of life of a new people (cf. 1 Cor. 5:7).

Who Was Jesus?

Behind the news announced by the early Christians, there was a man. He was the one in whom these events happened. But who was this man? Now ordinarily, when we ask this question about any historical person we set about to answer it by gathering all the facts we can about the person, as objectively as possible. We want to know where and when he was born, what his parents were like, what his education was, what social and cultural forces influenced his development, what were the psychological turning points in his life. When we have pieced together as many of these clues as we can obtain, then we can construct an overall picture of this person's life. We can make up our minds what kind of man he was.

In modern times many authors have written "lives of Jesus" which tried to answer just the kind of questions we have suggested. But when we go to the New Testament itself with such questions, we are frequently baffled. The New Testament writers seem remarkably oblivious to things about which we are most curious. What did Jesus look like? We have no inkling. How did he spend his childhood? We have only the single story of a brief incident (Luke 2:41–51). What of his parents? We know their names, and that Joseph was a carpenter. But he has vanished from the scene before Jesus' adulthood; we do not know how. How long did Jesus live? Uncertain. We do not even know how long his public ministry lasted; Mark apparently thought he lived only about a year after his Baptism, while John describes a ministry extending over three years.

Why is it that the Gospels are so opaque to our curious questions? It is clear that they do want us to know "who Jesus was"; why are the facts we want so obscure? Could it be that our way of asking the question does not measure up to the problem? In Part One of this book we discovered how complicated it was to find out who any person "really" is—even if the person in question is your roommate or even yourself. Are we running into a similar problem here? Is it possible that even if we knew all the facts we want, we would still not know who Jesus really was? Pilate and Peter both had excellent access to the facts— but their conclusions were quite different. Caiaphas the High Priest and Paul the Pharisee both examined the evidence; one decided that Jesus ought to die for blasphemy, the other that he had been put to death as the Savior of mankind. Maybe the difference does not lie in what we regard as "the facts."

With this preliminary warning, let us turn back to our question. We can draw a bare sketch of Jesus' career with some certainty. But we have to remember that the books from which we derive this sketch are not called "biographies," but "gospels": good news. Every one of the four makes plain that not everyone who knew "the facts" knew who Jesus was, not everyone who heard the exact words of Jesus heard the Good News. There was something else involved in knowing and hearing. But the best way to get at that something else is to let the Gospels lead us through their own story to their own climax.

Somewhere between A.D. 26 and 29 a man named Jesus showed up in Galilee, a kind of backwoods area of Palestine

north of Samaria. He had been baptized by John the Baptist,
a wild sort of fellow who was going around dressed like Elijah
the prophet, urging the Jews to turn away from their sins. When
John was locked up because he got too specific about sins going
on in the king's household, Jesus stepped into the public eye.

After the fashion of rabbis, Jesus gathered around him a
group of "disciples." These people went with him from place
to place, carefully listening to his teaching, asking him questions, and in turn trying to answer the cryptic questions he
asked them. It was the classic method of teaching in the Orient.
Perhaps, we wonder from a later perspective, there was symbolic significance intended in the fact that he chose twelve of
them, the same number as the tribes of Israel, to be an inner
circle, sharing the "secrets" the others did not understand.

This rabbi—who had, so far as we know, no training to be a
rabbi—first attracted attention as a preacher. His message, as it
was remembered later, was summed up by Mark like this:

> The moment is fulfilled;
> God's kingly reign is imminent;
> Repent, and put your trust in the news.
>
> (Mark 1:15, author's translation)

The thing that impressed Mark about him was the urgency of
this message. Mark is always introducing the stories he records
with the word "immediately." Jesus was always saying to his
disciples, "Let us go on." He was in a great hurry to announce
his news to everyone possible.

Jesus also gained fame as an exorcist—one with the power to
liberate people who were in the grip of demonic forces—and as
a healer. Such exorcists were not uncommon in first-century
Judah, as elsewhere in the Near East, and demons were everywhere. The point of the healing stories is not that Jesus hung
out a shingle as professional demon-chaser. Instead, acts of healing were very closely related to his preaching. He announced
that the Kingdom (more accurately, the kingly rule) of God
was dawning. And he said, "If it is by the finger of God that I
cast out demons, then the kingdom of God has come upon you"

(Luke 11:20). It is worth noticing that the phrase "the finger of God" also occurs in Exodus 8:19, in connection with the miracles that were the prelude to the Exodus. The healings of Jesus, then, were the prelude to another mighty act of God. Wherever the Kingly Rule of God had begun to dawn, there the forces of evil—whether the evil of physical or mental sickness, or the evil of human sins, or evil personified in "demons"—had to stop ruling. Jesus not only proclaimed this, he acted it out. Where he appeared, a battle with evil ensued.

The works of healing were also connected with a radical claim of Jesus. To a paralytic who was brought to him, he said, "My son, your sins are forgiven" (Mark 2:5). That got him in trouble with the scribes, the professional religious lawyers. This is blasphemy, they cried. "Who can forgive sins but God alone?"

This was the beginning of hostilities between the professional religious leaders and Jesus. Even the rival Pharisees and Sadducees found something they could agree on: dislike of Jesus. Jesus, in turn, reserved some choice words for them, especially the Pharisees, whom he habitually called "you hypocrites." He incurred their wrath by his radical interpretation of the Law. "You have heard that it was said to the men of old . . . But I say to you . . ." Who did he think he was, someone greater than Moses? The common people, however, were amazed at his teaching. At the end of his first sermon in a synagogue, the congregation (if we may paraphrase the Greek into our everyday idiom) "were flabbergasted at his teaching, for he taught with the air of one who knew what he was talking about, not like the preachers" (Mark 1:22).

Even worse than his teaching, from the point of view of the Pharisees, was the company he kept. Like ourselves in younger days, they had always been taught:

> Shun evil companions,
> Bad language disdain.

The only way to be a pure Jew, truly obedient to the Law, was to be "separated" from evil, including bad people. Bad people were all those who did not keep the Law—or did not have the leisure or education that permitted the luxury of keeping it—as meticulously as the Pharisees did. Jesus did not come as a "separate one," but as a man deeply involved in life. He came "eating and drinking," and the Pharisees maliciously labeled him "a glutton and a drunkard, a friend of tax collectors and sinners!" (Luke 7:34.) "Well people don't need a doctor," retorted Jesus. "I came not to call the righteous, but sinners." As for the Pharisees, the streetwalkers would enter the Kingdom of God ahead of them! (Matthew 21:31.)

The animosity of Jesus' opponents grew steadily in proportion to his fame among the "sinners." At last the Pharisees, who hated him for religious reasons, and the Sadducees and Herodians, who suspected him for political reasons, conspired together to have him put out of the way. Taken treacherously at night, he was tried before the high priest and the Sanhedrin, found guilty of blasphemy, and sent to the Roman procurator on a trumped-up charge. When Pilate wavered, apparently unable to see clear proof of any crime, the conspirators stirred up a mob to help make up the governor's mind. Jesus was turned over to a battalion of soldiers, ridiculed and beaten, and then nailed to a cross. He died quickly.

That is the story of his life. It serves more to raise than to answer the question, Who was Jesus? That was a question that his contemporaries were pushed more and more to ask, and indeed, that was the question of his judges at the two rigged trials. The high priest demanded, "Are you the Christ?" and Pilate asked, "Are you the King of the Jews?" (Mark 14:61; 15:2.) It was the question which Jesus himself threw to his Disciples at the midpoint of his career. That was a very significant moment: let's read the account of it in Mark 8:27—9:1.

*   *   *

The people at large had strange ideas of who Jesus might be. Some thought he was John the Baptist come back to life. Herod, perhaps bothered a bit by guilty conscience, was one of them (Mark 6:16). But mostly Jesus was regarded as Elijah or "one of the prophets." Elijah was expected by popular tradition to come back to earth in time to announce the beginning of God's final kingdom. Others expected a prophet like Moses (Deut. 18: 15,18).[2] It was general belief that the gift of prophecy, dead since the time of Ezra the scribe, would flourish again in the last days (cf. Joel 2:28ff. and Acts 2:15–21). The masses then thought Jesus might be the forerunner of the Kingdom, after whom either God's Messiah or God himself would introduce the new age.

To his own Disciples, Jesus asks the question more pointedly: "But who do you say that I am?" Peter speaks for the group: "You are the Messiah."

Strangely enough, Jesus does not either approve or disapprove Peter's response, according to Mark, the earliest Gospel. He only cautions them that they must not tell anyone that he is Messiah. All through the Gospel According to Mark we find this same warning repeated. This "secret" points to a very significant fact that emerges from careful study of the Gospels. Jesus never made an open claim to be the Messiah expected by his people. When the disciples had their eyes opened by the events of Jesus' total life—and especially by his death and resurrection —so that they could confess that he was indeed the Messiah, the first thing they had to make clear was that "Messiah" now meant something completely new. When Jesus is called "the Messiah," then it is not Jesus who has to fit the going notions of "Messiah," but the notion of "Messiah" that has to be radically transformed to fit the events of Jesus' life and sacrifice. Jesus does not prove himself to us by fulfilling all *our* expectations of what the Son of God *ought* to be like; he does not have to pass *our* tests, so that then we will do him the favor of believing in him. No, when he comes he proves far greater than our expectations. All our dogmas are shattered by the marvel of his love. That is what the dialogue with Peter shows us.

Immediately after Peter's statement, Jesus "began to teach them that the Son of man must suffer many things, and be rejected by the elders and the chief priests and the scribes, and be killed." To Peter, all this was preposterous. The Messiah suffer, be rejected, be killed? This was nonsense. The Messiah

was a winner, not a loser. He was a king, who came to kill other
people, drive out the enemies of Israel, and set up the glorious
reign of a revived and purified Israel. But Jesus turned on Peter
and said, "Get out of my way, you Satan!" Jesus had heard that
temptation before. From the beginning of his ministry, he was
"tempted by Satan" (Mark 1:13). According to the story of
that temptation in Matthew and Luke, the temptation which
came as Jesus prepared himself for his mission was precisely to
put himself in the role of that victorious Messiah. Great miracles,
popular following, rule over "all the kingdoms of the world," all
this belonged to the picture. Now exactly this same temptation
came to him in the person of one of his own Disciples. Peter
had become "Satan," the Tempter.

The story of Peter's misunderstanding was told by disciples
who had had their eyes opened and their lives made over by
Jesus' death and rising and his continuing rule as their Lord.
From their new point of view illuminated by faith in this crucified yet living Lord, their former misunderstanding and unfaith
stand out starkly in Mark's Gospel. Now they comprehend that
Jesus' mission was completely different from their understanding of it. He had come, the King of the end-time, God's own
beloved Son, the new Redeemer, not to rule, but to take up into
his own life the sufferings, the hostilities, the sin of human life.
The image of the Suffering Servant, seen dimly and hopefully
by Second Isaiah, had come alive in human flesh. "For the Son
of man also came not to be served, but to serve, and to give his
life as a ransom for many" (Mark 10:45).

9

radical grace

The first Christians made the scene of history as town criers, proclaiming some news. Something had happened! This thing that had happened had happened to them; as a result of the happening they were different people. So we cannot blame them for being enthusiastic. But if, after almost twenty centuries, Christians keep on telling just the same old thing, it may be become annoying. So something happened in A.D. 29. So what? Why should that concern me, trying to puzzle my way through life in the last half of the twentieth century?

There is one man whom we meet in the New Testament who, more than any other, devotes his life to answering that question. Like ourselves, Paul of Tarsus first encountered the news when it was already "old," received it secondhand from the announcement of preachers. Like ourselves, he had to ask the question, "What does that have to do with me?" We are interested in him because he not only answered the question for himself, but pointed the way to answering it for all who would ever hear the news. That was the way Paul became the first theologian of the church. All Christian theology is just the attempt to answer the question, What have the events that happened, the things God has done in the history of his people, what have these to do with me and with my world?

Now Paul's reaction when he first heard the news from the Christians was not exactly a model for Christian behavior. He did not accept it at all, but attacked it for all he was worth. As he reminded the Galatian church later,

> . . . you have heard of my former life in Judaism, how I persecuted the church of God violently and tried to destroy

141

> it; and I advanced in Judaism beyond many of my own age
> among my people, so extremely zealous was I for the tradi-
> tions of my fathers.   (Galatians 1:13–14)

Then something happened:

> But then in his good pleasure God, who had set me apart
> from birth and called me through his grace, chose to reveal
> his Son to me and through me, in order that I might pro-
> claim him among the Gentiles.
>
> (Gal. 1:15f., New English Bible)

That "but then" is the point where Paul's life turned a corner.
The persecutor became an Apostle! What happened "then"? That
would give us a clue to our question. From Paul the Galatians
do not get a description of his experience at that turning point.
But these people knew him already. Let's turn to the letter he
wrote to strangers. The Letter to the Romans is really a letter of
introduction. Here he will surely give us the important facts
about his life.

Look at the beginning of Romans. How does Paul describe
himself? He is "a servant of Christ Jesus," "apostle by God's
call," "set apart for the Gospel of God." That's all. No more
description of his life. Instead his introduction turns to a recital
of the *gospel* (vv. 3–4)—yes, the same old news! But we wanted
to know about Paul! Yet it is just this recital of the news about
Jesus Christ that forms the basis of Paul's fellowship with his
readers. All they need to know about him is that his life is mo-
nopolized by the necessity to tell this news (1:5, 9, 14–16; 15:
16–21; cf. 1 Cor. 9:16f.). How can this be? What kind of news
can take over a man's whole life?

The New Righteousness

Verses 3–4 Paul quoted from some familiar creed of the
church. His own way of putting the news comes in verses 16–17,
which form the theme of the whole letter. (It will be helpful if
you stop here to *read the whole of Romans,* in a modern translation if possible. We shall work through the first eight chapters
together, but each passage needs to be seen within the context

of the whole letter. Some of it is not easy reading; some passages you will have to read twice—at least! But do not get bogged down in details at this point. Try to scan the entire letter to see what its patterns are.)

❉   ❉   ❉

The news is, the long-expected Son of David, God's Anointed, has come—though he came but to die. Nevertheless, his Resurrection reveals him as the one who reigns in power—far greater than merely a New David—the Son of God. Verse 17 presents the significance of this news for the life of the world: "God's righteousness is revealed from faith to faith."[1]

What does "righteousness" mean? Jot down some of the ideas that come to your mind when you hear the word "righteousness." Do you think of "goodness"? "Morality"? "Law-abiding," "justice," "self-righteousness," "righteous indignation"? Now try to put these everyday connotations of the word out of your mind so you can listen freshly to what Paul is saying. Paul is talking about "*God's* righteousness." What is that? Look at the way he develops his theme. The statement "The righteousness of God is revealed" pulls after it two very similar sentences: 1:18 and 3:21. These mark the beginnings of two significant steps in Paul's description of "God's righteousness." Now this is not just a theoretical discussion of a concept "righteousness"; what God's righteousness is *is revealed.* Where is it revealed? Look at verse 17. It is in the event of Jesus' death and resurrection as it is proclaimed, in the news of what God has done—and there alone.

Man Against Himself

The first step is verse 18: "For the wrath of God is revealed from heaven against all ungodliness and wickedness of men . . ." A new constitution is given, for a new king is ruling. The court's decree has been laid down; it is the law of the land. In its light, all the distortion, selfishness, and brokenness of human life stands exposed. To those who oppose it, it can bring only bitterness and destruction.[2] That is the wrath of God; that is the first side of God's righteousness.

There follows, in verses 19–32, a catalog of the wickedness of men. It is interesting to compare this catalog with the story in Genesis 3 (cf. chapter 3 of this book). Paul lays out the results of the refusal to "acknowledge God" as the Creator, because men were trying to be gods for themselves. What are the results? *Look at the developments in human life listed in verses 22–31 and compare them with the "curses" in Genesis 3:14–19. When man tries to live independently of God, when he centers his world in himself, what happens to his intellectual life? To his religion?* (Notice that man does not cease to be religious just because he does not acknowledge God—he only invents his own gods!) *To his sexual relationships? To his life in community?* Man wants to dominate the world—including other people—as if *he* were its lord. Ironically he becomes finally the slave of the destructive forces he has released.

Paul's argument may be theoretically denied, but its validity is oppressively obvious all around us. Do you remember when we decided to create ourselves a solid chunk of security by spending our defense money on nuclear weapons? Whatever became of that security we bought? Instead we find ourselves constantly trying to forget the precarious balance of terror as we teeter on the brink of insanity or destruction. Free? Secure? Rather slaves of the creatures we have devised.

Again, Paul illustrates his argument in the sphere of sex. Sex belongs to life as God created it. It can combine the ultimate respect of two persons for each other with a profound giving of each to the other. But when man "does not see fit to acknowledge God," he begins to use sex as an instrument of his self-exaltation or self-security, as if all things and all persons were at his disposal. In perverted sex, each partner becomes less than a person, first in the eyes of the other who seeks to use him, then in the blighting of his own highest possibility of personhood.

There is something else here. What is the theme that runs through this depressing account of the mess man makes of running his own life? "God gave them up . . ." (verses 24, 26, 28). Every man wants to be god, yet God is still God. He is still the Judge. All these "natural" and "inevitable" consequences of our distorted relationships are God's doing: these are the "wrath of God." He will not let us play our games, as if there were no better possibility, as if he did not exist.

The "wrath of God" belongs to God's judgment. It was a standard Jewish expression of the action God would take at the end of time "against all ungodliness and wickedness of men." But Paul speaks of this final wrath not only in the future (2:5, 16) but also in the present tense (1:18). To eyes of faith (v. 17) the final judgment of God can be seen already active wherever the news of Jesus' death and resurrection is heralded. That is why the Christians are the people "upon whom the end of the ages has come" (1 Cor. 10:11).

The Ungodly Religious

With chapter 2, Paul turns to his fellow Jews. Have they been following his description of the wickedness of the Gentiles with smug approval? "Yes, Paul is right. All those wicked people outside the church, all those poor sinners who had no proper upbringing, do not even *know* what is right. But Paul is right. They are absolutely without excuse." Can't you imagine the Adult Bible Class in the church at Rome, clucking their tongues and shaking their heads sadly over the fate of those outsiders? Can't you picture the Westminster Fellowship council discussing the lascivious life of the Greeks on campus? And then they turn piously to their closing devotions: "Lord, I thank thee that I am not as other men are."

"Therefore," says Paul to these superior ones, "*you* have no excuse, O man, whoever you are, when you judge another; for in passing judgment upon him you condemn yourself. . ." (2:1). God does not play favorites (v. 11). The religious people will not evade his penetrating gaze by standing conspicuously around his tribunal, pointing at the others. What God wants is not piety, but obedience. It will not do to turn Law and Covenant into an insurance policy offering blanket coverage (vv. 17–24). The ones who do this are not real Jews at all, though they have the name (2:25–29).

Chapter 2 unmasks hypocrisy. It is addressed to people who

put their trust in just *having* the Law—without troubling about obeying it. But what about those who *do* obey? What about the Pharisees, whose whole lives were dedicated to obeying the Law? Surely *they* could stand before God with heads erect.

Paul knew something about that; he had been a Pharisee. The predominant characteristic of the Pharisee was his *confidence*, confidence in himself, as Paul recalled to the Philippians:

> If any other man thinks he has reason for confidence in the flesh, I have more: circumcised on the eighth day, of the people of Israel, of the tribe of Benjamin, a Hebrew born of Hebrews; as to the law a Pharisee, as to zeal a persecuter of the church, as to righteousness under the law blameless.
> (Philippians 3:4–6)

In a world filled with evil and uncertainty, the Pharisee was good and certain. He knew where he stood. Not only did he know the Law, he knew he could obey it and that he *did* obey it. The poor sinners and Gentiles, all those "lesser breeds without the Law," lived a life ultimately rent with insecurity, but the Pharisee was secure. God himself was his security, because he was keeping the covenant God had given.

To this Pharisee Paul, the demand of the gospel, "Repent and believe," must have come as a threat to his life. To believe the news which these Christians were announcing would mean to accept their claim that God's final kingdom had begun, but that God had not brought it to his faithful Pharisees. It would mean to confess that the Messiah had come, not to the separated ones, the guardians of the Law, but in one who involved himself with the sinners and outcastes of the world, with those who lived outside the Law. It would mean to accept the preposterous assertion that the Messiah had come, not to establish the secure reign of law over all people, but in a man who had no security, but who had poured himself out, defenseless and weak before the powers of the world and the Law, yes, who had let himself be killed by those very guardians of the Law. If these things were true, then Paul's former life had not been true. If the reign of God meant not might, except in weakness, not victory, except through suffering, if the Messiah came not to rule in glory, but to die, then all his grounds of confidence had become just "so much garbage" (Phil. 3:8, New English Bible), replaced by "the surpassing worth of knowing Christ Jesus my Lord." In the face of the gospel, then, a self-centered religiosity can be the worst sin of all.

God's Own People

Do the Jews have any special advantage then? In 3:1–20, Paul takes up the election of the Jews, which he seemed to reject in chapter 2. Does their "chosenness" mean anything? To this question Paul answers Yes in verse 2 and No in verse 9. *Yes*, the Jews had an advantage. They were chosen as the custodians of God's word to the world. They were the concrete, specific community through whose life God entered history in the great events that added up to salvation for all mankind. The "story" of these events, their meaning, the "oracles of God," were entrusted to the Jews. That was their advantage, and that advantage stands fast, for the promise of God cannot be canceled. God remains faithful to the Jews (Paul returns to develop this statement in chapters 9–11). But as a matter of fact, God had to preserve his word in their history in spite of their unfaithfulness (v. 3). Hence the Jews, though they are the Chosen People, are *no better off* than the Gentiles, for "all men, both Jews and Greeks, are under the power of sin" (v. 10).

Through this discussion, Paul has shown that the real function of the Law is entirely different from the use to which the Pharisees put it. The Law is not a ladder for climbing into heaven. Whoever makes that his concern will stumble over Christ's word, "Whoever would save his life will lose it." But the purpose of the Law is just to unmask the selfish foundation of all human striving:

> . . . so that every mouth may be stopped, and the whole world may be held accountable to God. For no human being will be justified in his sight by works of the law since through the law comes knowledge of sin.   (3:19b–20)

In the light of the Crucifixion of the only truly obedient man, the eyes of faith see that the Law serves only to show that man cannot *earn* God's approval. The Cross is God's No spoken in judgment over all the illusions we build, all the dream-fortresses we erect against the unknown, all the artificial piety we offer up to a god of our making, all self-deceiving "goodness" by which we only compare ourselves with the weaker and poorer. Only when we hear that No can our ears be unstopped to hear also the Yes that was spoken at the same time.

The Pivot of History

The second major section of Romans begins with a pregnant phrase: "But now . . ." (3:21). We must pay strict attention to those two little words. The "but" is a decisive conjunction, drawing a sharp contrast between what has gone before and what follows, but nevertheless a conjunction, holding the two sides together in tension. What has gone before is a description of man under "wrath"; what follows is man under "grace." But wrath and grace are two sides of the same event, as we have suggested. Wrath unmasks sin, so that grace may prevail.

The "now" is equally decisive. It points to the moment which is absolutely new; this "now" has never been before. By this "now" Paul means the New Age, the Age of the End and of God's kingly rule, which has "now" broken into history and taken effect in the affairs of men (cf. 1 Cor. 10:11). For this reason, "now" refers first to the moment of Christ's death-and-resurrection. Secondarily, however, it means the moment in which that death-and-resurrection invades *my* life, putting to death my illusory goodness and offering me as a gift real life as a forgiven sinner. For this reason, although Paul can speak of the event of Christ's death-and-resurrection quite factually as *past*, he can also speak of it as *present*. To live by faith is to live always in the "now" of the New Age, to live as always "present" to that event which happened in the past.

What has happened "now" is that "the righteousness of God has been revealed."

The first two chapters told about the negative side of God's righteousness, his wrath. But righteousness is also positive. It is, as the New English Bible translates it, "God's way of righting wrong" (1:17). What is new in the "now" of Christ's reign is that the positive side of God's righteousness, the caring, vindicating, self-communicating side of his righteousness, is accessible "through faith." The righteousness of God not only condemns man's unrighteousness, it changes it; it "rights" man.

The Judge Who Justifies

The righteousness that comes to the man of faith is not his own. As the Reformers used to say, it is an *alien* righteousness. It comes as a gift (3:24). The man of faith stands before the judgment seat of God "now" and knows that here finally his pretended goodness, his "better-than-thou-art" is transparent. Then comes the surprise. The verdict is "Not guilty." Has there been some mistake? No, the judgment is accurate. Why? Because God is not only "just," he is a "justifier" (v. 26). He has taken action to put sin out of the way, to get rid of this barrier between man and himself, between man and genuine life. That is what Christ's death accomplished (3:25).

The righteousness that comes through faith is not to be confused with morality. It is a legal term: acquittal. "It does not mean the ethical quality of a person. It does not mean any quality at all, but a relationship."[3] This may be an exaggeration, but it points to a truth: Even when I have been acquitted by God, that is, when in faith I have received his righteousness, I may still not yet be helpful, loyal, clean, friendly, brave, and the rest, but I am free! I no longer have to prove anything to anybody, not even to myself, for before God my life is an open book. Now, in my new freedom, genuine goodness will begin to emerge. But this goodness then is not the *cause* of God's "justifying" me, but the *result*.

"Then what becomes of our boasting? It is excluded" (3:27). Of course, for what do I have to brag about? Because I am a Christian, does that mean I am better than that murderer or this prostitute or that arrogant atheist over there? Not at all. Tomorrow I may find that they have all gone into the Kingdom of God ahead of me. In God's eyes I may be no *better* at all than they; but I stand in a different relationship to him. But that was not *my* doing. "No one can give himself faith, and no more can he take away his own unbelief; how, then, will he take away a single sin, even the very smallest?"[4]

Promise Never Failing

In chapter 4, Paul shows that he is not contradicting the teachings of Israel's traditions. The very father of Israel, Abraham, was not a man renowned for good works, but a man of faith. Abraham was not a "religious genius" who went searching for God. He was minding his own business in Haran when God came looking for him. God did not promise Abraham that he would become a mighty people because Abraham was a good, loyal, circumcised Jew. He was circumcised only as a sign of the promise God had already given him. The only thing that made Abraham's life significant was his faith. He found the meaning and security of his existence only in the fragile, intangible word of God. When God promised Abraham that which was absurd— that he and Sarah, old and barren, would have a son—then Abraham believed. He believed even in the face of what was tangibly and obviously impossible; the word of God was more real to him and more dependable than all that was tangible and obvious. By recalling Abraham's story, Paul shows that, even in the most ancient traditions of Israel, it was God's free grace that was operating, not any sort of self-originated righteousness. Grace always preceded law. The covenant which bound Israel to God was not a contract to get God on Israel's side, but only a structure for the response Israel ought to make to God's gracious deliverance.

Look at 4:5: God is the one "who justifies the ungodly." There is a shocking statement! What kind of judge is this, who goes around acquitting guilty people? This is precisely the same language used in Exodus 23:7 (in the Septuagint, Paul's Bible) and Isaiah 5:23 to describe the unjust judges whom God condemns. Now does God himself act like that? Why, this will make chaos of the legal order.

But God's "justifying" does not stop with acquittal. It does not merely turn the criminal loose, with a few stern words, "Don't let me catch you doing that again." The justifying act of God—that is, Jesus Christ's death and his exaltation as the living Lord—*creates new life* in those who receive the event by faith. "For he who through faith is righteous *shall live*." It is this "shall live" that is the subject of chapters 5–8. (The way the new righteousness works itself out in the concrete decisions of everyday life is the subject matter of chapters 12–15, which we shall not have space to discuss.[5])

Living the Gift

Look now at 5:1–11. Notice that three times Paul repeats, "We rejoice . . ." The Greek reads, "We boast . . ."—the same verb that is used in 3:27, "Then what becomes of our boasting? It is excluded." How can "boasting" or "rejoicing" be excluded in one place and permitted in another? In 3:27 Paul is talking about a man's boasting in his own deeds, his own accomplishments, his own goodness—like Paul's previous "confidence in the flesh" (Phil. 3:3–6). That is excluded by faith. But in what does the "justified" man rejoice? In hope (5:2), in suffering (5:3), "in God through our Lord Jesus Christ, through whom we have now received our reconciliation" (5:11). The statements lead in a circle that begins and ends with hope (vv. 2, 5) and with the act of God in Christ (vv. 1, 6–11). The present sufferings of the Christians (v. 3) are thus completely encompassed by God's act and the resultant hope. That is why the Christian can rejoice even in suffering: not because he has some kind of martyr-complex and *enjoys* suffering, but because in the very midst of persecution that snatches away all visible security, the Christian becomes most aware of the "endurance" that God gives him. Through the endurance of suffering, he is led step by step to hope, "and hope does not disappoint us, because God's love has been poured into our hearts through the Holy Spirit which has been given to us" (v. 5).

The "pouring out" of God's love came through the death of Christ, as Paul now reiterates (vv. 6–11). God did not wait for us to become "good" or even "just" before taking his decisive act for us. Rather, it was at "just the right time," "while we were yet helpless . . . sinners . . . enemies . . ." that Christ died for us. It was precisely "the ungodly" for whom he died (cf. 4:5). Through his death, we are now "reconciled to God." The opposite of "reconcile" is "estrange" or "divorce." Christ has come to remove the estrangement between God and his rebellious creature. (Does this remind you of Hosea and his astonishing love?) Notice that it is not an angry God who has to be reconciled, but a consistently loving God who himself acts by giving his Son to reconcile man.

But this loving act of God was not only "at the right time," it is for all time, since the Holy Spirit is constantly at work in the Christian community to create life in keeping with God's love (v. 5). It is this "life of the Spirit" that is the subject of chapter 8. Notice that every one of the themes mentioned in 5:1–11 is taken up again and spelled out in chapter 8. This shows that chapters 5 and 8 form a close unity in Paul's thought. Together they show what life is like when God's new righteousness is in control.

A New Mankind

In 5:12–21 Paul compares Christ with Adam. Adam, as we saw in Genesis 3, is "Everyman," that is, he is the representative of mankind (cf. chapter 3 of this book). His sin was disobedience (v. 19), the attempt to be his own god, and that sin all mankind has repeated (v. 12). But now a New Man has come, a new representative, who did not seize the prerogatives of God, but submitted obediently to God (v. 19, cf. Phil. 2:6ff.). The result of rebellion was the destruction of man's real life (v. 12, cf. Gen. 3:19); the result of Christ's obedience is righteousness and eternal life for all who belong to the new humanity (vv. 19, 21).

So far the argument sounds like a mechanical process, like some kind of strange celestial bookkeeping or hocus-pocus. Once upon a time Adam did something that spoiled man's life, but again upon another time, Christ did something that made it all right, so now I can go my way. Is that what Paul is saying?

Hardly! In fact he goes out of his way to unbalance his own argument to keep anyone from reading it so mechanically. Verse 13 breaks the train of thought, and so does verse 15. Paul wants to show that "the free gift is not like the trespass," because the free gift is God's superabounding grace (v. 20f.). To make this clear, he inserts into the argument a statement about the Law. Isn't the Law given to man so he can live as God intended? Far from it: "Law intruded into this process to multiply law-breaking" (v. 20, New English Bible). Man-in-rebellion seizes on God's own law and uses it as an instrument against God and against his neighbor (cf. ch. 2). But this "multiplication of law-breaking" is not outside God's power. "Where sin was thus multiplied, grace immeasurably exceeded it" (v. 20), so that sin, having finally overplayed its hand, could be done to death.

A Transplanted Life

"Law intruded . . . to multiply law-breaking." "Where sin was thus multiplied, grace immeasurably exceeded it." Now that is the last straw! Any Jew listening to Paul would by now be holding two rocks ready to throw. And not only any Jew, but anyone concerned for basic morality and decency, for law and order; indeed, most Christians would be offended. Paul has snatched the foundation out from under the moral life and blasphemed against God's law, hasn't he?

Paul is not unaware of these objections. Had he not persecuted the church because of his own zeal for the traditions of the Fathers? Now he takes up the two questions in turn: "If we are under grace, then why not sin?" and "What about the Law?" The former is answered in 6:1—7:6, the latter in 7:7–25.

If grace comes as a gift, regardless of my relative goodness or badness, then why not sin all I please, and give grace more opportunity (6:1)? That such a question could and did arise is demonstrated by the Letter of James, which apparently argues directly against such a popular misunderstanding of Paul's teaching (James 2:14–26). But for Paul the question is really absurd. The asker of such a question might have followed Paul's argument superficially, but he would have totally failed to perceive what "grace" or "faith" meant. The Christian, Paul says, is a man who has *already died;* therefore neither death nor sin can control him.

Paul uses Baptism as the symbol of the re-creation of every believer's life when Christ was crucified. Again, take as an example Paul's own conversion. When Paul believed, he "died." That is, he was no longer the same person, for his whole Pharisaic-legal self-understanding, his whole structure of security, was shattered, and that meant the destruction of his *self.* Now he lives again—but not really he! (Cf. Gal. 2:20; 2 Cor. 5:14–17.) It is Christ who now lives in him, that is, in his "body." Before, his "body" was a "body of sin" (6:6), a "body of death" (7:24); now he belongs to "the body of Christ."

"Body" for Paul does not mean just the material body. It means the whole *self* as seen from one perspective: the self-in-relationship. Paul, unlike Greek philosophers, did not think of a good "soul" trapped in an evil body. Man is always body-and-soul. But the body, that is, the whole self, can be perverted. It can become a "body of sin," that is, a self-in-relationship to sinful striving. The body of sin is at the same time a "body of death," because it is trapped in the network of relationships which will all be destroyed by death.

The Christian is one whose "old self" (literally, "old man," v. 6), the "body of sin," has been crucified in Christ's crucifixion. But he has been brought to life anew, like an organ transplanted from a dying body into a new, healthy body. Now he is a member of "the body of Christ." Therefore he is no longer enslaved (vv. 6, 9, 10). Mixing the metaphor, Paul says that the dead-and-risen Christian now has a new master; he is no longer a slave to sin, but of righteousness and of God (vv. 12–23).

In answer to the first question, whether I may not do just as I please, since God has picked up the check, Paul thus answers, "By no means!" You are free: assert your freedom. You are alive anew: live! You have been bought by a new Master: obey him now from the heart. The timeworn arguments about faith versus good works are all absurd. Only when man is liberated from himself does he really become free to do what is truly good.

If the Christian has died with Christ, he has died to sin. But he has also "died to the law" (7:4). Paul illustrates this by an example from the divorce law (7:1–6). The single point is that someone else's death can make a radical difference in a person's status under the law. The result of Christ's death is that "we serve no longer under the old written code, but in the new life of the Spirit."

What about the Law then? Is it evil? That is the question of 7:7–25. Paul's answer (vv. 7–12) is clearly No! The Law is still *God's* Law, and as such is "holy and just and good" (v. 12). The Law expresses the demand of God for obedience, and man never has real life until he does obey his Creator.

But the Law did *not* bring this true life to man, as Paul has made clear again and again (v. 9; cf. Gal. 3:10, 21f.). Instead it became the instrument of self-righteousness (10:3) in which the whole vicious circle of trying to be gods, of judging one another and ourselves, of basing our lives on our own pride, is active. And that, seen from the standpoint of Christ's cross, is the real function of the Law. It is just a "warden" that binds us up in our sin (Gal. 3:24) until Christ comes, exposes our pretenses, and gives us a new life. In 7:13–25 Paul lays out the hopeless self-contradiction in which the man is trapped who is trying to get life by means of keeping rules. From the situation of faith, the real hollowness of his "goodness" is evident.

More Than Conquerors

Chapter 8 takes up anew the themes of 5:1–11, elaborating them in the light of chapters 6 and 7. Its theme is "the new life of the Spirit" (7:6, cf. 8:2). The life of the Spirit is distinguished from the "life of the flesh." "Flesh" for Paul does not mean physical life. It means life in rebellion against God. The self-righteousness of the Pharisee, which is certainly not physical, is a "fleshly" sin. And the "life of the Spirit" is not an otherworldly, antiphysical life. When Jesus washed the Disciples' feet, that was, as Luther says, a "spiritual" act. The life of the Spirit is life led by the Spirit of God in the midst of all the day-to-day, concrete decision-making of life.

The new life of the Christian is a life of freedom, but it is not life on a roller skate. It is a life which includes "sufferings," "groaning in travail," waiting, hope, weakness, fear. The Christian is a man who has died and who has been raised to new life. How strange the world looks to such a man! All the things that gave security to men who had not tasted death are gone for him. His new life is tender, unprotected, open and sensitive to all the attacks of life. The Christian will suffer. His new life is identified with the life of Christ, and Christ fulfilled his life in suffering service. The Servant Lord controls the Christian's life. If he faces the world with wonder and love, the world will attack him, as it attacked and killed his Master. The world cannot know that love is triumphant, and therefore the world hates goodness, hates it for the mirror it always holds up to the world's face.

But it is just in the midst of his insecurity that the Christian finds unshakable security. If he is attacked, what can he say? "If God is for us, who is against us?" "Who shall separate us from the love of Christ?"

> No, in all these things we are more than conquerors through him who loved us. For I am sure that neither death, nor life, nor angels, nor principalities, nor things present, nor things to come, nor powers, nor height, nor depth, nor anything else in all creation, will be able to separate us from the love of God in Christ Jesus our Lord.

10

faith for a frightened world

The Problem of Success

"The power of God is made perfect in weakness"; but what happens when the church is strong? In the first century the Christians were mostly "little people," the craftsmen and laborers, slaves and small businessmen, who could live out their lives in the crevices of the sprawling organization of the Roman Empire. They seldom attracted the attention of the ruling classes or the intelligentsia, and when they did, the "big shots" of the world were hardly inclined to come to the Christians with problems of state. Nevertheless, in a remarkably short time, Christian congregations had sprung up in every major town of the empire, and they could no longer be ignored. There was something about these little groups that set them apart from all the variety of cults and clubs and philosophies that had been multiplying like mushrooms. Soon people from every class of society were coming to hear what the Christians were saying. They came curious for the secret of the Christians' life, attracted by the strange freedom with which they walked through a world which felt itself increasingly to be bound by fate and luck; envious of the self-discipline and mutual concern which contrasted with a society whose lost weekends were stretching into a continuous binge; awed by the Christians' fearless life in the face of a world that was choking with fear of death and nothingness. Often the reaction of the Roman world was to despise these Christians it could not understand, then to seek to exterminate them. But more and more the Good News which these crowds of anonymous witnesses whispered was heard and listened to, till the church included thousands of men and women from every class and vocation, in every corner of the empire.

The story of that miracle of growth, of the centuries in which "the blood of the martyrs became the seed of the church," is an exciting one, but one we cannot tell again here. What we want to notice is that the very success of the Christian mission brought new problems for the church. The time came when Christians themselves held high posts in the empire, faced with decisions of war and peace, justice and injustice, inflation and depression. The time came when the empire itself felt its foundations tottering, saw the future clouded into anxious uncertainty, and came to the church with its questions and its fears. In this new situation, God raised up a new spokesman in the church, one with the keenest mind and at the same time the most intimate knowledge of the world since Paul himself: Augustine, Bishop of Hippo. In many ways he was the first of the church's leaders really to understand Paul, but the situation in which he found himself was very different from Paul's. So, while trying to understand Paul's insights into God's radical grace in Jesus Christ, he had to apply these insights to the problems of a dying empire.

Augustine: The Tardy Saint

In Augustine two powerful worlds, the classical world of Roman politics and Greek philosophy and the Christian world of the Bible and the church, met head-on. The collision produced in Augustine himself a long and intense struggle, but at the end this struggle developed a mind and personality uniquely equipped to address the problems of his age.

Augustine's mother, who was a devout Christian, had a great influence on him. When he went away to school in the big city of Carthage, however, he decided her faith was impossibly naïve and her morals too narrow. He took a mistress and plunged into the gay social life as well as the sophisticated intellectual circles of the city.

Endowed with enormous curiosity, Augustine wanted to be a philosopher. First he was carried away with the exotic ideas of the Manichean religion, a strange mixture of Persian ideas and some biblical language that claimed to be the thinking man's Christianity. Life, said the Manicheans, was the battlefield in a struggle between a good god and an evil god, who were evenly matched. The same battle went on in every man, as his good soul tried to escape from the dark world in which it was trapped. Augustine was intrigued by the Manichean doctrines for eight years before he gave them up as fantastic.

Augustine's next intellectual love was Neoplatonism, which taught almost the opposite from Manicheanism. Everything that was really real was good, they said. Evil was not real. God is another name for what is really real, that is, pure being and pure mind. Like the sun, which sends its rays into the world, God radiates being from himself. The rays of being that issue like light from God make the world. Since the world comes from God, it cannot be evil. It seems evil, however, because it is not pure mind, but mixed with matter. Matter is not real. The more mind and the less matter anything contained, the more real it was and therefore the nearer to God. Man, for example, is more real than animals. Because man is basically mind, he can teach himself to rise above matter, that is, above the mere appearances of things. By reasoning, he can be reunited with God, first gaining the dazzling, mystical vision of this intellectual sun, then losing himself altogether in the ocean of Being.

Augustine found Neoplatonism a congenial philosophy, but he began to doubt that reason alone could solve man's problems. The Neoplatonists taught him that anyone who *knew* what was good could *do* what was good. Augustine, however, when he looked honestly at his own life, found himself described better by Paul's complaint, "I can will what is right, but I cannot do it. For I do not do the good I want, but the evil I do not want is what I do." In this state of mind, he moved to Milan, where he was appointed to public office and worked as tutor for aristocratic youths. He was impressed by the vigorous preaching and by the courage of the bishop of that city, Ambrose. After a profound emotional turmoil, Augustine at last found the end of his search in the letters of Paul—the very letters he had once thought barbarous. At the age of thirty-two, the sensitive young intellectual was baptized by Ambrose. In a short time he became a priest and then was named Bishop of Hippo, in North Africa.

In that strategic position Augustine could see the effects of the dying Roman Empire on its citizens. He began to work out answers that the church could speak to people who were seeing all their familiar securities dissolve.

The Decay of Rome

In A.D. 413, when Augustine began to write his greatest book, he may not have been aware that he was living at the end of one political age and the beginning of a new one. But he knew quite clearly that the "eternal city," as Rome had been called, belonged to "the form of this world" which was "passing away." That Rome was neither eternal nor invincible had been demonstrated to everybody only three years before, when Alaric and his army of Goths had marched into the paralyzed city, burning and pillaging, sparing only the Christian churches and those who fled to them for refuge. The defeat stunned the empire, but when the first shock was past and Alaric had withdrawn from the city, the popular reaction was only to try to forget that such a thing had happened. When Augustine's first chapters dealing with the defeat had been published, a fellow churchman wrote to complain that such painful memories should not be kept alive. In its declining years, Rome seemed to want only to turn back to the dreamworld of its mighty past, living by visions of ideals that had never been realized. But Augustine, both as a pastor ministering to the hordes of refugees who streamed into Hippo from Rome and as a theologian trying to proclaim the biblical word for his time, knew that men had to find their hope in something more sturdy than those wilted dreams. Rome was no eternal city, but there was another city, "whose maker and builder is God."

Rome's genius had combined native Latin political shrewdness with Greek idealism. The result was a society whose goals were peace, justice, and community. The peace of Rome was an armed peace, the peace of a stockade in the wilderness. Inside the boundaries, which were established and defended by Rome's famous fighting legions, men had security to cultivate business, art, and learning, but outside were the "barbarians," locked in continual struggle for survival. Justice for Rome meant the rule of law, law which guaranteed the rights of all within the "stockade," that is, all who were citizens of the Republic. Ideally the law was supreme, even to the emperor. It guarded a private sphere of life and property for every household against encroachment by others. The community of Rome meant basically sharing responsibility for safeguarding property. But it meant sharing the ideals as well. The whole system depended on one ideal standing fast: the ideal of the "eternal city."

When Alaric broke through the "stockade," he shattered Rome's *peace*. But more important, by the light of the flames he lighted, it became obvious that both *justice* and *community* had already decayed inside the fort. In their fear of invasion and subversion, the citizens had been persuaded to give up the rights of individuals under the law. Consequently, the state had become totalitarian. As justice and individual freedom disappeared, the economy also crumbled. The mutual trust which was necessary for economic community had been undermined. The community disintegrated as fear, suspicion, and greed divided neighbor from neighbor.

This was the Rome in which Christianity had finally been legalized, in which masses of people now looked to the church to show them the way out of a world falling to pieces. Constantine, the first of the Christian emperors, had tried to use Christianity as a kind of glue to hold together the realm he had reassembled by force. The sign of the cross and the monogram of Christ, carried into battle by Constantine's troops, seemed to bring good luck, and the church was now the single institution holding the loyalty of men in all parts of the empire. But in the long run Christianity could not be used successfully as a rabbit's foot or a prop for patriotism. Constantine's patronage of the church, though it brought a welcome change from the former persecutions, ended in such corruption for both empire and church that Constantine's high-minded successor, Julian, turned back to paganism in disgust.

By the time Augustine was writing, however, a member of the church was again reigning as Caesar. For most of Rome's leaders, the old gods were finally dead. Into the church's lap the question was tossed again, Can you give us a new justice, a new peace, a new community?

Concerning the City of God

Augustine was driven to write his famous book, *The City of God*, first of all to answer the pagans who blamed the Christians for the sack of Rome. It had happened, they said, as vengeance by the old gods, who were angry because the Christians had forbidden sacrifice to them. Augustine disposed of this charge easily enough; in the bulk of his book he works painstakingly but brilliantly through far profounder questions. To the longings of his contemporaries for a new justice, a new peace, and a new community, he proposes a threefold answer: (1) a theology of grace, (2) a theology of history, and (3) a theology of community.

The classical world had always proposed a "bootstrap" approach to human problems. That is, the evil in the world could be overcome by hard work and positive thinking. Under the influence of Neoplatonism, Augustine had already tried this approach and found it ineffective. When the same kind of teaching showed up in the church, especially in the teachings of a British monk named Pelagius, Augustine was infuriated. Pelagius and his followers (a good many are still lurking in our modern churches!) taught that man's freedom could never be taken away from him. He needed only a little help from God and the good example of Christ in order to save himself. Augustine had had a long controversy with the Pelagians, which served to open his eyes more and more to Paul's teaching about God's radical grace. To be sure, Augustine said, man had been created by God with a free will. But in his freedom he had pridefully rebelled against God, thereby sliding into an unreal world, a neurotic self-centeredness, from which he no longer had the freedom to escape. But in Jesus Christ God had come to reveal his own reality, wisdom, and power, and to *re-create* man, restoring his freedom.

On the other hand, there was a more pessimistic strain in all classical thought, which Augustine equally repudiated. From Plato on, idealists divided the world into mind, which was essentially good, and matter, which was, if not evil, at least not good. Salvation consisted basically in *escape* from the limits imposed on man by his physical nature. The body, they taught, was the tomb of the soul. Some religious sects, like the Manicheans whom Augustine had once joined, carried this "dualism" to an extreme, saying that matter was made by an evil god, spirit by a good god. Augustine saw that this kind of thinking ran squarely against the Bible's teaching that "God created the heavens and the earth . . . and . . . it was good."

Augustine's theology of history was even more revolutionary compared with the common thought of Greece and Rome. The classical man saw history in terms either of luck or of fate. The most common view of time was that it moved in a circle. If Rome had enjoyed a Golden Age, then it must inevitably decline to an Age of Bronze, an Age of Iron, an Age of Clay. Hence many of Augustine's contemporaries stared at the passing events with utter despair, sure that civilization was on the "down" side of the wheel of time. Popular superstition thought individual lives were controlled with the same rigid fate, determined by the stars under which they were born. Others, however, saw no pattern at all in history, but only the whimsy of chance. As Rome's fear of the barbarians increased, her citizens tried desperately to change their luck, pouring out sacrifices to more and more gods, until the Pantheon showed signs of a divine housing shortage. Significantly, luck itself was elevated to deity in the goddess Fortuna. For Augustine, however, history has no place for either luck or fate, for history is the realm where God is working. The things which happen take place through the Wisdom of God, the same Wisdom who became flesh in Jesus Christ. He who knows Jesus Christ, therefore, knows the meaning of history. He knows that history moves hiddenly toward an end which is determined by God's love, wisdom, and power.

For the Roman, community meant citizenship in the Republic, shared power, shared property, shared interest. But Augustine saw that real community cannot be defined in terms of what people *own,* but in terms of what they *love.* That is why, though there had been many empires, many cities, they composed in reality only two communities, two "cities," the "city of the world" and the "city of God." The latest example of the city of the world was Rome, which was bound together by the love of power, glory, and liberty. But the city of God, which is to be found in the church, is bound together by the love of God and the love of the brethren. In short, the city of the world is created by the love of *things*—even though some of the things may be ideas or ideals—while the city of God comes into being in the love of *persons.*

But it is time to let Augustine speak for himself. *The City of God* is a very long book; the following excerpts are only some brief samples of its ideas.

Evil in the World and the Goodness of God

"There is no Creator higher than God, no art more efficacious than the Word of God, no better reason why something good should be created than that the God who creates is good. Even Plato says that the best reason for creating the world is that good things should be made by a good God. . . .

"The explanation, then, of the goodness of creation is the goodness of God. It is a reasonable and sufficient explanation whether considered in the light of philosophy or of faith. It puts an end to all controversies concerning the origin of the world. Nevertheless, certain heretics remain unconvinced, on the ground that many things in creation are unsuitable and even harmful to that poor and fragile mortality of the flesh which, of course, is no more than the just penalty of sin. The heretics mention, for example, fire, cold, wild beasts, and things like that, without considering how wonderful such things are in themselves and in their proper place and how beautifully they fit into the total pattern of the universe making, as it were, their particular contributions to the commonweal of cosmic beauty. . . ."[1]

"Should anyone say that the cause of vices and evil habits lies in the flesh because it is only when the soul is influenced by the flesh that it lives then in such a manner, he cannot have suffi-ciently considered the entire nature of man. [Here Augustine cites scriptural verses on both sides of the issue: Wisdom of Solomon 9:15; 2 Cor. 4:16; 5:1–4.]

"On the one hand, our corruptible body may be a burden on our soul; on the other hand, the cause of this encumbrance is not in the nature and substance of the body, and, therefore, aware as we are of its corruption, we do not desire to be divested of the body but rather to be clothed with its immortality. In immortal life we shall have a body, but it will no longer be a burden since it will no longer be corruptible. . . .

"Virgil, it is true, seems to express a different idea, following Plato in his luminous lines:

A fiery vigor of celestial birth
Endows these seeds so slowed by weight of earth
Or body's drag; and so they ever lie
In bondage to dull limbs that one day die.

And, as if he wanted us to believe that the four most common emotions of the soul—desire, fear, joy, and sadness—which are the causes of all sins and vices, spring from the body, he con-tinues with the verse:

Thus do they fear and hope, rejoice and grieve,
Blind in the gloomy jail they cannot leave.

"So Virgil. Our faith teaches something very different. For the corruption of the body, which is a burden on the soul, is not the cause but the punishment of Adam's first sin . . . .

"Now, since the Devil has all these vices [enmities, conten-tions, jealousies, anger, and quarrels, which Augustine lists in a paragraph omitted here] but has no flesh, they can only be the works of the flesh in the sense that they are the works of man. Actually as I have mentioned, Paul often refers to man under the name of 'flesh.' It was not by reason of the flesh—which the Devil does not possess—but by reason of a man's desire to live accord-ing to himself, that is, according to man, that man made himself like the Devil. . . ."[2]

At this point maybe it would help to take a breather from Augustine's argument to see if some of the things he has said so far do not help to clarify some issues that are as lively for us as for the people in Hippo then. *Can you think of any points of view today that imply, consciously or unconsciously, that the world is bad in itself? Have you read any books or articles that express this kind of total despair about the world? How would Augustine answer such a view?*

Or take a narrower problem, say one of the questions about sexual morality that agitate so many of those dormitory bull sessions. What guidelines for right and wrong would be adopted by someone who believed that the body was bad just because it was body? How would Augustine's view differ? What does Augustine mean when he says it is not our flesh that makes us sinful, but our desire to live according to ourselves? What biblical passage is he thinking of? Compare this view of sin with that of Paul as we saw it in Romans.

History Does Not Go in Circles

"It was this controversy [why the world did not begin at some other point in eternity] that led the natural philosophers to believe that the only way they could or should solve it was by a theory of periodic cycles of time according to which there always has been and will be a continual renewal and repetition in the order of nature, because the coming and passing ages revolve as on a wheel.

❀   ❀   ❀

"Why, there are some people who want to twist even a famous passage in the book of Solomon, called Ecclesiastes, into a defense of these recurring cycles of universal dissolution and re-evocation of the past: 'What is it that hath been? The same thing that shall be. What is it that hath been done? The same that shall be done. Nothing under the sun is new, neither is any man able to say: Behold this is new, for it hath already gone before in the ages that were before us.' . . .

"Far be it from us Christians, however, to believe that these

words of Solomon refer to those cycles by which, as these philosophers suppose, the same periods of time and sequence of events
will be repeated; as if, for example, the philosopher Plato having
taught in a certain age at the school of Athens called the
Academy, even so, through innumerable ages of the past at long
but definite intervals, this same Plato and the same city, the
same school and the same disciples all existed and will all exist
again and again through innumerable ages of the future. Far be
it from us, I say, to believe this.

"For Christ died once for our sins; and 'having risen from the
dead, dies now no more, death shall no longer have dominion
over him'; and we after the resurrection 'shall ever be with the
Lord,' to whom we say, as the holy Psalmist reminds us: 'Thou,
O Lord, wilt preserve us: and keep us from this generation
forever.' And the verse which follows, I think, may be suitably
applied to these philosophers: 'The wicked walk round
about.' . . .

"No wonder, then, that they keep wandering around and
around in these circles and can find neither the entrance nor the
exit—neither the origin nor the end of our mortal human race.
The trouble is that they cannot penetrate the depth of the
wisdom of God, who, though eternal and without beginning,
caused time to have a beginning and, in time, created a man,
who had not been made before, and He made man, not by a
new and sudden resolution, but according to His unchangeable
and eternal plan."[3]

The question what meaning history has—or whether it has
any meaning at all—has been forced upon us by the events of
this century, just as fourth-century events thrust the issue upon
Augustine and his contemporaries. *Is the cyclical view of history
which Augustine opposed a live alternative today? What are
some other ways of understanding history? For example, a
Marxist might say, "If you have read Marx and Lenin, then you
know what is going to happen in history." What is his idea of
history? How would Augustine reply? Did Augustine "know
what was going to happen"? In what sense? What had happened*

that made it impossible for Augustine, as a Christian, to go along with the view that history had no real meaning?

The Story of Two Loves

"What we see, then, is that two societies have issued from two kinds of love. Worldly society has flowered from a selfish love which dared to despise even God, whereas the communion of saints is rooted in a love of God that is ready to trample on self. In a word, this latter relies on the Lord, whereas the other boasts that it can get along by itself. The city of man seeks the praise of men, whereas the height of glory for the other is to hear God in the witness of conscience. The one lifts up its head in its own boasting; the other says to God: 'Thou art my glory, thou liftest up my head.'

"In the city of the world both the rulers themselves and the people they dominate are dominated by the lust for domination; whereas in the City of God all citizens serve one another in charity, whether they serve by the responsibilities of office or by the duties of obedience. The one city loves its leaders as symbols of its own strength; the other says to its God: 'I love thee, O Lord, my strength.' . . ."[4]

"Actually, I think I have said enough on the really great and difficult problems concerning the origin of the world, the soul, and the human race. In regard to mankind I have made a division. On the one side are those who live according to man; on the other, those who live according to God. And I have said that, in a deeper sense, we may speak of two cities or two human societies, the destiny of the one being an eternal kingdom under God while the doom of the other is eternal punishment along with the Devil.

"Of the final consummation of the two cities I shall have to speak later. Of their original cause among the angels whose number no man knows and then in the first two human beings, I have already spoken. For the moment, therefore, I must deal with the course of the history of the two cities from the time when children were born to the first couple until the day when men shall beget no more. By the course of their history, as distinguished from their original cause and final consummation, I mean the whole time of world history in which men are born and take the place of those who die and depart.

"Now, the first man born of the two parents of the human race was Cain. He belonged to the city of man. The next born was Abel, and he was of the City of God. Notice here a parallel between the individual man and the whole race. We all experience as individuals what the Apostle says: 'It is not the spiritual that comes first, but the physical, and then the spiritual.' The fact is that every individual springs from a condemned stock and, because of Adam, must be first cankered and carnal, only later to become sound and spiritual by the process of rebirth in Christ. So, too, with the human race as a whole, as soon as human birth and death began the historical course of the two cities, the first to be born was a citizen of this world and only later came the one who was an alien in the city of men but at home in the City of God, a man predestined by grace and elected by grace. By grace an alien on earth, by grace he was a citizen of heaven. In and of himself, he springs from the common clay, all of which was under condemnation from the beginning, but which God held in His hands like a potter, to borrow the metaphor which the Apostle so wisely and deliberately uses. For, God could make 'from the same mass one vessel for honorable, another for ignoble use.' The first vessel to be made was 'for ignoble use.' Only later was there made a vessel for honorable use. And as with the race, so, as I have said, with the individual. First comes the clay that is only fit to be thrown away, with which we must begin, but in which we need not remain. Afterwards comes what is fit for use, that into which we can be gradually molded and in which, when molded, we may remain. This does not mean that every one who is wicked is to become good, but that no one becomes good who was not once wicked. What is true is that the sooner a man makes a change in himself for the better the sooner he has a right to be called what he has become. The second name hides the first.

"Now, it is recorded of Cain that he built a city, while Abel, as though he were merely a pilgrim on earth, built none. For, the true City of the saints is in heaven, though here on earth it produces citizens in whom it wanders as on a pilgrimage through time looking for the Kingdom of eternity. When that day comes it will gather together all those who, rising in their bodies, shall have that Kingdom given to them in which, along with their Prince, the King of Eternity, they shall reign for ever and ever."[5]

It might be interesting to compare these paragraphs of Augustine with the remarks made about different kinds of community in chapter 2 of this book. *Is he dealing with similar problems? Take Augustine's notion that the real nature of a community is determined by what or who it loves and try it out on some of the groups you belong to. What holds these groups together? What are their reasons for existing?*

Augustine's description of the "City of God" is a glorious one. *Is there really a community like that?* Notice that Augustine is careful *not* to identify that City with the church, although he evidently regards the two as very closely related. *In what ways does the church live the life of the City of God?*

In what sense is every Christian an "alien" in the world? What are some dangers in that way of thinking? What keeps Augustine from becoming otherworldly? To put it another way, how can it be that his conviction—that his true citizenship is in another world altogether—liberates him to take seriously the problems of this world and to take effective action in coping with them?

11

the divine empire

Merging the Two Cities

In the centuries after Augustine the "city of the world" fell apart rapidly. By the end of the sixth century the end was obvious. In Rome itself, whose population a short time before had been well over one million, not more than sixty thousand inhabitants remained. For those who were left, life contrasted pitifully to the comfortable efficiency of former times. The new barbarian masters were good soldiers, but poor engineers and managers. Soon the city's aqueducts crumbled, the sewers clogged, the malarial swamps went undrained. The great system of roads running to every corner of the empire fell into disrepair; the mail service stopped. It was clear that the empire in the West was dead.

This dreadful development would not have surprised Augustine, who had written calmly that the kingdoms of this world come and go, the city of Cain taking ever new forms. What would have surprised Augustine, however, would have been the suggestion that the City of God, in the form of the visible church, might take over the city of the world and run it. That, however, is precisely what was to happen.

At first it was a simple matter of practical necessity. The barbarian rulers who had replaced the imperial court in Rome were like backwoodsmen presented with a Cadillac: they admired the magnificent machinery of Rome's civilization, but they had no notion how to make it run. When the water stopped running in the public fountains, how did one make it start again? When the city ran out of grain for bread, how did one go about ordering more? How did one organize a merchant marine? a police force? a city government? The civil service of the empire was dissolved; the tribes of the Goths and the Lombards had nothing to take its place. There was, however, one surviving institution which had kept intact its organization, its discipline, its law, its communications. That institution was the church.

In A.D. 590, during an outbreak of bubonic plague which added still further miseries to Rome's plight, a man was made Bishop of Rome, or Pope, who was ideally fitted to lead both government and church: Gregory, later known as "the Great." Born in a devout Christian family of high rank, he had received a good education and had served in the imperial civil service before he became a priest. In fact, in 573 he had been prefect of the city, the highest office left since the imperial court had fled to Ravenna. Like Augustine, Gregory yearned for a life of contemplation in a monastery, but his administrative experience was too sorely needed and his flair for politics too natural for so quiet a life. As pope, he took over more and more of the functions of government. The enormous bookkeeping involved in importing grain from Sicily and Egypt was turned over to monks and priests: they alone could read, write, and do arithmetic! To maintain some degree of law and order in the towns, the law of the church increasingly had to take the place of the law of the empire. Diplomacy and even military defense were abandoned by the remnants of the empire, whose officers were secure in Ravenna. On one occasion Gregory himself had to interrupt his lectures on the book of Ezekiel long enough to take command of the militia and defend the city against a Lombard attack. He developed a policy of playing off the Lombards against the emperor in Constantinople, a process which not only brought peace to Italy, but also established the church as the real political power in the country.

The crisis in Rome thus brought about a blending of Augustine's two cities until the two were indistinguishable. The church continued to speak of itself as a "spiritual" commonwealth, but it had no inclination to give up the "temporal" power it had inherited. On the other hand, while the church, and especially the papacy, grew stronger and stronger, the secular rulers in the West soon came of age, too. The result was a continuous tug of war between kings and pope throughout the Middle Ages. The church fought back with great shrewdness and every weapon—"spiritual" and "temporal"—at its command. At the same time, its scholars were put to work to rationalize the pattern suggested by Gregory's reign, that the church ought to outrank the government. The ultimate expression of this claim, written when the tide had turned in favor of the secular authority, came in the bull "Unam Sanctam" published by Pope Boniface in 1302:

> We are obliged by the faith to believe and hold—and we do firmly believe and sincerely confess—that there is one Holy Catholic and Apostolic Church, and that outside this Church there is neither salvation nor remission of sins. . . . In which Church there is one Lord, one faith, one baptism. At the time of the flood there was one ark of Noah, symbolizing the one Church; this was completed in one cubit and had one, namely Noah, as helmsman and captain; outside which all things on earth, we read, were destroyed. . . . Of this one and only Church there is one body and one head—not two heads, like a monster—namely Christ, and Christ's vicar is Peter, and Peter's successor, for the Lord said to Peter himself, 'Feed My sheep.' . . .
> And we learn from the words of the Gospel that in this Church and in her power are two swords, the spiritual and the temporal. For when the apostles said, 'Behold, here' (that is, in the Church, since it was the apostles who spoke) 'are two swords'—the Lord did not reply, 'It is too much,' but 'It is enough.' Truly he who denies that the temporal sword is in the power of Peter, misunderstands the words of the Lord, 'Put up thy sword into the sheath.' Both are in the power of the Church, the spiritual sword and the material. But the latter is to be used for the Church, the former by her; the former by the priest, the latter by kings and captains but at the will and by the permission of the priest. The one sword, then, should be under the other, and temporal authority subject to spiritual. For when the

apostle says 'there is no power but of God, and the powers
that be are ordained of God' they would not be so ordained
were not one sword made subject to the other. . . .
Thus, concerning the Church and her power, is the prophecy
of Jeremiah fulfilled, 'See, I have this day set thee over the
nations and over the kingdoms,' etc. If, therefore, the earthly
power err, it shall be judged by the spiritual power; and if a
lesser power err, it shall be judged by a greater. But if the
supreme power err, it can only be judged by God, not by
man; for the testimony of the apostle is 'The spiritual man
judgeth all things, yet he himself is judged of no man.' For
this authority, although given to a man and exercised by a
man, is not human, but rather divine, given at God's mouth
to Peter and established on a rock for him and his successors
in Him whom he confessed, the Lord saying to Peter himself, 'Whatsoever thou shalt bind,' etc. Whoever therefore
resists this power thus ordained of God, resists the ordi-
nance of God. . . . Furthermore we declare, state, define
and pronounce that it is altogether necessary to salvation for
every human creature to be subject to the Roman pontiff.[1]

A Sacramental Universe

Despite the often bitter struggle between pope and kings for
supremacy over their world, neither would ever have questioned
the basic unity of that world. The modern concept of separation
between church and state would have been completely foreign
to the Middle Ages. The pope claimed to head both, with the
right to crown or to depose kings, while the new German empire
called itself "Holy" as well as "Roman," and insisted on its right
to appoint and install bishops. For the Middle Ages, all of life
was woven into a seamless fabric, with "spiritual" and "secular"
aspects intertwined throughout.

The most complete symbol of the unity and ultimate spir-
ituality of the medieval man's world is the Gothic cathedral. It is
the unity of one of these buildings which stops us and makes us
catch our breath when we first get sight of it. We may be surrounded by the swirling traffic of Paris or the throbbing business

of Cologne, or filled with a hundred distracting thoughts, but this massive, delicate structure lives in a stillness of its own. It draws our eyes to it, focuses them, moves them unhurriedly but irresistibly upward. The building is an organism, in which every part flows into the whole, supports its single, overpowering impression.

Yet the unity of the Gothic is very complex, not simple like the massive, plain towers of its Romanesque predecessors. The longer we gaze, the more we become conscious of the elaborate detail in even the smallest part, of the tensions and rhythms in its lines. We come nearer and discover that this is more than a building; it is an encyclopedia and a storybook, which is grand enough and detailed enough to include all of life in its images.

It is, as the medieval scholars would say, the "mirror of nature." And all of nature is reflected. The lacy fretwork we saw from a distance on doorways, cornices, pilasters, pinnacles, on closer examination turns out to be a zoo, a botanical garden, and Grimm's fairy tales, all scrambled together in the carved stone. Here is a symbolic panel showing God creating the world—he makes lions, goats, and sheep, fig trees and wine stocks, calls up fantastic creatures in the sea, and, when all is finished, leans on his staff and rests. This scene gives the context of the remainder, for every nook is filled with lively images: twining vines laden with grapes, raspberries and wild roses, birds singing among oak leaves, lions, elephants, and camels, squirrels, hens, and rabbits. Yes, and other creatures no zoo ever held: unicorns and dragons, sea serpents and griffins. Hideous monsters leer at us from the drain spouts; grotesque dwarfs and grinning demons smirk from cornices. For all things, ugly or beautiful, common or exotic, belong to God's creation, and this building stands for his world in all its abundance of life.

Not only nature, but the whole life of man which is lived out in the realm of nature is reflected in these stones. The daily round of work finds its place: there is a bas-relief of a peasant, sharpening his scythe; he represents the month of July. Here is a window donated by the guild of wool-merchants; it depicts the whole process of manufacturing cloth! Here is a group of statues which are allegories of the courses taught in the medieval school: rhetoric with her scalpel to sharpen the tongue, geometry with her compass, measuring the earth, and all the rest. Work and learning both had their places as steps on the road to salvation in the Middle Ages. The inner life of man was also depicted: on a portal we see carvings of the seven Cardinal Virtues, each doing battle with her opposite, a Cardinal Vice. The priests recognized the fact that it is always a struggle to be good, but the carvings also express their certainty that, if worked at hard enough, the virtues will always win out.

Despite the earthy practicality of some of these small scenes, however, the mood of the whole building is one of mystery. The flying buttresses seem to defy gravity, thin fingers of stone reaching across airy heights. A subtle engineering has so balanced hidden forces that apparently delicate pillars support towering walls. Sharp edges are broken by vines, grapes, and grotesques, and heavy structural members are delicately carved, till the solid stone of the towers seems to melt into the clouds. Inside, a forest of columns rises in the silent gloom of semidarkness, relieved by the multicolored rays of light that filter through the high windows and seem to fill the air itself with color. The lines of the columns lead our eyes upward, only to confuse them in the dim lacework of ribs in the vaulted ceilings, draw them down and forward and up again, until finally our whole attention is led steadily to the raised, half-screened chancel, the massive altar standing under its golden canopy, the eternal lamp glowing eerily in the twilight, casting a dim light on the figure of the Crucified who hangs there in perpetual agony. The whole setting says to us that all of the so firm realities carved in these stones—the celebration of daily life, of learning, of nature, and of fancy—all these only point beyond themselves, as the great towers point to the sky, to a world more real than that which is seen.

For the Middle Ages, every thing in the world is symbolic. ". . . the world is a book written by the hand of God in which every creature is a word charged with meaning."[2] Even some of these fanciful animals which seemed to belong only to the world of fairy stories turn out to be allegories of salvation. For example, the unicorn, one of the favorite beasts of the Middle Ages, was a symbol of Christ. In popular folklore, there was only one way to catch a unicorn. First one must find a pure virgin; if she would only sit down in the woods, the unicorn would come at once and put his head in her lap. Since the medieval theologians had never read Freud, they saw at once that this was a beautiful allegory of the Incarnation. The eternal Word of God could never be "caught" by philosophical systems, but he humbled himself to be born of the Virgin Mary and then to be killed for our salvation.

Of course the main symbols were not to be found in nature or in folklore, but in the Bible and in the lives of the saints. These together form the "mirror of history," which provides the framework for the mystery of salvation. Rows of imposing statues surround the main doorways of the cathedral, like the "great cloud of witnesses" of Hebrews (12:1). There are three groups of these figures: first, the great personages of the Old Testament, patriarchs, kings, and prophets. Second, there are the apostles and Gospel writers of the New Testament. Finally, there are the saints and martyrs of the church. Together, they symbolize the three stages in the history of salvation: the ages of mankind looking forward to the coming of Christ, the period of the Incarnation, and the epoch of the church, in which men try to live by the New Law which Christ brought, assisted by the grace he purchased by his death, and look forward with trembling to the final judgment. These figures out of the past usher us into the place where the mystery to which they all point is to be unfolded.

Inside, we find the "mirror of history" continued in the stained-glass windows. For us, the details of these windows are a puzzle, but for a thirteenth-century man, they were clear as a book—indeed, they were his book, for not many thirteenth-century men could read. "For what writing supplieth to him which can read, that doth a picture supply to him which is unlearned, and can only look," writes one of those who could. When we compare this "Bible" of the medieval man with our Bible, we are equally amazed by what was left out and by what was added.

Left out were all the momentous events we find in the Old Testament, and even all the events in the life of Christ, except for a very few chosen scenes which are repeated over and over. Added are fabulous scenes for which we look in vain in our Bibles. These were drawn from legends that grew up about the Apostles and especially about Mary's childhood. Obviously it is a strange kind of "history" which is reflected in this "mirror."

For the church of those times, the Bible was treated as allegory, in the same way that nature and popular stories were. Thus Moses stands at the entrance not because the church is impressed by the historical significance of the Exodus, but because Moses is seen as the "type" of Christ, a symbol which stands for some of Christ's characteristics. A window has a panel showing the sacrifice of Isaac by Abraham—but its meaning is shown by the fact that the wood Isaac carries to the altar is drawn in the shape of a cross. Isaac is merely a symbol of Christ. A statue of Isaiah is prominent, but no one was familiar with the actual message of Isaiah to the people of his own time. So far as the medieval church was concerned, Isaiah might never have uttered any words except, "Behold, a virgin shall conceive and bear a son . . ." and "There shall come forth a shoot from the stump of Jesse . . ."

Because the Bible was squeezed into the mold of such elaborate allegory, the reality of its history dissolved. Even though the theologians insisted that the events of the Bible actually happened, still their meaning was never contained in their happening. The meaning consisted in timeless truths, which had been revealed to the church by Christ and the Apostles. Apart from the crucifix, one of the most common statues of Christ in the cathedrals shows him holding a book, the "New Law" which he brings, his hand uplifted in admonition. He is the "Teaching Christ," who speaks through his personal representative, the pope. Even the crucifixion, which dominates all the other pictures of Christ's own life, is allegorized. In a typical window, Christ hangs on the cross. Above, the sun and moon appear, in eclipse. On his left stands a woman, blindfolded, a broken staff in her hand, a crown falling from her head. She represents the synagogue, which in rejecting Jesus has fallen from God's plan of salvation. On the right of the cross stands another woman, wearing a golden crown. She is, of course, the church. In her upraised hands she holds a chalice which catches the blood and water flowing from Jesus' side. The meaning of the window is perfectly clear: Jesus' death is the founding of the church and the institution of the Sacrament of the Mass!

The one theme which this building and all of its ornaments wants to drum into our heads, then, is that all of history, just like all of nature and of human life, is drawn together and given its meaning by the one overpowering event of Christ's death. But that event is seen less as something which happened once for all than as something which happens here and now, again and again. It happens within the ordered life of the church, and in its happening the eternal fate of our souls hangs in balance. That is why the very architecture of this place pulls our attention to the high altar, where the ultimate mystery is enacted under the shadow of the gaunt body, continually suffering there for our sins.

The Mystic Drama

Imagine yourself standing in this cathedral we have been picturing, but six centuries earlier. You stand shoulder to shoulder with a great crowd, for this is a feast day. There are murmurs here and there in the crowd, and the shuffling of wooden-shod feet on the stone floor. There is a craning of necks, a standing on tiptoe to peer toward the sacred altar. You are here to witness a miracle.

The choir of monks or of lower orders of clergy files into the chancel, raised above the nave in which we stand and separated from us by a screen. They begin the opening song, chanting the Psalm antiphonally, that is, each half of the choir alternating verse by verse. This chorus represents the yearning expectation of Israel for the coming of Christ. From the sacristy, which symbolizes the womb of the Virgin Mary, the bishop emerges, representing Christ entering the world. The elaborate vestments he has put on there represent Christ's "robe" of human flesh. Before him marches a long procession of clergy, all having symbolic functions. There are seven torches, standing for the Holy Spirit; two acolytes, representing the Law and the Prophets which preceded Christ; and four bearers, for the four Evangelists, holding a canopy above his head. He proceeds to the altar, and ascends his throne. He is silent, as Christ was before his public ministry began. The book of the Gospels lies closed before him. Act one of the drama of salvation has begun.

The center of this first act is the reading of the Scripture lessons. The ceremonial builds up solemnly to this point. After prayers for the faithful, one of the clergy takes up the book of the Epistles—this contains selections from the Old Testament, chosen for their allegorical meaning, as well as New Testament lessons outside the Gospels—and turning to the north, symbolic of the Old Testament, he begins to read. He represents John the Baptist, preaching to the Jews. When he has finished the lesson, he bows low to the bishop, for John must yield to Christ.

Now the choir begins a "gradual" or "Psalm of ascent," for the drama is rising to the first climax, when the Holy Gospel will be read. A priest or deacon goes to the altar and lifts from its case the Gospel Book, bound in gold or silver and ivory, and studded with jewels. He carries it folded in his stole: it is too holy to be touched with bare hands. Now he turns and marches to the pulpit. Two torchbearers go before him; he is followed by acolytes with censers, silver pots containing glowing coals and incense. Swung from side to side by their chains, these fill the air with the pungent smoke of holiness. The priest chants:

> Cleanse my heart, and my lips, O Almighty God, who didst cleanse the lips of the prophet Isaiah with a burning coal: vouchsafe so to cleanse me by thy gracious mercy that I may be able worthily to proclaim the holy Gospel.
>
> Through Jesus Christ our Lord. Amen.
>
> Lord, give me thy blessing.
>
> Lord be in my heart, and on my lips; that I may worthily and in a proper manner announce his Gospel. Amen.
>
> The Lord be with you.

The other clergy respond: "And with thy spirit." The priest continues: "The beginning of the Holy Gospel according to . . . Glory be to thee, O Lord." The priest makes the sign of the cross on his forehead, mouth, and breast. The people of the congregation stand rigidly at attention. The men remove their hats; if there is a prince present, even his crown must come off. The knights draw their swords and hold them at "present arms," for they are willing to fight for the Word of God! The priest sings the Gospel. The laymen listen in hushed attention to the strange cadences: surely this is the Word of God—though not one can understand its Latin! An acolyte sings: "Praise be to thee, O Christ." The priest kisses the book, saying, "By the words of the Gospel may our sins be blotted out." It is solemnly returned to the altar, presented to the bishop to be kissed, and replaced in its little casket. The clergy all sing the Nicene Creed, which marks the end of act one of the drama. In earlier times, this was said or sung by all the people; it symbolized their faith in response to the Good News of Christ they had heard. Now, however, all responses are sung by the clergy. The laymen have become only spectators to a play in which they cannot participate, whose words they cannot begin to understand, but on which their own lives intimately depend.

Now, while an offertory is chanted, the second act begins. The celebrating priest goes to the altar to prepare for the sacrifice itself. He takes up the paten, a small plate on which is laid the bread, or host (*hostia:* a sacrifice) which in a few moments will be miraculously changed into the very body of Christ. He lifts it with the words:

> Receive, O holy Father, Almighty eternal God, this unspotted host, which I thy unworthy servant offer to thee my living and true God, for my innumerable sins, offenses, and negligences, and for all here present, as also for all faithful Christians living and dead: that it may be available for me and them to life everlasting. Amen.

He pours wine and water into the chalice, reminding us of the blood and water which flowed from Christ's side. The wine will shortly become that very blood; the water represents the people, the members of the church, for in this sacrifice their lives are mingled with Christ's and offered up with him.

The priest swings his censer over bread, wine, and altar: the incense is the "fire of divine love." He washes his hands, for only one with "clean hands and a pure heart" dare touch God's holy mysteries. He prays for all the faithful, living and dead. Then comes again the solemn dialogue which marks a significant point in the service:

> The Lord be with you:
> And with thy spirit.
> Lift up your hearts:
> We lift them up unto the Lord.
> Let us give thanks to the Lord our God:
> It is worthy and just.

A "preface" is sung, while torchbearers form a procession and range themselves in front of the altar as if for a grand reception. As they chant "Holy, Holy, Holy, Lord God of Hosts. The heavens and earth are full of thy glory," the choir fall on their knees. "Hosanna in the highest! Blessed is he that cometh in the name of the Lord! Hosanna in the highest!" From this moment, complete silence reigns, for man has nothing further to say. Now God himself is the actor in this drama; his holy Son comes down again to the altar, his death is acted out for us by the priest, who whispers the almost magical words so softly that no one else can hear. Every step of the Last Supper is acted out by the gestures of the priest: "In the person of the priest, Christ Himself stands at the altar, and picks up the bread, and lifts up . . . 'this inebriating chalice' . . . it is Christ Himself who is now active, and . . . it is by virtue of power deriving from Him that the transubstantiation which follows takes place."[3]

We strain on tiptoe, eyes fixed on the altar. The tense silence is at last broken by the bell of the altar boy, taken up by the great tower bells. The words of the miracle have been pronounced: *Hoc est enim corpus meum:* "For this is my Body."

The priest holds the host on high, and a gasp bursts from the crowd as they catch sight of the small white wafer. They gaze in awe—this is their one moment of participation in the drama which is enacted on their behalf. There in the priest's hands, hidden beneath the external form of bread, is the body of Jesus Christ, "the very flesh which was born of Mary, and suffered on the cross and rose from the tomb . . ."

The drama is ended. The priests receive Communion, both bread and wine. The wine has long been denied to laymen, for fear the precious blood of Christ might be spilled and desecrated. The "whole Christ," according to the theologians, was present in even the smallest particle of bread. For the laymen, however, merely to *see* the host is more than enough; they dare not come near that awesome table more than once a year, and then only when they have carefully confessed their sins and done the penance prescribed for them.

The Dread of Hell

We have seen God's mighty act of man's redemption enacted again before our eyes. As the clerics recite their final prayers and gospel, we kneel, make the sign of the cross, and join the throng pushing its way out of the church. Certainly, after we have experienced the emotional catharsis of this moving drama, we must all leave with a sense of peace, sure of the forgiveness of God and carrying an inner renewal into our daily affairs. But the evidence is that such a typical congregation would go forth beset by deep anxieties, which in the Middle Ages frequently swept through the whole society. It is not like the anxieties to which Augustine addressed his *City of God*, the anxieties of a disintegrating culture which found its life meaningless and empty and dreaded death as the terrible prospect of nothingness. These people know the meaning of life, the meaning symbolized in all these pictures and in this drama we have witnessed, but it is a meaning which fills them with dread.

As we pass from the church, we look back to the magnificent relief carving over the western entrance, put there so that it is lighted by the rays of the setting sun to remind us that our earthly lives, too, must be extinguished as inevitably as the daily sun. The scene is the Last Judgment. Christ sits enthroned as the last trumpet is blown. He holds up his pierced hands; his robe falls open to reveal the wounded side. At the sight of these wounds, the souls of the saints, pouring out of their tombs, turn toward the throne in worship. They are ushered forward to his right hand by the archangel Gabriel. But on the other side cower the naked and twisted souls of the wicked, who hide their eyes from the terrible sight. The artists, who had little to work with in the serene faces of the saints, have outdone themselves in the figures of the damned and of the fantastic demons who seize them, chortling gleefully, to tear them with giant claws, seethe them in huge caldrons of bubbling sulfur, or hurl them into the gaping jaws of hell. It is an awesome picture, and utterly real to the man of the Middle Ages. On which side shall we stand at the Last Day? To be sure, we are completely convinced that Christ has given to the church the power to save us from all our sins. We know that the sacraments are the very pipeline of grace, and that the church can open the valves to a healing flood for all who are in good standing. But who can say whether he is really in good standing? It is common knowledge that all of us who must live in the world with its vices and temptations have scarce chance of avoiding mortal sin. Only the monk, who flies from the world to spend his time in ceaseless devotion and prayer, can hope to escape. And has the artist not drawn even some monks, even bishops and a pope or two in the crowd of the damned? Who can be saved? Even if we are fortunate enough to die with all our mortal sins confessed and forgiven, it is still necessary to make temporal satisfaction for them—part in this life by fasting, pilgrimages, and almsgiving, and part in the next life, by the suffering of purgatory.

We shudder as we turn away from the Judgment scene and walk into the dusty street. But even there we may suddenly be confronted anew with the terrors of hell. What is this weird procession approaching us through the narrow street, weaving and stumbling, accompanied by the chanting of hymns that is almost like the howls of a wounded animal? The worshipers shrink back from this awful mass of men, women, and young people who writhe slowly toward us. Stripped to the waist, each carries a leather whip with many thongs, weighted at the end with iron spikes. In rhythm to the chant, each lashes the back of the marcher in front of him. These are the Flagellants, driven to a frenzy of penitence by the fear of the Black Death which is sweeping through Europe. They believe that if they continue their bloody march for thirty-three and a half days, they will surely be spared the pains of hell.

The church condemned the Flagellants, though it finally had to burn them to stop the movement. Not only were their neurotic excesses repulsive, they were outside the control of the clergy, which was perhaps more important. The church had its own remedies for the dread of hell.

On this sunny day after a festival mass, it might happen that we would also see the church's remedy in action. There on the corner of the cathedral square a new wooden platform has been built and over it flies the papal banner. A black-robed monk stands on the platform, announcing something to the gathering crowd with all the manner of a carnival barker. What is he selling? Indulgences, or letters of pardon from the pope. Whenever a man sinned, he must make use of the Sacrament of Penance. If he felt sorrow for his sin—even if only because he feared hell—he could go to the priest to confess. The priest pronounced forgiveness for his sin—"I absolve thee, in the name of the Father, and of the Son, and of the Holy Spirit"—which canceled *eternal* punishment, that is, hell, for the sin. Nevertheless, he must make a *temporal* "satisfaction" for the sin, for the discipline of his own soul. Part of this "satisfaction" was done in this life, part after death, in purgatory. At an early time, indulgences began to be granted for satisfactions in this life. For example, a sick person might be granted an indulgence which permitted the giving of a certain sum to charity rather than fasting for a certain time, which might endanger health. But in the late Middle Ages, indulgences began to be offered also for time in purgatory. For taking part in a Crusade, an eleventh-century knight could have his total time in purgatory commuted!

The indulgences were made possible by the treasury of merit, which had been established by the good works of Christ and added to by the works of the saints. Since they did not need these good works themselves for salvation, their merits were left over for use as needed by others. The pope controlled them, for the "keys of the kingdom" given Peter by Christ could unlock the treasury.

The use of indulgences became more and more widespread in the fifteenth and sixteenth centuries, as the anxiety of the people was increased by threats from the Turks and the Plague, and the popes, building the monumental St. Peter's Church in Rome, became strapped for funds. Here is a contemporary description written by an incensed Franciscan monk who later became a Protestant:

Anno 1512. Tetzel [an indulgence salesman licensed by the Pope and by the Bishop-Prince Albert of Mainz, who split the profits between them] gained by his preaching in Germany an immense sum of money which he sent to Rome. A very large sum was collected at the new mining works at St. Annaberg, where I heard him for two years. It is incredible what this ignorant and impudent monk used to say. . . . He declared that if they contributed readily and bought grace and indulgence, all the hills of St. Annaberg would become pure massive silver. Also, that, as soon as the coin clinked in the chest, the soul for whom the money was paid would go straight to heaven. . . . The indulgence was so highly prized that when the agent came to a city the bull [the papal proclamation] was carried on a satin or gold cloth, and all the priests and monks, the town council, schoolmaster, scholars, men, women, girls, and children went out in procession to meet it with banners, candles, and songs. All the bells were rung and organs played. He was conducted into the church, a red cross was erected in the centre of the church, and the pope's banner displayed. . . .

Anno 1517. It is incredible what this ignorant monk said and preached. He gave sealed letters stating that even the sins which a man was intending to commit would be forgiven. He said the pope had more power than all the apostles, all the angels and saints, even than the Virgin Mary herself. For these were all subject to Christ, but the pope was equal to Christ. After his ascension into heaven Christ had nothing more to do with the management of the church until the judgment day, but had committed all that to the pope as his vicar and vicegerent.[4]

The bases for ethics and personal religion in the Middle Ages were *amor et timor:* the love of God and the fear of God. In its last centuries, fear more and more swallowed up love. The announcement of the miraculous grace of God, which had been poured out in Christ's sacrifice "while we were yet sinners," was twisted into the ominous teaching of the "new law," to which every man was accountable at the Last Day. And the church itself, custodian of that law, having been identified with the City of God, declined into a power-hungry and often vulgar monarchy of this world.

12

the freedom of faith

The System

The human personality cannot digest raw life, just as it pours in upon us. We have to filter life through the screen of our mind, refine it, force it into patterns, let it trickle through the little channels carved out in our experience, wearing them only slowly into broader or deeper courses. Otherwise, if these protective devices were to break down, the whole stream of things would hit us right in the face, and we would be swept away, carried along, or drowned.

Every age has its system, its way of seeing things. But sometimes in the life of an individual, and sometimes, perhaps once in five hundred years or so, even in the life of a whole civilization, the system breaks down. Either it just wears out internally, or something tears into it from outside, something it can neither explain nor withstand. In those moments, the system no longer protects us; it stifles us.

Back in Augustine's time, when the magnificent Roman cosmos was disintegrating, men in desperation dug in with the only defenses they knew, the only concepts by which they could make sense of the world: fate and luck. But these two blind forces, so far from liberating them, hemmed them in so tightly they could no longer really see what was happening. For these frightened, trapped people, marching lockstep in a circle, the Christian gospel quietly opened a door and pointed out a new world. That world, as Augustine so brilliantly proclaimed, was neither hitched to a runaway fate nor thrown on luck's roulette wheel. It was directed by the very God who had given himself to mankind in Jesus Christ.

The story of the Middle Ages is largely the story of the way that Good News itself was developed into one of the most

188

fantastic of all systems. It did not start out that way, of course. At the basis of the whole development lay that same sense of the "glorious liberty of the sons of God" which Augustine taught his contemporaries. Indeed, the purpose of the system itself was always to communicate that liberty to every individual, from the pope in Rome to the humblest peasant, to bring them all together, with every aspect of their lives, into a great, integral, rational world, and to lead them to salvation.

But, as we have seen, the church itself, the very institution which existed to proclaim and mediate that freedom to men, became a tyranny, its system a prison of the mind. The teachings which were expounded to make the way of salvation understandable and accessible became instead a source of the terror of damnation. The sacraments, established as channels of grace, became weapons for political control and economic exploitation. By the sixteenth century a heavy air of dread hung over all northern Europe. In countless ways, men began to feel an acute thirst for freedom—freedom from the system that was throttling their life—but at the same time an intense anxiety lest a demonic world swallow them up if they dared to break out of that system.

The system itself had begun to split apart when one school of theologians, the Nominalists, called into question the whole ability of human reason to grasp ultimate truth. Then at the end of the fourteenth and beginning of the fifteenth century, John Wyclif in England and John Hus in Bohemia attacked the abuse of power and general corruption that pervaded the church. Together with many less well-known figures, both tried to break the joyful news of the gospel free from the choking tangles of scholastic dogma and ecclesiastical vested interests. Despite the power of their words, though, the system smothered them. Hus was burned at the stake in 1415, though his influence remained alive in his books and in the Czech Brethren (Unitas Fratrum, later known in English-speaking countries as the Moravian Church).[1]

The man who was finally to take an ax to the system was one who had embodied the terrible tensions of its decline in his own life. Martin Luther was born among the common folk of

Germany, and he never ceased to feel his kinship with them, even when his brilliant scholarship and intuitive genius had carried him far beyond a level that would be "common" in any century. His parents were peasants, though his father had become a miner and worked his way up to the middle class. From him Martin inherited a robust, no-nonsense feeling for life; from his mother he received a rootage in deep personal religion, as well as a good supply of fearful superstitions.

In July, 1505, Luther, then twenty-two, was caught in a thunderstorm and knocked to the ground by lightning. Terrified and stunned, he cried out, "St. Anne help me! I will become a monk!" What could be more natural? St. Anne, legendary mother of Mary, was the patron saint of miners and therefore of Luther's father. And in the Middle Ages, a physical lightning bolt was only a symbol of the bolts of God's judgment which would be unleashed on the Last Day. Earthly terrors and eternal terrors were never far apart. It was the fear of judgment more than the fear of death, then, that called forth Luther's vow to become a monk. The vow was not just rash words; two weeks later he was entering a cloister of the Augustinians.

The surest way to salvation was the life of a monk. Thomas Aquinas taught that when the monk received his cowl, he became as pure as a baby just baptized. Shutting all the cares and temptations of the world outside the cloister's thick walls, a monk devoted himself to the only thing of real importance, the saving of his own soul.

Luther tried to work his way to God on the medieval ladder. Indeed, no one ever tried harder! In later years he said:

> I was a good monk, and I kept the rule of my order so strictly that I may say that if ever a monk got to heaven by his monkery it was I. All my brothers in the monastery who knew me will bear me out. If I had kept on any longer, I should have killed myself with vigils, prayers, reading, and other work.[2]

But these exercises in the long run only proved to Luther the complete futility of trying to make himself acceptable to God.

The system started cracking for Luther when he was sent to Rome in 1510, on business of his Order. Here was the center of the church and, for the devoted, the center of the means of salvation. So many bones of holy martyrs had been gathered there and so many indulgences granted for visiting them, that a pilgrim to Rome could easily hope, by any reasonable count, to keep himself and all his dead relatives out of purgatory. Luther stood at the *Scala Sancta*, the stairs Christ was supposed to have walked up to Pilate's palace, and remarked that it was too bad his parents were not dead, so he could get them out by climbing up. Since they were not, he went up for his grandfather, on hands and knees, a *Pater Noster* on each step. But at the top he straightened his aching limbs and murmured, "Who knows whether it is so?"

The Fresh Air of Freedom

It was not as a pilgrim but as a scholar that his question was answered. Luther was sent by the Augustinians to do more study. He received his doctorate and became professor of Bible at the new University of Wittenberg. He began lecturing on the Psalms in August, 1513. As he prepared his lectures, a quiet revolution began. In the face of his patient scholarship, his common sense, his clear-eyed intuition, the stained-glass spectacles through which the medieval churchman read his Bible shattered. Luther found himself face to face with the words of the Bible itself, groping not for what the theologians said they said, but for what they really said. In Psalm Thirty-one (or Seventy-one) he read, "In thy righteousness, O Lord, deliver me!" Deliver? By his righteousness? How? Was it not precisely God's awful righteousness, the righteousness of those horrible Last Judgment pictures, from which one wanted to be delivered? Could it be that the righteous God was different from those pictures, different from the face which the church, with its mechanics of damnation and grace, had shown Luther?

The full light did not break until Luther took up the book of Romans, two years later. Here is what he says:

Night and day I pondered until I saw the connection between the justice of God and the statement that "the just
shall live by his faith." Then I grasped that the justice of
God is that righteousness by which through grace and sheer
mercy God justifies us through faith. Thereupon I felt myself to be reborn and to have gone through open doors into
paradise. The whole of Scripture took on a new meaning,
and whereas before the "justice of God" had filled me with
hate, now it became to me inexpressibly sweet in greater
love. This passage of Paul became to me a gate of
heaven. . . .[3]

The fresh air of freedom, the freedom of the gospel, streamed
into Luther's little study. He hastened to start opening the
windows of people's minds to its winds, in his lecture room and
in the pulpit. At first it did not occur to him that he might also
have to knock down some walls of the ecclesiastical institution
before the people could really breathe. His assault on the walls
began when John Tetzel, Bishop Albert's supersalesman of
indulgences arrived in the neighboring electorate. (Saxony was
a "dry county" for indulgences, but Luther's parishioners were
soon bootlegging them across the line.) Luther, infuriated at
Tetzel's claims and by the ruthless way the ordinary people of
Wittenberg were being robbed, nailed up his famous *Ninety-
five Theses* on indulgences on the door of the Castle Church.
This door was the bulletin board of the university, and Luther's
theses, written in academic Latin, were an invitation for all
comers to debate the issue with him. But they were terse and
angry statements, and when a student translated them into
German and they were printed as a pamphlet, eager men bought
them up all over Germany. Almost overnight Luther became a
center of controversy, for some the champion of liberty, for
others a dangerous threat to the church.

In the midst of this controversy, when the pope had already
issued a bull condemning Luther as "a wild boar in the vineyard
of the Lord," and Luther had replied that the papacy was the
institution of Antichrist, Luther wrote a little essay in which he

summed up what he had learned about the freedom which God had given to men in Jesus Christ. He wrote it for the pope himself, and sent it along with a conciliatory, almost pastoral letter. It is not certain whether the pope ever received it, but it is certain that, translated into German, it was read by princes, scholars, and ordinary people all over Germany. Here it is for you to read, too. It is hardly less relevant for our own quest for real freedom.[4]

THE FREEDOM OF A CHRISTIAN
by Martin Luther, 1520
Jesus

1. So that we can thoroughly understand what a Christian is and what manner of freedom Christ has won and given to him —the freedom of which Paul writes so much—I present two propositions:

A Christian is a free lord over all things, subject to no one.

A Christian is an obedient servant of all things, subject to everyone.

These two propositions are clearly found in St. Paul (1 Cor. 9:19): "I am free in all things, and I have made myself everyone's servant." Again, Romans 13:8, "Do not be under obligation to anybody in any way, except to love one another." But this love! Love is always obedient and subject to that which it loves. Thus Galatians 4 says even of Christ: "God sent forth his son, born of a woman and made subject to the law."

2. If we are to understand these two contradictory statements about freedom and servitude, we will have to remember that every Christian is of two different natures, spiritual and bodily. As a soul, he is called a spiritual, new, inner man. As flesh and blood, he is called a bodily, old, and outer man. And because of this difference, things are said of him in the Scripture which exactly contradict each other, like the things I just said about freedom and obedience.

3. Let us consider then the inner, spiritual man, to see what it is that makes him a righteous, free, Christian man, in fact

and in name. Now it is obvious that no external thing, whatever it is called, can make him either godly or free, for his righteousness and freedom—or, on the other hand, his sinfulness and bondage—are not bodily and external. What good does it do the soul if the body is free, hale and hearty, eats, drinks, and does as it pleases? On the other hand, what harm is done the soul if the body is imprisoned, sick, and weary, hungers, thirsts, and has to suffer things against its will? These things cannot touch the soul, to free it or to bind it, to make it godly or to make it sinful.

4. Therefore it does not help the soul in the least if the body puts on sacred vestments, as the priests and the clergy do, not even if it is in the churches and holy places, not even if it occupies itself with sacred affairs, or prays, fasts, goes on pilgrimages, and does every good work that could ever possibly take place in and through the body. It takes something completely different to give to the soul righteousness and freedom . . . On the other hand, it does not hurt the soul for the body to wear secular clothes, to be in worldy places, to eat and drink, to skip the prayers, pilgrimages, and all the other works which even hypocrites perform.

5. The soul has nothing else, in heaven or on earth, by which to live and to be righteous, free, and Christian, than the holy gospel, the word of God preached by Christ, as he says himself (John 11:25): "I am the life and the resurrection; he who believes in me shall live forever". . . Thus we must be certain that the soul can do without all things except the word of God, but without the word of God nothing else can help it . . .

6. If you ask me now, "What is this word which gives such great grace, and how am I to use it?" Answer: It is nothing other than the proclamation which took place through Christ, as it is contained in the gospel. And this ought to be preached—and in fact is—so that you hear your God speaking to you, announcing that all your life and work is nothing before God, but must ultimately perish, with everything that is yours. Once you believe this rightly, aware of your guilt, you will surely despair of yourself and see the truth of Hosea's saying, "O Israel,

in you is nothing but ruin; only in me lies your help." But so that you can escape out of yourself and from yourself, that is, out of your ruin, he sets before you his dear son Jesus Christ and says to you through his living, comforting word: Surrender yourself to him with firm faith, and trust him boldly. Then for the sake of this faith all your sins will be forgiven you, all your ruin overcome, and you will be righteous, true, serene, and godly, all commandments will be fulfilled, and you will be free from all things. As Paul says, "A justified Christian lives only by his faith," [Luther's paraphrase of Romans 1:17] and (Rom. 10:4), "Christ is the end and the fulfillment of all commandments for those who believe in him."

7. Therefore the single reasonable work and exercise of all Christians ought to be this: to let the Word and Christ himself take form within them, by continually exercising and strengthening such faith. For no other work can make a Christian . . .

8. But now, if faith alone can make one righteous, and without any works can give such superabundant riches, how does it happen that so many laws, commandments, works, and directives are prescribed for us in the Scripture? Here you must pay close attention and earnestly remember that faith alone, without any works, makes one righteous, free, and blessed—more about that later. At the same time you must know that the whole Bible is divided into two kinds of statements: commandments or laws of God and his promises or pledges. The commandments teach and prescribe for us all kinds of good works, but these never get done. They direct, but do not help; they teach what one should do, but do not give the strength to do it. Their only use is to help man see his incapacity to do good so that he can learn to despair of himself. That is why they are called the Old Testament and all belong in the Old Testament. Thus the commandment, "Thou shalt not covet" [literally, "have sinful desire"] shows that we are all sinners, for no man can be free of sinful desires, no matter what he does. By this he learns to give up on himself and look elsewhere for help, so that he will be without sinful desire and therefore will fulfill the com-

mandment through someone else, which he cannot do by his own power. In the same way all the other commandments are equally impossible for us.

9. Now when man has learned and discovered from the commandments his own incapacity, he becomes anxious how he can ever satisfy the commandment, since he has to fulfill the commandment or be damned. As a result, he is really humiliated and ruined in his own eyes; he finds nothing in himself which will make him righteous. At that moment there comes the other word, the divine promise and pledge, and announces: "Do you want to fulfill all the commandments, be free from your perverted desire and sins, as the commandments demand and require? Lo! believe in Christ, in whom I promise you all grace, righteousness, peace, and freedom. If you believe, you have: if you do not believe, you have not. For what is impossible for you with all the works of the commandments which are so many, yet useless—that you have easily and quickly through faith. I have summed up everything in faith, so that whoever has faith has everything and is blessed, while whoever does not have faith has nothing." Therefore the promises of God give what the commandments demand and accomplish what the commandments order, so that everything belongs to God, both command and fulfillment. He alone commands; he alone fulfills. That is why the promises of God are the words of the New Testament and also belong in the New Testament.

✽   ✽   ✽

10. We can readily see why faith is able to do so much and that no good work can equal it. For no good work clings to the divine Word as faith does, and no good work can exist in the soul, but only the Word and faith rule in the soul . . . Thus we see that in faith a Christian has everything he needs. He no longer needs any work, so he is liberated from all commandments and laws. If he is liberated then he is certainly free. That is the Christian freedom: faith alone. Faith brings it about, not that we can loaf or do evil, but that we do not need works in

order to achieve righteousness and blessedness—we will have more to say later about that.

*   *   *

12. Not only does faith give so much that the soul becomes like the divine Word, full of all grace, free and blessed, but it also unites the soul with Christ as a bride is united with her bridegroom. From this "marriage" it follows, as St. Paul says, that Christ and the soul become one body. The goods, fortune, unfortune, and everything that belongs to each they now hold in common. What Christ has becomes the faithful soul's own; what the soul has becomes Christ's own. As Christ has all goodness and blessedness, these now belong to the soul; as the soul has all faults and sins, these are taken on by Christ. Here there arises a joyful exchange and contest. Christ takes over the sins of the believing soul by means of the wedding ring, which is faith, and makes them his own sins, as if he had done them himself. But since he is God and man, who has never sinned, and since his righteousness is invincible, eternal, and all-powerful, the sins are of course swallowed up in him and drowned. For his invincible righteousness is too strong for all sins. Therefore the soul is set free from all her sins, solely through her dowry, that is, because of faith, and is presented with the eternal righteousness of her bridegroom Christ, as a gift. Now isn't that a joyful transaction? The rich, noble, righteous bridegroom Christ takes the poor, despised, wicked little whore as his wife, sets her free from all evil, adorns her with all good things . . .

13. Here you see again why so much is rightly ascribed to faith that it fulfills all commandments and makes people righteous without works. For you see that faith alone fulfills the First Commandment, "Thou shalt honor thy God." Now if you were nothing but good works from head to heel, you would still not be righteous, and you would still not honor God, so you would not fulfill even the very First Commandment. For God cannot be honored without ascribing to him truth and all good, which are truly his alone. But no good works can do that, but only the

faith of the heart. That is why faith alone is the righteousness of man and the fulfillment of all commandments. For anyone who fulfills the First Commandment fulfills without doubt every other commandment. But works are dead things which can neither honor nor praise God . . . Faith is the head and whole essence of righteousness. That is why it is such a dangerous and blind teaching, to assert that the commands of God are to be fulfilled by works, while the fulfillment must first take place through faith, before all works, and the works then follow after the fulfillment, as we shall hear.

14. [By Old Testament allegories, Luther shows that Christ is both king and priest.]

15. Now Christ has the honors and prerogatives of a first-born son. These he shares with all his Christians, so that they also must all be kings and priests with Christ, as St. Peter says, (1 Peter 2:9): "You are a priestly kingdom and a royal priesthood." Thus it happens that a Christian is exalted by faith so high above all things, that he becomes spiritually lord of all, for nothing whatever can threaten his salvation. Yes, everything has to be subject to him and to contribute to his salvation, as St. Paul teaches (Rom. 8:28): "All things must help the elect toward what is best for them," whether life, death, sin, piety, good or evil . . . What a high and honorable dignity this is, and what a genuine, all-powerful reign, a spiritual kingdom, since nothing is so good or so evil but that it has to serve me for the good, so long as I believe. Yet I do not need anything, for my faith is sufficient for me. See what a precious freedom and power the Christian has!

16. Besides this we are priests, which is far greater than being kings, because the priesthood makes us worthy to come before God and to pray for others. For to stand and pray before God's eyes is a right given to no one except priests. This privilege Christ has obtained for us, that we can spiritually intercede and pray for one another, as a priest, in the bodily realm, intercedes and prays for the people . . .

17. Now you will ask me, "If everyone in the church is a priest, what then is the difference between the priests and the laymen?"

Answer: An injustice was done to such little words as "priest," "pastor," "spiritual" when they were transferred from the common mass of Christians and applied to that little group who are now called "the spiritual class." The Holy Scriptures make no distinctions, except that they call those who are educated or ordained *ministros, servos, oeconomos,* that is, servants, slaves, and stewards, since these are supposed to preach to the others Christ, faith, and Christian freedom. For although we are all alike priests, still we cannot all serve or minister and preach. Thus St. Paul says (1 Cor. 4:1): "We want people to think of us as nothing more than Christ's servants and stewards of the gospel." But now this stewardship has been turned into such a worldly, external, proud, fearsome rule and force that the legitimate secular authority cannot equal it in any respect, just as if the laymen were something other than Christian people! By this turn of events the whole understanding of Christian grace, freedom, faith, and everything that we have from Christ, and even Christ himself, has been swept away. In exchange we have received many man-made laws and works; we have become slaves of the most worthless people on earth.

18. From all this we learn that it is not enough to preach Christ's life and work merely as historical facts, a chronicle of events. Much less is it enough to ignore him altogether and to preach instead ecclesiastical rules and other human laws and doctrines. There are also plenty of those who preach and read about Christ just to stir up sympathy for him, anger against the Jews, or some other childish emotion. Instead he should and must be so preached that faith will be produced and maintained for you and for me. This faith is produced and maintained when I am told why Christ came, how we can benefit from and enjoy him, and what he has brought and given to me. That happens when one correctly explains the Christian freedom which we have from him, and how we are kings and priests, in command of all things, and that everything we do is pleasing and accepted in God's sight, as I have said before. For when a heart hears of Christ, it must rejoice to its very foundations, receive comfort, and be struck with a tenderness toward Christ, to love him in

return. It can never get to that point by laws or works! For who can hurt or frighten such a heart? If it is attacked by sin and death, it believes that Christ's righteousness is its own, and its sins not its own, but Christ's. Then sin has to vanish in the face of Christ's righteousness which is present in faith, as I said above. And the heart learns with the Apostle to scoff at death and sin and to say: "Where now is your victory, O death? Where is your lance, O death? Your lance is sin. But praise and thanks to God, who has given us the victory through Jesus Christ our Lord. And death is swallowed up in his victory," and so forth.

19. That is enough about the inner man, about his freedom and the real righteousness, which needs no law nor good work . . . Now we come to the second part, to the outer man. Here we want to answer all those who take offense at what we have said so far and go around saying, "Well! Since faith is everything and is sufficient all by itself, to make a person righteous, why then are good works commanded? We will just have a good time and do nothing." No, dear man, you have missed the point. That would be fine, if you were only an inner man, if you had become completely spiritual and inner, but that will not happen till Judgment Day! On earth there is only a beginning and growth, which will be completed in the other world. Therefore the Apostle writes of the *primitias spiritus,* the firstfruits of the spirit, and in this context the statement we made before belongs, "A Christian is an obedient servant, subject to everyone." In other words, insofar as he is free, he need do nothing; insofar as he is servant, he must do all sorts of things. We shall see what that means.

20. Although man is inwardly, as a soul, sufficiently justified by faith and thus has everything which he should have—except that this faith and sufficiency must continually grow throughout this life—still he remains in this bodily life on earth and must rule his own body and have dealings with people. At this point works enter the picture. He must not loaf, because the body has to be controlled and exercised with fasting, watching, labor, and every moderate discipline, so that it will be obedient to the inner man and to faith, and conformed to them, instead of hindering

and opposing them, as its habit is if not kept under control . . .

21. But we must not do these works with the idea that they can make man righteous before God, for faith cannot tolerate this false opinion, since it alone is and ever must be the real righteousness in God's sight. Rather, these works are to be done with the understanding that the body will become obedient and cleansed from its sinful desires . . . For once the soul is pure through faith and loves God, it wishes that everything were pure, above all its own body, and that everyone loved and praised God as it does. Thus it happens that for the sake of his own body, man cannot afford to be idle, but must perform many good works. Nevertheless, the works are not the basic good, by which he is righteous and upright before God, but he does them gratis, out of his free love, to please God, whose will he does gladly to the best of his ability . . .

❁ ❁ ❁

23. Therefore these two sayings are true: "Good, righteous works never make a good, righteous man, but a good, righteous man does good, righteous works," and "Sinful works never make a sinful man, but a sinful man does sinful works." Thus the *person* must always first be good and righteous, before any good works, and good works follow and proceed from the righteous, good person, just as Christ says: "A bad tree does not bear good fruit; a good tree does not bear bad fruit." . . . We see the same in every craft: A good or bad house does not make a good or bad carpenter, but a good or bad carpenter makes a good or bad house. The work never makes the workman like itself, but the workman makes the work like himself. It is the same way with the deeds of man. It depends on his condition of faith or unfaith whether he does good or evil deeds, and not the other way around, as if his righteousness or faith depended on his deeds . . .

24. Now once again, for the man without faith, no good work helps produce righteousness and salvation. On the other hand, no evil deed can make him evil and damned, but it is rather unfaith, which makes the person and the tree bad, which does evil and

damnable works. Therefore, if you want to be good or bad, begin not with deeds, but with faith, as the Wise Man says, "The beginning of all sin is to depart from God and not to trust him." So Christ also teaches that a man must not begin with works, and says, "Either make the tree good and its fruit good, or make the tree bad and its fruit bad." That is to say, if you want to have good fruit, you must start with the tree and plant it right. So whoever wants to do good deeds must not begin with the deeds, but with the person which is to do the works. But nothing makes the person good except faith alone, and nothing makes it bad except unfaith alone. Now of course, in the eyes of men, it is the works which make someone righteous or wicked, that is, they show outwardly who is righteous or wicked, as Christ says (Matt. 7:20): "From their fruits you shall recognize them." But all this is a matter of appearance and externalities, and the appearance has fooled many people . . . Whoever wants to avoid the errors of these blind men will have to look further than works, commandments, or doctrines of works: he must look into the person above all, to see how it becomes righteous. The person becomes righteous and is saved not through commandment and work, but through God's word (that is, through his promise of grace) and through faith. Thus God's glory stands firm, because he saves us not through our works, but through his gracious word, freely, and purely because of his own mercy.

*   *   *

26. So much for works in general and for those which a Christian is to do toward his own body. Now we will speak of other works, which he does for other men. For man does not live alone in his body, but among other men on earth. Therefore he cannot avoid activities which involve others, he must converse with them and work with them, even though none of these activities is necessary for him, for his righteousness and salvation. For this reason in every activity his attitude should be free, directed entirely toward serving other people and being useful to them, thinking of nothing else than what the others need. That is truly a Christian life, and for this cause faith goes to

work with all its might, as St. Paul teaches the Galatians. To the Philippians, too, whom he had already taught that they had all grace and sufficiency through their faith in Christ, he teaches further: "I admonish you, by all the comfort you have in Christ, and by all the comfort that you have from our love for you, and by all the fellowship which you have with all spiritual, godly Christians, that you make my joy perfect in this way: henceforth be of *one* mind, showing love for each other, each serving the other and every one being concerned not for himself or for what belongs to him, but for the others and their needs." See, there Paul clearly sets forth the Christian life: that every work is to be intended for the good of the neighbor, since every individual already has enough for himself in his faith. He has no need for any other life or work, so he can serve his neighbor out of unrestrained love. Paul sets up Christ as an example of this: "Be of the same intention then that you see in Christ, who, although he was fully in the form of God and had everything he needed and though his life, action, and suffering were not necessary for him to become righteous or blessed, nevertheless he emptied himself of all that and took on the role of a slave, did and suffered everything, thinking of nothing except what was best for us. Thus, though he was free, for our sakes he became a slave."

27. Therefore a Christian, like Christ his head, ought to be more than satisfied just with his faith, and always increase that faith, which is his life, righteousness, and salvation, and which gives him everything that Christ and God have—as was said above and as St. Paul says in Galatians 2:20: "The life I still live in the body, that I live in the faith of Christ, the son of God." And since he is now utterly free, he ought then willingly to make himself a servant, to help his neighbor, to deal and act with his neighbor as God has acted with him through Christ. And this he ought to do freely not looking for anything except God's approval. He should think, "Well now, in and through Christ my God has given to me, unworthy, condemned man that I am, without my earning anything but absolutely free, from the pure goodness of his heart, the full wealth of righteousness and salvation. Thus from now on I need nothing else but to believe, and

all is done. Lo! For such a father, who has thus overwhelmed me with boundless good things, surely I in turn will freely, gladly, and without expecting reward, do what pleases him. And for my neighbor I will become such a Christian as Christ has become for me.[5] From now on I will do nothing except what I see to be needful, useful, and wholesome for him, since I already have plenty of everything through my faith in Christ." See, thus there flows from faith, love and joy in God, and from love a free, willing, and joyful life, to serve one's neighbor for nothing. For just as our neighbor suffers want and needs what we can spare, in the same way we have suffered want in God's sight and needed his grace. Therefore, as God has helped us through Christ without price, so we ought to do nothing else with our body and its works than to help our neighbor. Thus we see what a high and noble life a Christian life is! But unfortunately at present it is not only laid low throughout the world, it is not even known or preached.

*   *   *

29. From what we have said, everyone can make up his mind and distinguish between all the different works and commandments. He can also tell which prelates are blind, which are foolish, and which are right-minded. For any work which is not intended to serve the other person or to submit to his will (so long as he does not demand something against God) is not a good Christian work. For this reason, I am afraid, few of the endowments, churches, cloisters, altars, masses, and bequests are Christian, nor even the fasts and prayers, especially the ones said to various saints. For I fear that in all of them everyone seeks only his own benefit, mistakenly thinking that by this means he can atone for his sins and win salvation. But this opinion stems from ignorance of faith and of Christian freedom. Now there are various blind prelates who lead the people to this and praise this kind of conduct, sweetening it with indulgences but never teaching faith. But I advise you, in case you want to set up an endowment, to pray, or to fast, not to do it with the thought that you will thus do yourself some good, but give it

away freely, so that other people can enjoy it and so you will do them good. Then you will be a real Christian . . . See, thus God's good things ought to flow from one to the other and become common to all, so that each one would be concerned for his neighbor as for himself. From Christ they flow into us, who has taken us up into his own life, as if he were what we are. From us they are to flow to those who need them, even so completely that I must present to God even my faith and righteousness on behalf of my neighbor, to cover his sins, to take his sins upon myself and to act as if they were my own, just as Christ has done for us all. You see, that is the nature of love, when it is real love. Hence the Apostle tells us it is the property of love to seek not its own, but the neighbor's.

30. From all this follows this conclusion: A Christian man does not live in himself, but in Christ and in his neighbor: in Christ by faith, in his neighbor by love. By faith he ascends to God; by love he descends from God again, though he remains still in God and in God's love, just as Christ says (John 1:51): "You will yet see heaven standing open and the angels ascending and descending upon the Son of Man." See, that is the genuine, spiritual, Christian freedom, which makes the heart free from all sins, laws, and commandments, which excels every other freedom as heaven excels the earth. May God grant that we truly understand it and keep it! Amen.

PART THREE

help my
unbelief

Sooner or later the pilgrimage of every Christian student takes him to that part of the road marked, "Abandon all preconceived ideas, all ye that enter here." Here is the stretch guarded by sentries in button-down uniforms, ready to pounce on every statement with the challenge, "Prove it!" It is the business of the college to teach its members to question, probe, analyze, and dissect. Does this mean that you must check your faith at the campus gateway? Or is it true, as one of the church fathers said, that "Faith seeks understanding"?

Before we can discuss seriously the relation between faith and the intellectual quest that so often takes the form of doubt or skepticism, it will be helpful to find out just what is going on along this stretch of our road. Why is it that doubting accepted beliefs is taken for granted as part of the very method of a college education? Why is it that this doubt is not just a classroom exercise, but often stirs the depths of our personality, muddying the whole stream of our thinking, our hoping, and our trusting? These things do not happen to you and me in a vacuum. They are the result of our interactions with the people around us, and with their ways of thinking and doing. They are also the result of our interaction with our past, with the way men have thought and acted before us and the living framework they have built into our society. We will begin by taking a look at the environment of our doubt and the history of our doubt. Then we can go on to talk about what faith is and how it is different from other things that pretend to be faith. Finally we can ask the question whether God is not leading us through this particular stretch of road because he has a special assignment for us, a job for people who have learned to love the Lord their God *with all their minds.*

✿ ✿ ✿

13

an anatomy of doubt

That's Not the Way I Heard It

Important as are the new ideas you encounter in college, they probably have less impact upon you than the new *people* you meet. It was all very interesting when your high school youth group had a series of programs on "What Different Faiths Believe," but somehow the effect was not quite so real as having a Buddhist from Japan living at the end of the hall, a suitemate who is a Roman Catholic, and a Jewish student across the hall, not to mention the fellow who sits behind you in English 101, who told you he was an existentialist. Here are real, live, intelligent people who take for granted things that are flabbergasting to you, while your accepted beliefs strike them as absurd. Their arguments make about as much sense as yours do. How can you know who is right? Maybe nobody is; maybe there is no truth. Maybe "it doesn't matter what you believe, so long as you're sincere." Not just religious ideas, but questions of right and wrong come up for review. For the circle your family moved in, there were some things that simply "were not done." The use of chewing gum, let us say, was regarded as terribly sinful. But your roommate says that even his minister uses chewing gum and once they served it at a church social. What's right? Maybe nothing. Maybe "everything is relative," and "anything is all right if it seems right to you."

The result of your new encounters is that your horizons are suddenly lifted. You discover that there are a bewildering number of possibilities, any or none of which could be right. The temptation is to play it cool: commit yourself to none of these, but taste them all. This would seem to be a pretty normal reaction, and one which is encouraged by the additional fact that you probably have a good bit more freedom, both for thought and for action, than you had in high school.

Good-bye, Mamma

There is a further, more personal, reason for the blossoming of doubt in college. The parental thumb is gone. Oh, it is still there in some ways—on the checkbook, in the warnings and advice, in those occasional tense scenes when you go home for the week-end—but never again in the effective control, the curfews and the deadlines and the inquiries, not if you can help it. They may still be footing the bill, but they're not going to tell you what to think and what you can and cannot do anymore! In short, you are undoubtedly engaged in some degree of rebellion against the dated older generation. That, too, is par for the course.

The exhilarating escape from parental authority carries over into matters of belief as well. There is not only the simple fact that there is no one around to drag you out of bed on Sunday morning, but the more important fact that the church itself is rather Mom-shaped in the popular teen-age eye. The way our society is wired up, young people get the capacity and the energy to do all kinds of interesting things long before Society—that is, parents—think they can be permitted to do them without blowing the whole civilization apart. All of this energy has to be controlled and channeled somehow, so it falls the lot of the church, along with parents, schoolteachers, football coaches, and other kinds of policemen, to keep the lid on. At least that is the way the picture looks to most teen-agers, and there is some truth in it. I think it is rather natural, then, that you rebel against the church, for the same reason that you may dislike "cops."

Now I hope you will not think me unkind or unfair when I suggest that some of your sophisticated reasons for doubting the teachings of the church are a rationalization for your rejection of an institution that reminds you too much of parental control. This is nothing to be ashamed of or surprised at. Our motives are almost always mixed, and we shall see that even great scientists have sometimes thought with their feelings more than with their minds on the subject of religion. But it is important that you try to sort out the various kinds of motivation behind your opinions.

That is the first step toward being honest with yourself as well as being fair to the reality proclaimed in the gospel.

HISTORICAL REASONS FOR DOUBT

Man Against the Dogma

The history of challenges to established beliefs is of course a very long one. The phase which affects us most directly had already started at the end of the Middle Ages. The Reformation itself began, as we saw in chapter 12, by taking an ax to an established system for the sake of the liberty given by faith. Even before the Reformation, the Renaissance had swept through Italy and had begun to bring even to northern Europe a powerful sense of human freedom and a suspicion of ecclesiastical authority. Fed by the rediscovered ideals of the Greek and Roman Classical Age, the Renaissance glorified nature and reason. The goal of the "Renaissance man" was to obtain the highest possible development of his own powers and talents—self-expression and self-fulfillment. In many ways the Reformation and the Renaissance joined forces to attack the medieval system of life and belief.

Yet the two movements were very different. The Reformation proclaimed that every individual was responsible to God, dependent upon him for all things. Renaissance humanism announced that every individual was responsible only to himself, free to create his own world. For the Reformation, God is the measure of all things, communicating himself to his people through his word. For the Renaissance, man was the measure of all things, by his unaided reason solving all mysteries. It was inevitable that these apparent allies would come into conflict. Unfortunately when the major conflict came, it was a hardened and stultified Protestantism that met a vigorous, self-confident humanism.

The Hardening of the Arteries

The Reformation was never a movement of unlimited individualism, as it is often advertised. Luther and Calvin did not intend to replace the dogmatism of the medieval church by the anarchy of uncontrolled private opinion, or give free rein to every crackpot who might decide that he had the one true interpretation of the Bible. One great contribution of John Calvin to the Reformation was a system of doctrine, spelled out in his extraordinary *Institutes of the Christian Religion*. Its purpose was to explain the liberating insights of the Reformation so clearly that they could never again be swamped by human pride, institutionalism, and superstition. But there were influences at work in his followers and even more in those of Luther that would soon turn explanations into law.

It was mainly a matter of self-defense that caused the Protestants to solidify their positions in dogma. On the one hand, they were plagued by the hordes of eccentrics and self-appointed founders of new sects who sprang up as medieval society became looser. The threat of anarchy often seemed real. On the other hand, a long, extremely bitter struggle was taking place between Protestants and Roman Catholics, even reaching the point of bloody wars of religion, and driving each side to make its position as clear and as rigid as possible. Against the sectarians and against each other, therefore, both the Protestants and the Roman Church began to draft creeds which were far more detailed and comprehensive than anything the church had needed in ancient times. To see the difference, you have only to compare the Nicene Creed, which you can write on half a page, with the Westminster Confession or the Heidelberg Catechism for example, or the Roman Church's canons of the Council of Trent, each of which would need a small book. Each side, fearful of being backed into a corner by the relentless debate, felt compelled to get everything down in black and white, to build a paper wall around its position.

The Roman side seemed to have an advantage in the enforceable discipline it exercised over its clergy and especially in its pope, who had the power to establish doctrine (although his infallibility was not made dogma until 1870). The Protestants had only the Bible, though that had proved a mighty weapon. "It was the Word of God," said Luther, "that made the Reformation." For Luther and Calvin, that word was not a mechanical transcription rumbling out the thought for the day if you dialed the right number. Christ himself spoke through the Scriptures, but not without the Spirit's activity in the heart of the believer. The Reformers insisted, to be sure, that a bartender or a housewife might understand the Bible as well as the parish priest, but they were not so muddleheaded as to imagine that it could be understood without diligent study—as their own commentaries show. The word was living, dynamic, never to be simply embalmed in human words. As the successors of Luther and Calvin had to fight their battles, however, they retreated more and more into the fortress of literalism, till the Bible became not only the word, but the very *words* of God. Some (both Catholics and Protestants) even revived an old view that the human writers of the Bible had been only passive instruments in the hand of God, God having dictated the very words they wrote down.

With their verbally inspired Bible and their elaborate creeds to interpret it, the second-generation Protestants lost the flexibility of the pioneers. They came to think more and more as the scholastic theologians did against whom they had been fighting. For both sides the Christian faith came to be regarded as a set of authoritative doctrines which had to be accepted for salvation—only the content of the doctrines differed. No wonder historians have called the Protestants of the seventeenth century "Protestant scholastics."

The Assault of the Mind

At the same time that Protestant and Roman scholastics were building their walls of doctrine, formidable forces were shaping up for an assault against them. As Protestant theology had grown stodgy, the Renaissance humanism had become robust. The seventeenth century, which produced most of the creeds our churches still use, also produced the outbreak of a violent rebellion by human reason against every kind of authority.

The battle between humanism and Protestant orthodoxy was fought out for the most part on the field of two main questions: whether miracles were possible and how to interpret the Bible.

The battle went on from the middle of the seventeenth century until the beginning of the twentieth, yet in all this time surprisingly few new arguments were raised. One of the seventeenth-century skeptics would probably find himself almost at home in many a freshman bull session even today, although the scholastics have become a rarer breed. Consequently the main argument can be summarized quickly.

Put on the defensive, the scholastics felt it necessary not only to assume that the Bible's every word was literally true, but to go back a step and prove that it was true. The standard proofs were miracle and fulfillment of prophecy. Jesus, said the orthodox, not only worked many astonishing miracles, he rose from the dead, which was the most inconceivable miracle of all. Therefore what the Bible says about Jesus, that he is the Son of God, must be true. If that is true, then the Bible is infallible (so the argument goes), and you should also believe what it says, for example, about the creation of the world in six twenty-four-hour days. Furthermore, the Bible is shown to be true because it contains many prophecies which were fulfilled centuries after they were made. This shows that it could not be a merely human book, but must have been divinely inspired.

The first attack by the humanists was directed against miracles, which offended their sense of the mathematical order and consistency of nature. Well, said they, if miracles were still taking place so that we could see one with our own eyes, we would gladly believe that they took place in Jesus' days. But you Protestants say that miracles ceased in the time of the Apostles. Now the only way to investigate something which is supposed to have happened in the past is by means of sources, that is, by the testimony of people who said they saw it happen. But look at the witnesses to biblical miracles! Not one of them trained in scientific techniques of observation, most of them poorly educated, all living in a superstitious age! Hence it is much more probable that these witnesses were mistaken, deluded, or even lying than that things happened then which never happen now.

The attack on the proof-from-prophecy argument began on

the same level as the attack on miracles, but led to debate and research which were to be far more productive. First of all, the idea of prophecy and its fulfillment itself demanded a belief in miracle, for it meant that a supernatural power could intervene in the course of historical events, just as a miracle demanded supernatural intervention in the realm of natural law. For the humanists, this was clearly impossible, because they saw history as an unbroken chain of causes and effects in the same way that scientists had begun to see the universe. A student of ancient history, trying to explain why Cyrus was able to capture the Neo-Babylonian Empire, would not be impressed by Cyrus' own statement that the god Marduk had given it to him. What the historian wanted to know was what social conditions enabled Cyrus to raise such a large army, what economic conditions let him pay for it, what political unrest in Babylonia gave him his opportunity, and so on. Now when the same historian read in the book of Isaiah that Yahweh had controlled Cyrus, was he meekly to drop his search for "real" causes? For a science of history that was more and more modeled after the science of physics, there simply was not room for God.

In recent years, the more thoughtful historians have largely repudiated such a rigidly closed system of history, so that historical events are seen in a much less mechanical way. But the old attack of the brasher, naturalistic history led to a revolution in the approach to the Bible which has had lasting effects. Scholars began to insist that passages of the Bible must be read in the light of the historical situations in which they were written, asking such questions as who wrote them? For what purpose? To what audience? What would these particular words have meant to that special audience? To take a single example, Isaiah's prophecy, "Behold, a virgin shall conceive and bear a son, and shall call his name Immanuel," was regarded by Christians from very ancient times as a clear prediction of Christ's birth. But is it reasonable to suppose, said the humanist critics, that in a time of national crisis in Judah this prophet gave his people a message which no one could possibly comprehend until more than seven hundred years later? And to imagine that these people were so impressed by that (to them) utterly meaningless message that they wrote it down and carefully preserved it? Nonsense. The message must have had an immediate meaning for their own time and situation—in this case, the meaning which is clearly and literally seen in the next two verses if they are read with unprejudiced eyes: "Before the child knows how to refuse the evil and choose the good, the land before whose two kings you are in dread will be deserted." With a little knowledge of Judah's history, the meaning is obvious and quite concrete.

Now such a naturalistic approach to the Bible cut the ground from under the prophecy-fulfillment scheme of scholasticism, but it also had a very positive effect. It forced Christian scholars to take the biblical text with new seriousness. No longer could they think of it as golden, isolated words sent down from on high to reveal timeless truths. They had to see that if God had revealed himself, it was in specific happenings among flesh and blood people. This criticism, then, paved the way for the rediscovery of the Bible in our own time as a book able to stand on its own, still confronting persons with a lively and demanding message. Such an approach to the Bible, however, requires more work than the neat scheme of scholasticism. As a result, many people prefer either to assume that criticism has proven that "the Bible is myth," or else, rejecting criticism altogether, to assume that every word is inspired, even though they do not know what most of them mean.

Science and Scientism

The outgrowth of the humanist movement which has most thoroughly soaked through every pore of our daily life is modern natural science. And of course it is with science that orthodoxy fought its most dramatic and most tragic battles—tragic both because, in retrospect, they seem so unnecessary, and because they produced so few good results. The starting point of modern science was embedded just as much in the Christian doctrine of a good creation separate from God and made for man's dominion, as in the classical thirst to know and understand. At least it is

certain that most of the pioneers of modern science were devoted Christians, seeking, like Kepler, to "think God's thoughts
after him." But orthodoxy was so frightened that the new ideas
of the scientists would drive God right out of his universe, that
they took up arms to protect him. Unfortunately, when the
smoke of battle had cleared, the giants with which orthodoxy
had been jousting often turned out to be windmills. The scientists, in the meantime, had gone their own way and God, presumably, had managed somehow to take care of himself.

Still, we can perfectly well understand why orthodoxy—
indeed, just about everyone—was shaken by many of the
changes in the world picture science has proposed. What could
have been more upsetting in 1543 than the proposal by Nicolaus
Copernicus that the earth *moved!* This was ridiculous to Roman
Catholic and Protestant alike. Everyone knew that the earth was
stationary, in the exact center of a round universe. All the planets
were attached to spheres which revolved smoothly around it.
Outside them was another sphere, to which the stars were
fastened, and surrounding the whole onion was heaven, where
God lived now and to which everyone aspired. Now along came
this Copernicus claiming that not only was the earth not the
center of the universe, but that it actually moved around the sun!
Why we would all be thrown off! Furthermore, the notion was
clearly against the Bible, which not only said "Thou hast established the earth; it shall not be moved," but also related that
Joshua told the sun to stand still one day.

But Copernicus politely said that he had *tried* a round, earth-
centered universe, and it just did not work. If the planets all
move in circles around the earth, any schoolboy could write
equations for their motion. With a little skull work, an astrono-
mer could use these equations to predict where a certain planet
would be on a certain night. But when Copernicus looked, it
was someplace else. That meant either that mathematics could
no longer be trusted, or that planets did not move in circles
around the earth. Since nobody wanted to throw away mathematics, Copernicus went back to the library. Sure enough, there
had been some ancient philosophers who thought the earth

might move around the sun. It was worth a try, at least, so Copernicus worked out new equations, and lo, they fitted! There were the planets, just where they ought to be by his calculations —well, at least a lot closer than by the old calculations.

The essentials of the modern scientific method were already clear in Copernicus' work. It demands that any view of natural events be reasonable—in the same way that mathematics is reasonable—and that it fit all the specific facts that we can gather with our five senses. As the use of this method gathered steam, then, it not only reinforced the Renaissance idea that the human mind was the ultimate judge of all truth, but it also led to the growing prejudice that the things which were really real were those that could be seen, touched, tasted, heard, or smelled, observed through a telescope or put in a test tube. So when Kepler, working out Copernicus' equations more carefully, said that he was looking for "true causes," he meant *physical* causes. Though Kepler was a quite faithful Christian, he was not satisfied to say that the planets moved because God wanted them to. Newton completed the scheme by showing that the forces that moved the earth around the sun were exactly like the forces that made his famous apple fall. There was nothing "spiritual" about either. Thus the universe became a huge machine. Newton could not account for all its motions, so he still thought it needed a mechanic: God had to step in from time to time to set it straight. But it was on its way to full automation. When Napoleon asked Laplace, the great mathematician, where God fitted into his system, Laplace is said to have replied, "Sire, I did not need that hypothesis."

It seemed that the worst fears of the orthodox had been realized. In the new picture of the universe, God was the victim of technological unemployment. It is hardly suprising that many Christians reacted in desperation by opposing science altogether, as if it were a work of the Devil. The very desperation, of course, led to hasty attacks on positions which were not really understood, producing such debacles as the notorious "monkey trial" at Dayton, Tennessee. There, in a test that resembled a circus more than a court trial, the anti-science Fundamentalists won their fight, but lost a war. Although they succeeded in keeping the teaching of evolution illegal in Tennessee schools (it is still illegal, though of course it is taught everywhere), they made the church a laughingstock, while the assistance rendered to God is at least open to debate.

On the other hand, there were a great many thoughtful people who wanted to go along with the new science, at the same time keeping the heart of the Christian faith. The most eloquent of them, however, were often so rebuffed by the literalistic interpretation of the Bible that they lost sight of the Bible's unique content altogether. They were trying to work out, as it were, a "thinking man's religion." Any number of essays were written on "the reasonableness of Christianity," the most famous of which was John Locke's treatise by that title. There was no contradiction, he found, between the teachings of the New Testament and reason. In fact, reading his essay, I have the impression that any fairly intelligent fellow, with a day off and pencil and paper, could work out all the important points for himself. The only remaining question is, if that is all the New Testament has to say, why bother? Still, we cannot afford to look down our noses too placidly at either the literalists or the rationalists. They had to find their way through a maze of conflict and misunderstanding into a new world. In many respects most of us have to repeat the same journey.

The journey was not made any easier by some of the scientists and their supporters, who, after all, were human beings. If the literalists attacked the new science, it is also true that science was very often used as a stick to beat religion. This is perfectly natural; it is like the inevitable small town gossip about preachers and organists. Since preachers usually try to be better than they are and the church usually claims to know more than it does, the opportunity to deflate them is only too tempting. The attacks range from demolition of churches in the French Revolution to the satirical remarks by teachers of sophomore psychology. It was perhaps also inevitable—at least from the Christian perspective that recognizes man's sinful pride—that the very success of science would lead to an unbecoming arrogance, a kind of intellectual imperialism which saw science as the final answer to all human questions. Our adulation encourages the pride. If scientists can construct a nuclear bomb, then let us ask the scientists to decide for us whether it is morally right to incinerate our enemies. Only the greatest of them have had the humility to reject such misplaced faith and to throw that kind of question back into our common human lap.

The World Inside Us

A good example of a scientist's stepping outside the realm of his competence can be seen in Sigmund Freud's almost neurotic attack on religion. At the same time his authentic and brilliant discoveries have had a permanently revolutionary effect on the way we understand ourselves and certainly on the way we understand our faith as well. For both these reasons, it is worth our while to give special attention to him.

The enduring contribution of Freud is that he opened up the hidden world of the unconscious. He showed us that a great part of our personality is unknown to us, but goes on functioning secretly with a logic all its own. He was able to show that our most carefully reasoned beliefs are often merely a mask, a "rationalization," to make acceptable the fulfillment of wishes that arise from basic instincts that our conscious minds will not recognize. Even if our beliefs become irrational, they are quite logical to the unconscious, for they satisfy wishes in symbolic ways. The key to the understanding of personality Freud found in the "Oedipus complex," the unconscious desire of every boy to kill his father and marry his mother. Since this desire was too terrible to be consciously admitted but too strong to go unexpressed, it produced all kinds of unreasonable fantasies, fears, and obsessions in children. These "childhood neuroses" enabled the child to make a kind of sense of his feelings without admitting the awful truth behind them. If he were fortunate enough to grow up in an affectionate and stable home, a healthy boy would outgrow these illusions and come back to reality, but Freud met many people in his examining room who had never been able to shake free from the childish obsessions. They went on living in a world of illusion, because only in that world had they found fulfillment for their hidden but powerful wishes.

Freud saw that the illusions of the neurotic not infrequently took the form of a religion. Many were terrified by a God who threatened the most sadistic punishments if one did not please him, yet whom one was somehow supposed to love. It was obvious to Freud that this God was nothing other than a blown-up image of the father whom the boy, writhing in the unconscious agony of the Oedipus conflict, had both hated and admired. Again, he often treated obsessive neurotics, people for whom the most commonplace of daily actions had to be performed with elaborate ritual: if the left shoe were not removed before the right one, and the socks placed in the form of a *T*, or the hands washed meticulously after touching anything whatsoever, or some other such apparently meaningless procedure enacted, then a horrible dread would assail them. Were these mechanisms of neurosis any different, asked Freud, from the rituals of the church? Were not both designed for the purpose of relieving the pangs of unconscious and groundless guilt-feelings?

Freud's model of personality was so helpful in making sense of complex individual problems that he could not resist applying it to much broader fields. In a series of books on religion, he undertook the solution of problems of biblical criticism, anthropology, religious history, the origin of religious institutions and dogmas, and a host of other matters. His answers have the boldness of genius and the power of simplicity, though later research has called most of his "facts" into question. Religion, Freud said, serves the same purpose for a whole civilization that illusion or neurosis does for an individual. Primitive man was faced with a very threatening world of nature, which seemed utterly incomprehensible and uncontrollable. To live with this world, man imagined that it was personal, that it had the same kind of emotions that his father had. Hence, while thunder was terrifying, just as Dad was, like him the Thunder-god could be appeased and, so long as he was on man's side, would protect him against other dangers. Eventually the con-

fusing world in which everything was personal was simplified
into just one, all-embracing father-figure, called God or Allah
or Brahman or some such. This was simply a return to the
Oedipus starting point in a disguised form. All religion was just
"wish-fulfillment," "the universal obsessional neurosis of humanity." But just as a healthy child outgrew his early neuroses,
civilization would inevitably, Freud trusted, outgrow the illusion
of religion.

Freud's legacy affects our pilgrimage through doubt in two
ways. First, there is that frightening spotlight he has thrown
on our unconscious life. We squirm with the realization that
some, maybe a great deal, of our personal religion does stem
from wish-fulfillment. We do find it very difficult to break
through our "father-images" to the Father of Jesus Christ. We
have to admit that many of our pious practices are done because
we feel guilty, vaguely and neurotically guilty, and that we
have been unable boldly and openly to confess that "We have
left undone those things which we ought to have done; and we
have done those things which we ought not to have done . . ."
Surely we ought to welcome the contribution of psychology at
this point, as it helps us to strip away the gods we are ever and
again constructing in our own images, though it can neither
reveal nor hinder the God who made us in his image.

But the other legacy of Freud is also still with us. Freud
hated religion. Born one of a hundred Jews in a town of five
thousand Roman Catholics, he hated the Christianity whose
representatives despised his race and had often butchered his
ancestors. But perhaps he also hated Judaism, which somehow
symbolized the inferior position the Jews held in his society.
At any rate, it is clear that his passionate opposition to religion
obscured his keen sense of fact and reason when he approached
this subject. Many of his hypotheses—like the existence of two
Moseses, one of them an Egyptian—were fantastic. His theories
about primitive society have been rejected by specialists in
anthropology, and he ventures into biblical criticism in a craft
that would not hold water. Nevertheless, some of these wonderful fantasies have won a lasting place in armchair psychology—

perhaps they fulfill hidden wishes—and it is not uncommon to hear Freud's *The Future of an Illusion* cited as "proof" that science has exploded Christianity.

Cosmopolitan Campus

The long history of conflict between reason and religion, of which we have seen only a few high points, has left its scars. In the church, it has left varying degrees of suspicion or even hostility towards science and learning. Among intellectuals and even in every man in the street, it has left the tendency to regard all theology as monkey business and a low-pressure skepticism toward anything that cannot be measured, photographed, or sold for cash.

It is not hard to see why this conflict, embedded in our culture, should break loose in an individual when he goes to college. The college or university exists precisely for this purpose: to pass on the culture, to boil down the discoveries of those who have lived before us, pull together their solutions to the old problems and the problems they left unsolved, and hand the whole mess on to a new generation. To become a college student means to stand in a special way at the focal point of history. The history of America, of Western culture, and, if yours is a very good college, the history of humanity, is trying to become your history. And since doubt has played so large a role in that history, doubt becomes part of your way of thinking; you learn a vocabulary and a framework that make your foggy suspicions and felt doubts jump into focus.

In a sense, the better student you are, the more intense your doubt is likely to become. That is because the university as such has inherited much more from the Renaissance than from the Reformation. Despite the fact that most of your professors are probably churchmen, and no matter how profound may be their faith, still the very tools of their profession are the methods developed by reason and science. The occupational stance of every successful scholar has to be a kind of skepticism, an openness to new possibilities, a willingness to abandon the most cherished assumptions if contradictory evidence turns up. If you learn these habits of thought, then the things you learned in Sunday school either have to be shut up in an airtight box, or thrown out the window, or else you have to take the hard and painful way of working through them for yourself.

Things Are So Complicated

We are living at one of those awful and wonderful times in the world's history when our whole way of looking at things is being shaken. A great many of the things which seemed so absolutely certain even for our grandfathers have been shown to be very doubtful. As members of a college or university, you and I are riding the leading edge of the shock wave. Sometimes we get dizzy. The combination of the complex history which has given us our spectacles for seeing the world plus the emotional equipment we bring along from our private and family histories produces confusion. We are tempted to commit ourselves to nothing, to ride the times, to wait and see what turns up. Maybe, for some of us, this is the best course. But if it means the easy way out, disengagement because we are afraid of getting hurt, apathy because we do not have the will to dig for what is real and alive, then uncommitment means commitment to immaturity, permanent suspended animation. On the other side, there is what the preacher calls faith. Can we get there from here?

14

faith and its counterfeits

In the last chapter, we admitted that doubt had become an occupational hazard for college students in our century. This is true, not because we are more sinful than students of past eras, but because we have, in a sense, had our world jerked out from under us. It is really much harder for you to believe the teachings of the church today than it was for your grandfather. But you should not jump to the conclusion that it is more difficult for you to have faith. It is exactly as difficult to have faith in our generation as it was when Paul wrote, "We preach Christ crucified, a stumbling block to Jews and folly to Gentiles . . ."

Faith Is Not Belief

Two words often used interchangeably are *faith* and *belief*. In this chapter we are going to use each one in one particular sense, out of the various meanings you can find in a dictionary. Belief is the grasping of an idea, a conviction that some proposition is true. Faith is a relationship to a person. You may believe that God "exists in three persons" without any change in your life; but to have faith in God means that he has done something to which you respond.

Much of the conflict between science and the church has resulted from a confusion of faith and belief. There can be no conflict between science and faith, unless someone tries to make science into a god. However, there is almost inevitably conflict between science and various systems of accepted beliefs. Beliefs are held on the basis of authority; you believe the world is round because your father told you it was round, and you believe that Jesus is the Son of God because your minister told you or because the Bible says so. Now good science, like most college students, always rebels a bit against authority. It does

226

not like to have someone decide in advance what is permitted or not permitted to be believed.

Furthermore, science does not have to depend upon authority, because it has other means at its disposal for deciding what is true. In physics class, for example, I learn that "for every action there is an equal and opposite reaction." Then the professor says, "Learn this law, because I'll ask for it on the final exam." Therefore I remember the third law of motion, and I believe it on the basis of the professor's authority. But I am not stuck with this. If I doubt the professor, I can set up my own experiment, perhaps with a bunch of marbles hanging by threads from a common support. Then I try pulling back various numbers on one side and letting them fall against the others, and counting those that fly off on the other side. I can try this as many times as I want, and I will see each time that the same number of marbles flies off as strikes the cluster. Maybe now, if I am an Isaac Newton, I can sit down and think about this fact until I decide that the same thing will always happen, even with forces that are very different from falling marbles. Then maybe I will agree that the professor and Mr. Newton are right. But now I do not believe it on the professor's authority alone, but on the basis of my own experience and my own reason.

The trouble with all this, from the church's point of view, is that people who get into the habit of checking up on science professors are likely to do the same thing with preachers and theologians. They are likely to respond to authoritative statements with "Prove it!" Is this habit good or bad? Well, if faith and belief are the same thing, then the habit is very bad, indeed quite dangerous, for it challenges the authority on which faith rests. Very often, the church has taken exactly this position. The *Catholic Encyclopedia* defines faith as "knowledge based on authority—whether human, and therefore fallible, or Divine and therefore infallible." It goes on to say:

> Divine faith, then, is that form of knowledge which is derived from Divine authority, and which consequently begets absolute certitude in the mind of the recipient.[1]

If anything happens to shake the "absolute certitude," then the whole system and the authority on which the system rests are called into question. The immediate authority in this case is the church, which delivers "the faith," that is, the system of beliefs, to the believer, but behind the church stands, according to this point of view, God himself as the ultimate Authority. To question the beliefs, then, is not only to question the church, but really to question God. No wonder then that the church had to squelch Galileo when he claimed, following Copernicus, that the earth moved around the sun. According to the system, the earth had to stand still in the center of the universe, for man was the center of God's providence. Take away the "fact" of the earth's majestic immobility, and the whole system started cracking. So Galileo had to be haled before the Tribunal of the Inquisition and forced to recant his "heresy" under threat of death.

In its more humble and, I might add, its more *faithful* moments, however, the church has not feared to have the system questioned. The Reformation proclaimed that "Councils and Popes do err," and Martin Luther remarked, "Every man must do his own believing, just as every man must do his own dying." Far from anxiously and authoritatively throttling doubt, faith welcomes honest inquiry and even skepticism. At heart the Protestant has much in common with the scientist who insists that every assertion, every hypothesis must be tested on the rock of experience. If we meditate for a little on some of our colossal *faux pas* of the past, such as the Roman Catholic attempt to stamp out the ideas of Galileo and our Protestant attempt to do the same with Darwin, we might develop a frame of mind receptive to Paul's clear statement, "Our knowledge is imperfect and our prophecy is imperfect," and again, "Now I know in part." Faith perceives that, though our beliefs may be attacked, he who is the Truth is not endangered. The man of faith knows that having faith is not the same thing as having God, nor does the greatest faith give me power to construct a comparative anatomy of God's nature.

When we have digested our humble pie, however, we may

want to suggest to the scientists, especially to the sophomore scientists, that their knowledge is also partial. Every genuine scientist lives with the awareness of his imperfect knowledge, but scientists, like theologians, are human and likely to be rather jealous of their systems. When something shows up that doesn't fit the system, they (like Galileo's inquisitors) are tempted to brand it as absurd.

The Power of the Absurd

Oftentimes it is the thing which appears "absurd" which leads us into new and more profound knowledge. The absurd has the power to break through the complacency of partial knowledge with the embarrassing reminder that here is something not yet known. The process is shattering! For example, there were many things that you "knew" by common sense before you took Psychology 111 or Introduction to Philosophy. Then you were introduced to some very foolish-sounding statements which, however, the professor was prepared to prove. As a result, perhaps the whole system of what you "knew for certain" fell apart temporarily. This can be a very rugged experience, until you assimilate the new ideas which appeared at first so foolish. But as a result you know much that you did not know before— and you have a modified "system."

In 1880, a prominent physicist remarked, "We have nothing left to investigate but the next decimal place." All the great discoveries of physics, he thought, had already been made; it only remained to perfect the tools of measurement. He must have been shocked by the developments which occurred in physics in the next fifty years: the basic laws of mechanics altered, the very structure of matter radically reinterpreted, the mathematics of physics revolutionized. Why did all this happen? Because, as Einstein said, he "challenged an axiom." That is, Einstein, Planck, Bohr, Schrödinger and the rest took seriously certain persistent facts which appeared altogether absurd. For example, it did not make sense—according to the system of Newtonian mechanics—that the speed of light seemed always constant. But Einstein believed the absurd, challenged the axiom, and was on his way to a whole new system. Such is the power of the absurd! If the absurd is true, then it becomes the hammer which shatters former ways of thinking and prepares the way for new and deeper truth.

> Can you comprehend
> That we're sometimes hoisted by the unbelievable
> On to the shoulders of truth?[2]

It is just this kind of "absurdity" which we find in the gospel. Let's listen to Paul again:

> For the word of the cross is folly to those who are perishing, but to us who are being saved it is the power of God. . . . For since, in the wisdom of God, the world did not know God through wisdom, it pleased God through the folly of what we preach to save those who believe. For Jews demand signs and Greeks seek wisdom, but we preach Christ crucified, a stumbling block to Jews and folly to Gentiles, but to those who are called, both Jews and Greeks, Christ the power of God and the wisdom of God. For the foolishness of God is wiser than men, and the weakness of God is stronger than men.   (1 Cor. 1:18, 21–25)

Jesus Christ, at the same moment fully God and fully man, Creator of the universe, yet hanging in slow criminal's death on a piece of timber, is absurd. The Jews stumble over him, for he does not fit their expectations of Messiah. For the Greeks, he is just foolish, to be scoffed at because, from their philosphy of what is universally and always true and real, he is impossible. But if he is real—then the portrait of Messiah has to be redrawn and what is possible radically revised.

If he is real, then here is a fact that shatters all our systems, changes all our knowing, transforms all our wisdom. But how can we test the fact, prove the reality? Einstein's facts were foolish and radical, but we could test them, given time and ingenuity. Here, however, we face something different. Jesus Christ is not, by definition, a phenomenon which always happens. There is no laboratory in which we can reproduce the right conditions for a Jesus to appear. There is no way we can reduce the reality behind the word "Jesus" to something you can measure with a scale or a meterstick, no mathematical equation for "Son of God." The fact, if he is a fact, is more radical than Einstein's, demanding a totally different dimension of "knowing."

Knowing Things and Knowing Persons

Perhaps, however, other dimensions of knowledge are not so strange to us. Back to our physics class, suppose that there shows up on the second row a blonde freshman co-ed of exceptional symmetry and unusually interesting distribution of mass. Now there occurs to each of the male members of the class a question *not* likely to appear on the exam: "How can I get to *know* this girl?" Are they using the word "know" in the same sense as the professor did when he said, "Know the third law of motion"?

Let us apply the scientific method. First, using sense perception, there are important facts you can discover: she is blonde, say, with brown eyes, about five feet two. But still, helpful as these statistics are, you are reminded that "beauty is only skin deep." If you are going to *know* her, you must go beyond superficial observation. You can now find out where she is from, what her family is like, what she studies, what kind of grades she makes, what her hobbies are, and so on. But you want to go deeper, so get really scientific. Call in a clinical psychologist and give her a battery of tests, from Kuder Preference to Minnesota Multiphasic. Find out her I.Q., her aptitudes, her goals and values; probe into her complexes and repressed desires.

Now you have learned a lot about this girl. You have the facts. If you are reasonably intelligent, you can sit down and put all these facts together until you have an overall picture of your fair lady. But will you know her? You know more facts about her than the average man ever discovers about his wife, but you do not know her as a person. You have not discovered the central mystery of who she is, a living, conscious individual. That mystery begins to be visible only when she reveals it to you, when you begin to take responsibility for each other by entering each other's world.

To know a person means to know his history. He *is* his history, the course of his life, the residue of all the interactions with his past, with his contemporaries, with his world, with the hopes, fears, and ideals of his future. To know a person, moreover, it is not enough to look at his history from the outside, as an objective observer. The history that he is can only be seen from inside. To know a person, therefore, I must *participate* in his history. When I say that my friend and I know each other, I mean that we have participated in events together. We together have a history that is both his and mine, but neither his nor mine exclusively. It is *our* history.

This is the way in which God lets himself be known. God has a history. That is the joyful news of the Bible. God has a history; we are privileged to share a small part of it, and so to know him. In a nutshell, it is the history of Jesus Christ, the story that the gospel tells. Faith is our response to these events, a response that can mean nothing less than our being pulled into them by God's Spirit, to participate in them with him.

Faith Is Not Feeling

We have said that in order really to get to know another person it is necessary to enter into a relation with that person, which, I suppose, we would call "love." But this word "love" has become very hazy, so that when I say "love" you probably think of that funny feeling in the pit of your stomach, the quickening pulse and rising excitement that occurred when you first saw that "stranger across a crowded room." For a long time, the ballad singers have been trying to convince us that this visceral stimulation, mixed with a stiff dose of sentimentality, is love. It is not. Every year a great many marriages collapse because they were founded on a feeling down inside and the feeling has worn off.

We have perpetrated exactly the same crime on the word "faith." Again and again I hear students say, "I can't explain exactly what I believe or why; I just know the way I feel." The trouble with this is that the feeling, like the feeling of romance, may wear off. Or some bright psychologist may come along and show you that this feeling does not necessarily have anything at all to do with God, but is only the projection of your idealized father-image onto the empty sky. Of course genuine faith is often accompanied by deep stirring of the soul, but when the faith is identified with the emotion, we are in trouble.

Behind the common tendency to regard faith as a kind of feeling lies the history of that peculiarly American movement, revivalism. In the revivals, especially in the later stages of the movement, attention was more and more focused on the creation of an emotional crisis in each of the participants. Every sort of stimulus was brought into play—music, chanting, rhythmic cadences of the preacher, the pressure of the crowd itself—to produce in an individual an overwhelming feeling of remorse, lostness, fear of death and hell, and finally surrender with subsequent exhilaration and ecstatic joy. The emotional experience itself came to be regarded as the essential sign of conversion, indeed as conversion itself.

It is obvious that such a preoccupation with one's own emotions is very far from the faith we find in the New Testament. A student came to a minister in great distress one day because on a retreat, during a vesper service at sunset on a beautiful hillside overlooking a lake, she had been overcome by a sense of union with God and had declared herself to be born again. But now the retreat was over and the hillside was gone and the only feeling she had left was something approaching a hangover. Now this girl was nearly hysterical because she thought she had lost her faith. She was sure that God would not love her if she did not maintain the same ecstatic feeling that came on the retreat. Faith, you see, had been turned into an emotional work that one had to do to win God's favor.

As a boy, I once slipped into a tent where a revival was in

progress and watched with great wonder as the woman evangelist and her assistant shouted at an apparently reluctant sinner who was seated in great misery on the platform between them. As the poor man remained unmoved after a long course of chanting and exhortation, she turned on him finally in exasperation and cried, "You're just too damned lazy to get religion!" That puts it exactly. It is really hard work to climb into the Kingdom of God on one's emotions. But the New Testament takes great pains to assure us that faith is not a work—neither a legal work nor an emotional work—but the gift of God.

There is another, more sophisticated source of the idea that faith is a feeling. This is the eighteenth-century attempt to discover room for God in a world increasingly dominated by "natural law" and mechanical causation. Against the prevailing rationalism of the day—the confident belief that human reason could ferret out all the secrets of the universe "as if God were not there"—many Christians urged a return to "heart-religion." The way to God was not through involved rational questioning, but through simple piety, gentleness, and trust.

A brilliant young man named Friedrich Schleiermacher was much influenced by this Pietist movement, as well as by the Romantic movement which was then beginning in literature. Schleiermacher went on to base a whole system of theology on feeling, seeing this as the one loophole through which a Christian might reach the "cultured despisers of religion." God is not to be found, he argued, by looking at history or by examining the processes of nature, but by becoming sensitive to the deepest feelings of one's own heart. Science and reason might have cleared the heavens of God, but within the human heart, there he could still be found. "But as often as I turn my gaze inward upon my inmost self, I am at once within the domain of eternity."[3]

But does faith turn my gaze "inward upon myself"? This sounds instead suspiciously like Luther's definition of the state of sin! The sinful heart, he said, is curved in upon itself. That, in the final analysis, is what is wrong with the identification of faith with feeling. Preoccupation with my feelings turns me in upon myself; faith, on the contrary, turns my being outward to God.

Faith Is Not Religion

The final and perhaps most deadly counterfeit of faith is "religion-in-general." We live in a period in America when religion is everywhere, but faith is just as rare as it ever was. This is nowhere more true than on college campuses. The militant campus atheist who used to harangue admiring sophomores in the student union has almost vanished; the atheists that are still around are very quiet ones. Almost everyone is in favor of religion in moderate doses. In a recent sampling, Dr. Rose K. Goldsen and associates report that eighty per cent of college students express a "need for religious faith" and forty-eight per cent are even willing to say "I believe in a Divine God, Creator of the Universe, Who knows my innermost thoughts and feelings, and to Whom one day I shall be accountable."[4] But Dr. Goldsen observes, after an objective appraisal, ". . . even if religious belief is widespread, religious commitment is rare."

If Paul were to show up on one of our university campuses today, I think he would not change very much the remarks he made in Athens, which was, after all, the center of intellectual life of his own day. "Men," he said, "I perceive that in every way you are very religious." Evidences of religious ceremony filled the city. There was even one altar, thrown up as a kind of hostage to fortune, not to take any chances, "To an unknown god." So far, Paul sounds like the normal Religious Emphasis Week speaker, sent in to Athens U. to keep the pot boiling for God. "I see here in the Catalog," he says, "that you say religion is a good thing." At this point, however, Paul departs radically from the Religious Emphasis text, with the words, "The times of ignorance God overlooked, *but now he commands all men everywhere to repent* . . ." Here the audience starts grumbling, because Paul is not playing the game. Religion-in-general is a great thing—if it is general enough—but Paul makes the mistake of getting specific. His proclamation becomes an attack on religion itself.

Paul's attack on religion is no surprise to anyone who has read the Old Testament. The Old Testament is filled with the constantly renewed skirmishes of the prophetic faith against every kind of man-made religiosity.

> "I hate, I despise your feasts,
>   and I take no delight in your solemn assemblies.
> Even though you offer me your
>   burnt offerings and cereal offerings,
>   I will not accept them, and the
> peace offerings of your fatted beasts
>   I will not look upon.
> Take away from me the noise of your songs;
>   to the melody of your harps I will not listen.
> But let justice roll down like waters,
>   and righteousness like an ever-flowing stream."
>   (Amos 5:21–24)

> "Stand in the gate of the Lord's house, and proclaim
>   there this word, and say, Hear the word of the LORD,
>   all you men of Judah who enter these gates to worship
>   the LORD. Thus says the LORD of hosts, the God of Israel,
>   Amend your ways and your doings, and I will let you dwell
>   in this place. Do not trust in these deceptive words: 'This
>   is the temple of the LORD, the temple of the LORD, the
>   temple of the LORD.'"   (Jeremiah 7:2–4)

The main function of religion in the ancient world was always to maintain the status quo, to purchase security, and to keep the society functioning smoothly. The Ba'al cult about which we hear so much in the Old Testament, for example, was a kind of fertility-religion designed to manipulate and appease the divine forces of soil and sky in order to keep the wheel of the seasons turning and make sure the crops would come up each spring. All religions aim to keep God on our side, and use God to sanctify what society wants to get done.

Very much of present-day American religiosity serves the same functions with different names. Goldsen and her investigators found, for example, that the more religious their students

were, the more closely they conformed to beliefs and actions of
the majority. Sometimes this led them into strange contradictions,
as in the case of cheating. When asked if they thought cheating
was wrong, students who could be identified as "religious" were
much more likely to say Yes than nonreligious people. But
they were also more likely than the irreligious to say, "If
everyone else cheats, why shouldn't I?"

> Religious believers seem to feel more integrated in society;
> non-believers seem more alienated from it. Religious be-
> lievers tend to testify to the kinds of behavior and belief
> that conform to the standards of propriety of American
> culture; non-believers are less likely to do so. Religious
> believers are more likely to respond to the pressure of a
> social norm, even on an issue that they regard as a moral
> question (such as cheating on examinations).[5]

Religion, you see, frequently serves as the icing on the status
quo, the oil on the social machinery.

How very different from such religion is the faith that can
hear God saying, "My thoughts are not your thoughts, neither
are your ways my ways." "Religion" strives to keep everything
running smoothly in the familiar way, but faith is alert for the
word from God which disrupts the familiar and creates something new. "Religion" always tries to harness God to satisfy
our needs; faith means being at God's disposal for his mission.
"Religion" tries to polish up guaranteed ways for presenting
our demands to God; faith is obedience to the unexpected and
absolute demand of God.

The Real Thing

Faith is not the grasping of ideas; it is being grasped by a
Person. Faith is a response to that which God has done, or, to
use the words of Emil Brunner, it is "a personal encounter with
the God who meets us personally in Jesus Christ."[6]

Faith is a relationship, not just an experience. And this
response, encounter, relationship, involves not merely *part* of
my personality—whether mind or my emotions or even my

"religious" life—but all of me, my total being and will. Finally, faith is not a work that I do—not a mental work ("believing what is unbelievable") nor an emotional work ("conversion experience") nor a religious work ("some time for God"). Faith is not a work at all, but a gift. It is really not even my grasp of God, but God's grasp of my life, not even my belief in Christ, but my discovery that Christ has seized me.

One of the most provocative statements about what faith means is in Paul's letter to the disturbed Christians of Galatia:

> I have been crucified with Christ; it is no longer I who live, but Christ who lives in me; and the life I now live in the flesh I live by faith in the Son of God, who loved me and gave himself for me.   (Galatians 2:20)

Faith is the form in which my life emerges when I have been crucified with Christ and raised with him to participate in his new life. Faith is the condition of awe, of wonder, and of joy when I get up in the morning and discover, here is my life. It is not really mine; I died, did I not, back there on the Hill of the Skull? But here it is, this life, and it is given me for this day. Shall I not receive it then, live it—just this day—with awe, with joy, with peace, and with freedom?

15

discipleship of the mind

The Desk and the Altar

There may be a unique little room in your church. It is called "the pastor's study." Now why should it be a "study"? Why not an "office"? The pastor's study is an institution, but it is not at all self-evident why it should be. What have all these books to do with faith?

Speaking of study, I observe that your room also has a desk in it, and I am quite sure there are *some* books lying around. The ones on top may be *Good Ol' Charlie Brown* and *Ten Ever-lovin' Blue-eyed Years with Pogo,* but there are others underneath which will have to be dug out at least by exam time. It is, after all, a *study* desk. Is there any connection between this desk of yours and the pastor's study? Between both and the holy table of the sanctuary? Is there any relation between your study and your life as a Christian?

Some people have said, emphatically No. Back in the third century a fellow named Tertullian, who was an intellectual himself, ironically enough, said, "What has Athens to do with Jerusalem, the Academy with the Church? What is there in common between the philosopher and the Christian, the pupil of Hellas and the pupil of Heaven? . . . We have no need for curiosity since Jesus Christ, nor for inquiry since the evangel." In more recent times, I heard a rather nonintellectual fellow, an elder in a little church where I had been preaching from time to time while I was still in college, deliver a sermon on "The Perils of an Educated Ministry." Looking back at the sermons I had preached, I think he was right about the "perils," though I doubt it was my education that was to blame.

Tertullian and my friend the elder have some truth on their side. We are all tempted to make our own ideas the yardstick for measuring everything, insisting that anything we can't get our minds

239

around cannot be true. Whether this temptation assails educated people more than uneducated is a question I shall leave open. On the other side, the pastor's study is a symbol for the central place that study has always had in the life of the church. Nothing is more characteristic of the history of God's people than the study group. Look at the Jews in Babylon. Jerked up and dragged out of their city, marched in chains those hundreds of aching miles into a strange and frightful country. Where was their God? Had they left him behind too? The Temple was gone—they had seen its demolished walls crumbling in the flames. No worship here, except for the polished pagan rites of Marduk. Was God gone? Then the word was passed around, among the laborers down at the new canal, among the Jewish group assigned to bookkeeping in the market, "We're meeting tonight. At Simeon's house." They came, huddling together into the tiny room, hardly able to make out each other's faces by the flickering little oil lamps. But no matter. Simeon needed no lamp to recite the books of the Law—they were engraved on his memory. In these little gatherings, to hear and discuss the *Torah*, earnestly trying to comprehend what God meant them to see in the things that had happened to them, the Jews gave birth to the Synagogue. No persecution has ever been able to destroy it.

Again, on a Galilean lakeshore, a man sits down to teach, and a great crowd gathers around him to hear what he has to say. A bit later, he leaves the crowd, and goes apart with a small band of men. As they walk, they ask him questions. "Teacher, what did you mean by those parables?" He explains; he pricks their minds with new questions. The crowds are amazed. "Where did this man get all this? What is the wisdom given to him? . . . Is not this the carpenter . . ."

A monastery in the ninth century: the monks sit hunched over those huge, handwritten volumes in their library. Hours on end they read, copy, deliberate, trying to keep some flame of knowledge alive through these Dark Ages. A small German university in the sixteenth century: students rush into a lecture room and scramble for seats. There is a buzz of excitement as the young professor strides in, opens his Greek Testament and begins to lecture, pouring out those pungent, biting sentences that are turning the church upside down. A spring evening in Aldersgate, England, 1738: a handful of Christians[1] have come together to study and pray. John Wesley, a visitor, hears Luther's preface to Romans and feels his heart "strangely warmed." America, the same century: new preacher arrives in a frontier town. The first thing he does is to build a home and a meetinghouse. The next year he starts a college in his home. How many of our great universities began that way! Mid-twentieth century, a cellar in East Germany: a group of Christian university students have gathered. The government has launched an all-out attack on religion; their futures are in danger if they admit that they are Christians. Their topic of study: what does it mean to love your enemy?

The Word That Happened

There is a good reason why the history of the church can almost be written as a history of study groups. The very nature of the Christian gospel is such that to understand it you have to know some things that happened once and to puzzle out what they mean.

You could have a religion that did not require that kind of knowledge. For instance, if the main thing about religion is its ritual, then the ordinary member does not need to know how the ritual got started, or even what it means. The professionals, the priests, may have to study so that the ritual will be performed correctly. But for the rest it is enough to observe or to participate. When someone is initiated into a fraternity, for example, he need not know *why* these ceremonies are done. Indeed, if no one knows why, they are all the more mysterious. The important thing is that a group feeling is produced when we all do them together.

If religion is seen primarily as activity, the more or less practical things that the church *does,* the result is similar. You may be a very active member of one of our churches—participating in the bowling league, the family night suppers, the fellowship meetings, and the rest, all without having to raise the question how the church got started or how all these functions are connected with Jesus Christ.

On the other hand, you might define religion as man's search for something to worship. In that case, *reason* would become the main tool for approaching God, and certainly some study would be necessary. But it would be a very different kind of study from that which occurred in those study groups I have mentioned. Reason begins with us and our world. It asks, if there is a God, then what kind of God must he be, to make sense of what we know about ourselves and our world? Whatever there is about human beings that seems disagreeable to us, God must not have, else he would not be perfect. But everything that seems good about man, God must have, except in greater degree. You can work up a picture of a God that way, and probably it would be helpful.

But this is not the Bible's way. It is the approach of reason. We must not, of course, fall into the blunder of crying down all reason as anti-God and anti-Bible. For "reason" is a blanket word, covering all the activities of the human mind; the whole point of this chapter is the importance of *thinking* in the Christian religion. Reason by itself will not save us; if it did, only Phi Beta Kappas would be saved. To be sure the exercise of reason belongs as much to the Christian life as to human life in general. We have had to stretch our brains and use all our powers of logic as we have tried to understand what the Bible is saying to us. But the Bible does not begin by asking what is reasonable, probable, or universally taken for granted. It does not have to stop to ask reason's permission before telling us its story. Its starting point is quite different.

What is the gospel? It is news: something has happened. That is the theme of the Bible. It is not the chronicle of man's religious growth, of the assorted ideas men have hatched about God— though these things are there—but it is the story of God's coming to man, again and again, the story of God's surprises and of men's responses, good and bad. Who is God? "I am Yahweh your God, who brought you out of the land of Egypt, out of the house of bondage." God's name is defined by the event, by his "mighty act," and man's life is called into responsible commitment to the God who acts in this way: "You shall have no other gods before me." The New Testament is equally emphatic: "For I delivered to

you as of first importance what I also received, that Christ died
for our sins in accordance with the scriptures, that he was buried,
that he was raised on the third day in accordance with the scriptures, and that he appeared to Cephas, then to the twelve"
(1 Cor. 15:3–5). Something has happened; there can be no Christian life unless we understand *what* happened and what it has to
do with us.

Even our worship is anchored in event. Every Jewish family,
from the most ancient times of the nation down to this day, re-
enacts the Exodus from Egypt every Passover. The Rabbis say,
"In every generation a man should look on himself as if he had
himself gone forth from Egypt." The ceremony is a drama that
makes the ancient history come alive, makes the event become
present before the eyes of the participants, as if "you were there."
To this corresponds our Christian Communion, "For as often as
ye eat this bread and drink this cup, ye do show forth the Lord's
death till He come." Our worship at this occasion is the celebration of the one momentous event, the central thing which God has
done, to which, we are thus reminded, our total life is to be a response.

But if we forget the *history*, if through ignorance we are unaware of what *happened*, of the event to which worship points,
then the drama lapses into ritual, routine, or even magic. That is
exactly what happened in the Middle Ages, when the common
laymen, having no Bibles they could read and unable even to
understand the language of the Mass, their minds filled with fantastic superstitions, legends of saints and martyrs, and a skeleton
selection of biblical stories, came to regard the Mass as a
spectacle of pure magic. Our language retains a memorial to
their captive ignorance: "Hocus pocus" is the illiterate's ab-
breviation of the Words of Institution, *hoc est enim corpus
meum!*

The Exile of Ignorance

Whenever the central events of God's dealings with men are
buried under the crust of institutions, legends, or misunderstandings, or simply forgotten by an ignorant age, then the church can

only be healed and renovated by the painstaking labor of someone to dig them out again. The prophets of Israel railed against the ignorance of their contemporaries: ". . . they do not regard the deeds of the LORD, or see the work of his hands. Therefore my people go into exile for want of knowledge . . ." The cry of the Exile Prophet was "Have you not known? Have you not heard? Has it not been told you from the beginning?" Israel had to be taught anew what God had done.

The Reformation had the same intent, and its method was, above all, the technique of the historical scholar. We often forget that the Reformation was a movement begun in professors' studies and university classrooms. It started, someone has said, as "an academic affair, a scandal in a university."[2] The deep stirring of soul that marked Luther's "evangelical conversion" came while he labored in his study to make sense of the letter of Paul to the Romans. His revolutionary recovery of the meaning of the gospel grew directly out of endless hours of drudgery he had spent mastering Greek grammar. To an even greater extent, John Calvin was the scholar of the Reformation, and the traditions which stem from his leadership have always valued education. Educated at the University of Paris in law and humanist philosophy, Calvin always felt himself cut out by nature to be a quiet, objective scholar—though his life was to take a far stormier course than that. Nevertheless, he produced "fifty-nine stout volumes," of high caliber. The *Institutes of the Christian Religion* which he published has been called the highest monument to Reformation scholarship.

Furthermore, the Reformers' scholarship was not designed merely for professionals. They did not write theology just to help ministers prepare sermons, but to liberate all the people from superstitions and misunderstandings. Every professor was "a doctor of the church." Calvin not only wrote his Institutes in a Latin version for fellow scholars, he also carefully translated each edition into French so that laymen could read them. Luther and Calvin swept away the elaborate machinery of regulated grace, and left all men, priest and layman alike, confronting God directly, standing no longer under the regulation of the church, but under God's word. Like Hus in Bohemia and Wyclif in England, they had a great zeal to translate the Bible into the language of the common people, so that "every ploughboy could recite Scripture to himself as he toiled." This conviction of all the Reformers that the layman must be permitted to read and interpret the Bible for himself, already implies *study* for the layman.

Since that time, we have turned that wonderful, liberating insight of the Reformers into the great Protestant heresy of the self-interpreting Bible. We have come to think that, since every man is responsible directly to God, he is always entitled to his opinion, even when that opinion is based on utter ignorance. As far as the Bible is concerned, it is no longer necessary to read it at all in order to expound at length on "what the Bible says." The Reformers were not so stupid. They were fully aware how difficult it was to read and interpret the Bible. That is why they all labored long and hard to provide commentaries and introductions, and urged the lay people so insistently to come to hear the explanation of Scripture by men who had been trained.

Every generation has to repeat, for its own time and in its own terms, the labor of the Reformation. Otherwise, the jungle of ignorance creeps back and takes over. I have the impression that a good many creepers of misinformation are mixed with the ivy on college walls today. An astonishing number of Christian students imagine that a junior high school knowledge of the data of our faith is adequate; indeed, they seem hardly to suspect that there *is* anything else to be known. Somehow they have not understood that the Bible was written for adults. The result of this creeping ignorance is that faith is often stunted or blocked altogether by the most incredible half-truths or complete nonsense masquerading as "the Christian faith" or "what the Bible says." A freshman co-ed will not be convinced by her campus pastor that a certain rather lurid scene is not to be found in the New Testament. It has to be, she insists; she saw it in a "biblical" movie that cost eight million dollars to make. Another conversation goes something like this:

Student: "You mean you still expect people to read that stuff? The whole Bible is full of myth. You know that bit about creation? It's all copied from an old Egyptian or Babylonian or some kind of myth."

Minister: "Have you read the Babylonian one?"

Student: "No, but one of my teachers told us about it in class. It's exactly the same."

Minister: "How about the one in Genesis. Have you read that?"

Student: "Sure, lots of times."

Minister: "When was the last time?"

Student: "Oh, in Sunday school . . . it must have been . . . I was about ten, I guess . . ."

The only defense against the endless variety of nonsense that gets promulgated in college bull sessions is a little hardheaded study and thought. The Reformation continues today where serious, biblical scholarship goes on. The church is being reformed wherever it is enabled to hear anew the word of God in the freshness and relevance that only study can break free from the clay of habit and tradition. Where preacher and people alike submit themselves to the discipline of study, trying to discover what is God's word to them, there the church shakes off her lethargy and stands again under the judgment and grace of God's mighty acts. Now the fact that you are a student means that you have a special opportunity and obligation to participate in the renewal both of the church and of the world.

Events That Speak

What kind of study is needed? If it is in history that God has revealed himself, then every Christian must be, in some sense, a historian. Just as passionately as the historian of the Punic Wars or of modern Europe, he wants to know "what really happened." Above all he must begin, as every good historian begins, with his primary source. That is to say, he begins by reading the Bible. That ought to be self-evident—both that it is *primary* and one should begin there, and that it is to be read as a *source*, with an open mind, expecting to understand something, and not as a pious exercise, a chapter a night like cranking a prayer wheel.

But it is true that the Bible is a difficult book. The latest parts of it are at least eighteen hundred years old, after all, and the whole thing written in languages that few of us understand, by people who lived in cultures very different from ours, who saw the world in a completely different way than we do. It is very difficult indeed to think ourselves back into the world of those people and to understand what their words mean. On the other hand we have today at our disposal better tools for understanding the Bible than any laymen in the history of the church. Of course much of the fine work is a job for specialists, but like the Reformers they have not been stingy with their findings. In any bookstore you can buy several translations which are far more accurate than was possible a century ago. Commentaries and introductions multiply, even in paperback!

We have excellent tools for getting at the biblical history, but something seems lacking. The Bible has a curious way of frustrating the historians. It seems strangely uninterested in things about which we are often curious. We come with all kinds of questions to be answered; we want to know what are all the causes, what led up to this and that event. But again and again the Bible is simply silent to our questions, or merely gives us some answer like "God spoke, and it happened."[3] We come trying to understand this man from Nazareth, this Jesus, and we find a puzzle. If only we could piece together the facts of his life, if we had a decent biography of him, then maybe it would all make sense. If we knew about his childhood, what kind of home life he had . . . But the Gospels hurry over all that. There is one momentous event toward which everything hurries, the one event we shrink from because most of all we do not understand it.

At this point we may learn from the best historians that the study of history is not just a matter of gathering facts. If we are really to understand the facts, we must be willing to put ourselves into the shoes of those people to whom the "facts" happened, to see, to the best of our imaginative ability, through their eyes. Real study involves the willingness to stop asking questions at a certain point, and to let those voices out of the past ask *us* questions. It is at this point that the events cease to be mere facts, mere happenings, and begin to be the word that is spoken to us.

All history is able to speak to us, insofar as it is human history and as we are able to recognize what we and the men of the past share, despite our differences of outlook. God's history addresses us in a special way, however, because it comes to focus in a person, a person who is still living. We come to know him as a historical person, as we may know Julius Caesar or Woodrow Wilson. But Caesar is safely "back there" and Wilson affects us, if at all, only by the strength of certain ideals he advocated, while Jesus Christ comes to meet us in our present and waits for us in our future. If one had a perfect biography of Wilson, then one would know all there is to know about him, for his history is done. But we cannot know all there is about Christ, for his history is not yet ended. He may have some surprises in store for us. Of course, he would still be meeting us and waiting for us, even if we did not do our homework, even if we did not study his past history. He is working in our times, in our world, whether we know it or not. The difference is that when we have understood the story of his life in Palestine, then we are prepared to recognize him when he meets us, to take our stand for or against him. The function of our study is to clear our eyes of the false images of him, so that we shall not be looking for the Christ of the sentimental art so popular in our churches, nor the gaunt and terrible revolutionist of the Orozco murals, nor the pure-white Aryan superman, nor any of the projections of our fantasies and dreams.

The Mill Hands and You

It would be easier, of course, if you did *not* know the story of Jesus Christ. Then you would not have to make the choice. Either a simple faith, inherited from your parents, or a simple disbelief, absorbed from your culture or copied from an honest skeptic, would be easier. Secondhand faith or secondhand doubt is less demanding than the do-it-yourself kind. But God has a way of refusing us the easy way out. He edges us along to crossroads where we have to make up our minds. The very fact that you are in college and that you know how to read and have a rudimentary equipment for thinking has already put you at such a crossing.

The faith of a pious mill hand or washerwoman seems so much simpler! Perhaps it is, perhaps it is not. At least it is different. But you are neither; you are a student, a member of that minority whose interest and abilities, combined with the necessary finances, have placed you where you can study. This is an opportunity not easily come by, even in affluent America. It is to be responsibly used and carefully cherished. God has a job for both kinds in his church, mill hands as well as students: "The eye cannot say to the hand, 'I have no need of you . . .'" You need the faithful mill hand to remind you that "God chose what is foolish to shame the wise," and the mill hand needs you, just as the sixteenth-century peasant needed Luther and his students, to keep trying to get the history pure, to prune away the nonsense, to break down the idols, to read the story for those who cannot read. Study is your vocation.

We students are members of the church in that peculiar place, the university or college. This ivy-covered parking lot, filled with people who do and people who do not want to learn something, dedicated to the pursuit of a good time as well as the pursuit of knowledge, this college is nevertheless a crucible of the future. It is a place where opposing views collide and mix. It is a place where questions are raised which have no easy answers. It is a place where the church confronts the world of ideas. It is a place where revolutions—but also Reformations—can start. What are we, the Christian students, doing in this place? Do we leave our faith carefully tucked away in the family Bible, like a pressed flower, so that no harm will come to it during these four delicious years, expecting to find it there waiting, a little brown but unhurt, when we "settle down"? Or, trying to make the best of two worlds, shall we run madly onto the campus each day, deftly sidestepping the serious questions which explode all around us, take down our notes with precision, and run home again, stopping our ears against the ideas that are fired at us, till we reach the spiritual refuge of the Westminster House, the

Wesley Center, or the warm security of a Moravian love feast? Or shall we concede that our study may be precisely the basic calling through which we can serve God in this place?

> And these were his gifts: some to be apostles, some prophets, some evangelists, some pastors and teachers, to equip God's people for work in his service, to the building up of the body of Christ. So shall we all at last attain to the unity inherent in our faith and our knowledge of the Son of God—to mature manhood, measured by nothing less than the full stature of Christ. We are no longer to be children, tossed by the waves and whirled about by every fresh gust of teaching, dupes of crafty rogues and their deceitful schemes. No, let us speak the truth in love; so shall we fully grow up in Christ.
> (Eph. 4:11–15, New English Bible)

PART FOUR

the church
in our world

The "modern world" began with the breakup of the medieval system of thought and life. Within the church, the disruption came in the form of the great division of the Reformation, followed by sharp conflicts between Protestants and Catholics and within each group. At the same time, broader changes were transforming all of society. Feudalism gave way to trade and the development of cities; modern nations emerged out of the fragments of old empires and small duchies and kingdoms; the new science was born amid growing confidence in man's ability to understand and to control his environment. These far-reaching changes resulted in a challenge of crisis proportions for Christianity. In earlier chapters we have talked a little about some of the effects.

Nevertheless, the crisis which involved the Western churches—that is, Roman Catholic and Protestant—at the end of the Middle Ages was merely backyard in scope compared to the changes which confront us in the twentieth century. The earlier crisis was confined to western Europe. So far as Europe's churches were concerned, the Christian world was identical with Europe. Outside, there were the Turks, but the church saw them in the same way that the Roman Empire once viewed the northern barbarians: they were the outsiders who did not belong to the real "world," the agents of evil, a threat alike to Christianity and to civilization. Of course, there was also the Eastern Church, but since the eleventh century it had been sharply divided from the West, refusing to accept the authority of the pope. The medieval

252

Christians were often so unequipped to think of people outside their own boundaries as even human beings, much less Christians, that one of the Crusades sent to drive the Turks out of the Holy Land deviated from its purpose in order to steal the richer prizes of Constantinople, looting the city and herding thousands of fellow Christians into their churches to be burned alive.

The story of the church since then has been the history of successive penetrations through the walls with which the church was surrounded. First the geographical walls, the boundaries of Europe and the "Christian West" were broken through. Then the walls which were erected between one group of Christians and another were painfully crossed or penetrated. Finally the walls of thought and feeling, of fear and incomprehension which separate us from the new things happening in our world have begun to give way.

These breakthroughs have never been easy. The church's story is always the story of Jonah. The reluctant prophet, sent to the strange place where he does not wish to go, where he fears to go, the place he hates, ever and again shrinks back and flees in the opposite direction. Only when cast by circumstances into the seething waters of chaos does the church learn the source of its true security, learn to cry out to its Lord for deliverance from the threatening abyss and, set free by him, to follow humbly where he sends, even though the results of its mission may be far different from what it expected or wanted.

❀　❀　❀

16

breaking through
to the world

The Church Discovers the World

Luke relates that Jesus, seen by his Disciples for the last time in the flesh, told them, "You shall be my witnesses in Jerusalem and in all Judea and Samaria and to the end of the earth." Luke spoke for a church which not only remembered this command of Jesus, but had gone an amazingly long way toward carrying it out for its own generation. The book of Acts itself is Luke's account of the miraculous way in which "the word of God grew and multiplied" in concentric waves, from Jerusalem to the capital of the Roman world. While the hero of this account is clearly Paul, Luke also makes it plain that that first-century miracle was carried out by a "cloud of unknown witnesses," thousands of unordained, unprofessional, everyday Christians. Traveling merchants who gave the Good News along with their wares, housewives and domestic slaves who "gossiped the gospel," soldiers and beggars, secretaries and schoolteachers, these were witnesses who learned "to give a reason for the faith that was in them," the leaven that set the whole Roman Empire in ferment.

By the end of the Middle Ages, however, the Great Commission of long ago seemed a dead letter. The "uttermost parts of the earth" had long since been reached, and the church's mission had boiled down to a holding operation: keeping out the Turks and hanging on for heaven. When in 1492 Columbus bumped unknowing into America and when six years later Vasco da Gama landed in Calicut, India, it suddenly became obvious that "the world" amounted to a lot more than people had suspected. At the same time that the Reformation was shaking and purifying the church, Roman churchmen responded to the new discoveries by

254

sending Spanish and Portuguese monks along with the fighting forces of the *conquistadores,* planting the cross alongside the national flags and seeking to convert the newfound "Indian" tribes to Christianity even while the soldiers were converting them to slavery. At about the same time, on the other side of the world, Francis Xavier and his companions were pioneering for Christ with a quite different motive. Instead of being a sort of auxiliary for an army of occupation, these men went to China and the Far East moved by the love of God and the love of man. Their memory is cherished by Catholics and Protestants alike, though the results were then few.

As for the Protestant churches just being born, it required two hundred years to discover the world. They were too busy trying to rediscover the meaning of the gospel and then too engrossed in defending their interpretation of it to notice that "the uttermost parts" to which it was to be preached had suddenly moved.

Nevertheless, there was something at the heart of the Reformation that sooner or later had to drive the Protestants into the world. Their rediscovery of the gospel as Good News, as God's ultimate word to all mankind, meant that they were obligated to tell this news to everyone. The serious Bible study that marked both the beginning and the result of the Reformation could not long miss the fact that the New Testament was a collection of missionary documents.

By the early years of the seventeenth century, the first Protestant missions were already underway. Dutch ministers had been sent to the East Indies, Swedish preachers to Lapland, and a number of missions had been established among the Indians in North America. In spite of the upheaval brought to Europe by the Thirty Years' War, German Lutherans had gone as missionaries to the Middle East. Several outstanding Christian thinkers urged the Protestant groups that they were obligated on theological grounds to minister to non-Christians. Among them were Bishop John Amos Comenius, the scholarly leader of the Moravian Brethren, and the philosopher Leibniz, who had been impressed while visiting Rome by conversations with Jesuit missionaries to China.

The real beginning of the Protestant march "into all the world," however, did not come until the eighteenth century, when some unusual things began to happen within the then tiny movement of the Moravian Brethren (Unitas Fratrum). The Brethren had had an international spirit from the beginning. The English Wyclif had strongly influenced John Hus, who had had much to do with the beginnings of the Brethren, and they had corresponded early with the Waldensians of western Europe. Even before the German Reformation they had sent delegates throughout Europe to establish contacts with Christians who were concerned to renew the life of the church. Beginning in the sixteenth century, however, a series of violent persecutions sent many of them fleeing from their homeland, and the struggle for mere survival threatened to overwhelm their concern for the world. When groups of the Brethren began in 1722 to settle on the estates of Count Zinzendorf in Saxony, the missionary concerns of Bishop Comenius had apparently long been forgotten. Instead they sang,

> Himself will lead me to a spot
> Where, all my cares and griefs forgot,
> I shall enjoy sweet rest.[1]

If they built the village of Herrnhut as a resting-place, however, they had not counted on the extraordinary zeal of Zinzendorf. The Count had been deeply influenced by German Pietism, which, like the Brethren, stressed the personal, transforming experience of the believer's encounter with Christ. The Pietists had become deeply interested in missions to non-Christians, partly as a result of Leibniz' essay, and Zinzendorf even as a boy had dreamed of going himself as a missionary to India. When the Moravians arrived on his estates, he found them congenial spirits. Almost at once he began to organize them into a tightly knit community and to engage them in an educational program whose central theme was an obligation to proclaim the gospel to all men. The resting-place of the refugees was quickly transformed into a home base for a missionary army that spread throughout almost the entire world. The persecuted bands who had come looking for quiet refuge found themselves permanently a "church of pilgrims."

The first two missionaries who went out from Herrnhut were Leonard Dober and David Nitschmann. They had been so moved by reports brought from the Danish West Indies by a Negro slave whom the Count had met in Denmark that they had resolved to go and preach to the plantation slaves in the Indies, even if it meant they themselves must become slaves. Though they were spared slavery, they had to overcome the extreme hostility and often outright persecution by the planters and the leaders of the white church on the islands. The Brethren persisted, however, and soon they had established colonies in the Indies for the sole purpose of creating communal centers for a ministry to the slaves. One of their most remarkable achievements was their early recruiting and training of leaders, including evangelists and pastors, from the slaves themselves.

By the end of the century, the Moravians had begun missions in Russia, India, the Nicobar Islands, Ceylon, North America, the British West Indies, Surinam, the Gold Coast, South Africa, Lapland, Greenland, and Labrador. Just as important as their own missions was their influence on other Protestants. For example, the entire Methodist movement can be said to have begun when John Wesley, terrified by a storm at sea, met the strangely calm Moravians traveling on the same ship. When Wesley said in later years, "The world is my parish," he was reflecting in part a view held by the Moravians. Another significant turning point in the relation of the Protestant churches to the world came when William Carey, meeting with a group of Baptist ministers called together at his own insistence, threw on the table a stack of Moravian missionary reports and said, "See what these Moravians have done!"

What the Moravians had done inspired Carey to do some remarkable things himself. Though he was only a frail-looking little shoemaker, part-time schoolteacher and Baptist preacher, in a tiny inland village of Britain, he was afire with a sense of obligation to the whole world. Against entrenched opposition, he conveyed this sense of the world to enough of his fellow Baptists to make possible the founding of the Baptist Missionary Society. In 1794 he landed with his family and one other minister in Calcutta, the first overseas representatives of that society and the first English missionaries in India.

The accomplishments of Carey and his associates are almost incredible. Carey, who had quit school in his early teens, became known around the world for his scholarship. With the help of two other missionaries and Indian assistants, he translated the Bible into forty-four languages and dialects. He wrote grammars and compiled dictionaries. He established a boarding school and a liberal arts college, the first to grant degrees in India. His efforts in the scholarly Asiatic Society led to publication of leading Indian literary classics in Bengali and English, the first step toward the emergence of Bengali as a literary language. Although he belonged to a denomination which construed the gospel very narrowly, his own understanding of Christ's commission was extremely broad. He labored to raise the standard of living of the Indians, becoming an expert botanist in his spare time and urging new methods of agriculture and reforestation of the country. He campaigned against slavery, infanticide, and *suttee*, the practice of widows' sacrificing themselves on the funeral pyres of their husbands. He urged the cooperation of all Christian denominations and even proposed worldwide conferences of Christian leaders. His whole life spells out the slogan he had proposed in a sermon of 1791: "Expect great things from God: attempt great things for God."[2]

Under Orders

The same sense of joyful obligation which controlled the lives of Nicolaus Zinzendorf, Leonard Dober, David Nitschmann, and William Carey, the sense of being commanded by Christ to proclaim the gospel to those who had not heard it, was characteristic of thousands of missionaries who went, literally, "into all the world" during the next century and a half. The conviction of all was summed up by Robert E. Speer, addressing the first World Missionary Conference at Edinburgh, 1910, when he said, "No one can follow Him without following Him to the uttermost parts of the earth."

The early missionaries had shown by their own actions that intellectual equipment was demanded for obeying Christ's rigorous commission. It was natural that the new movement of Protestant missions should find students in its forefront. The very colleges which, at the turn of the eighteenth century, were centers of skepticism and antireligious rationalism, became focal points of the new missionary movement. One of them, Williams College in Massachusetts, became especially important. In 1806 Samuel John Mills came to Williams as a freshman. Already interested in the mission to non-Christians, he discovered there a small group of students who had been strongly affected by the "awakening" then in progress in the colleges. The group used to go out once a week to pray for a renewal of Christian life in the college. During one such meeting in a meadow near Williams, the students were caught by a thunderstorm. They found shelter in a haystack and continued their conversation, which turned to the question of foreign missions. Before the storm was over they were convinced that only if Christian students dedicated their lives to the task could significant numbers of people in Asia and Africa hear the gospel. They became further convinced that the dedication had to begin with themselves. They vowed together to use their lives wherever God needed them.

Influences of that "haystack meeting" spread around the world. The Williams students visited and even transferred to other colleges to encourage similar movements. A petition from the Williams group persuaded the Congregational Churches' General Association of Massachusetts to organize the American Board of Commissioners for Foreign Missions, the first American organization for sending missionaries to foreign countries.

Many years after the "haystack meeting," nearly three hundred students gathered at Mount Hermon, near Northfield, Massachusetts, for a month-long conference—the first of those innumerable conferences that students have been going to ever since. At the insistence of leaders of the intercollegiate YMCA, the conference had been organized by Dwight L. Moody, the famous evangelist of that era. At that conference, which was partly the result of ideas set in motion by the Williams group long before, a new organization was born: The Student Volunteer Movement for Foreign Missions. Members of the new movement were men and women who had pledged, "It is my purpose, if God permit, to become a foreign missionary."

The Student Volunteer Movement has had a long and exciting history. Spreading to many other countries, it has recruited altogether well over twenty thousand students who have gone to mission fields under denominational boards and agencies. It has been the foundation of many other movements for cooperation among Christian students of different nations and different denominations. Today the American movement, now the Commission on World Mission of the National Student Christian Federation, is still a powerful force in the life of the student Christian movement. No other student organization has ever equaled the power of the SVM conferences, held every four years. In these conferences thousands of students have for the first time learned to think in the context of the whole world, as they have lived, studied, and worshiped together with other students from every nation. They have been brought face to face with the new problems created by a rapidly changing world, helped to wrestle with the new intellectual currents sweeping through each student generation, and confronted with the "new frontiers" of Christian mission and the demands for new responses and new dedication which they present.

The Great Adventure

The Protestant missionary movement shared much of the spirit of the American frontier. Those early student leaders knew themselves to be pioneers, venturing into places they did not know and taking on obligations whose consequences they could not understand in advance. To an extent which still seems unbelievable even in our Space Age, they were at home in the whole world. John R. Mott, the first secretary of the Student Volunteer Movement, and one of the founders of almost every one of the great worldwide organizations of Christians that have developed during the last century, was called by one astonished observer "the young man who thinks in continents." For Mott, a round-the-world tour was undertaken as casually as a trip to the beach. He and his colleagues in the early student Christian movements seized every opportunity to deliver addresses to audiences of skeptical students in every country in Europe, and in China, Japan, India, Indonesia. Some of them enrolled in foreign universities, carefully cultivating the language, for the sole purpose of organizing student Christian associations. Ruth Rouse, the first woman secretary of the World Student Christian Federation, tells of speaking to a thousand students, almost all revolutionaries of one kind or another, in Moscow, 1907, with armed czarist police officers occupying the front row.

For the missionaries who became residents of what we now call "underdeveloped countries," the frontier life was even more obvious. Pushing continually farther to the remotest places where people lived who had not heard the gospel, they have made use of every form of transportation known to man, from dugout canoe and pack-mule to airplanes. They have taught themselves languages for which no grammar book or dictionary existed. They have faced isolation and hostility, suffered diseases unknown to their home countries, and endured the long, lonely disappointments when no results showed from their work.

Looking back over the time since Dober and Nitschmann landed in the Indies, however, we see some very impressive results. The word scattered by the missionaries has often fallen on good soil and produced, some thirtyfold, some sixtyfold, some a hundredfold. The Moravian descendents of Dober and Nitschmann provide one of the most striking examples: of the 326,000 Moravians in the world today, nearly 213,000 of them are in areas once defined as foreign missions. Today, many of the "mission" churches are regularly sending their own missionaries abroad. They have often shown more vitality than their "parents." For years, to take a single example, the fastest-growing Presbyterian church has been one established by missionaries only one hundred years ago in Brazil.

But evangelism was not the only task of missionaries. From the beginning it was taken for granted that the love of Christ must not only be talked but also acted. Wherever missionaries went, they established schools: more than 60,000 of them by

1950. The whole modern literacy movement and its techniques were developed on the mission field. Languages never written before were given alphabets; by 1900 more languages had been given written form than in all the centuries before 1800.[3] Agricultural experiment stations and training schools were established; improved breeds of livestock and new crops were introduced. And of course medicine, nursing, and dentistry became a major activity of missionaries. Alert mission personnel had driven forcibly home to them the biblical truth that man is a unity, soul and body inseparable.

A similar lesson was being learned by the "home" churches where Christianity had been implanted longer. If the geographical expansion at the beginning of the nineteenth century enabled Protestant churches to discover the world outside their old boundaries, transformation of European and especially American life at the end of the century brought the discovery of a new world under their noses. New frontiers were discovered which were not geographical. The movement for the abolition of slavery had long exercised the churches, and when slavery had ended, peacefully in Britain but by tragic war in the United States, the church found itself increasingly involved in trying to solve the racial tensions which were to be slavery's lingering aftermath. Another complex and far-reaching frontier was created by the rapid growth of cities. In them institutions and morals which had grown up in rural life became meaningless or ineffective. Millions of new people, from every nation of the world, were flocking to the United States, dazzled by the glamour of the New World and longing for its promised freedom. These settled in the cities, where they often found their dreams painfully shattered, the new land strange and hostile. The rapidly developing industrialization of both Britain and the United States soon created enormous tensions between the laborers and their employers, tensions which reached their peak in this country in the depression years of the 1930's. The impact of the new growth turned many sections of the cities into slums, where impossible conditions destroyed family life. Youngsters reared in the "asphalt jungle" found expression for their bitterly frustrated energies in outbursts of violence. From these overwhelming problems, many of the leading Protestant churches fled away to the suburbs, leaving the "inner city" to further decay. But dedicated and open-eyed ministers and laymen saw here a frontier as tangible as the oceans, one which the church must find ways to cross.

Both in the old "home" lands and the old "mission" lands, these and many other new frontiers remain uncrossed. We shall have to look at some of these more closely later. At present it is enough to notice that through the modern mission movements the church has genuinely discovered the world, in new dimensions of both breadth and depth, and in many ways has come into effective encounter with that world, both proclaiming and working out concrete evidence that God loves the world and gave his Son for its salvation.

Missions Under the Cross

On the other side of the ledger, we have to face honestly and openly the failures and perversions of the Christian missionary effort. In 1952 the International Missionary Council met in Willingen, Germany, to consider the somber theme, "Missions Under the Cross." The theme was chosen deliberately and carefully, for the conference was planned under the heavy shadow of the successful Communist revolution in China. From that vast land, representing twenty-five per cent of the geographical area of foreign missions and at one time attracting the largest body of missionary personnel of any nation, almost every Christian missionary had been expelled, and virtually all contact between Chinese Christians and those outside the Communist bloc was broken off. Under the cloud of the China debacle, the cross at Willingen had a double and ominous significance. First, it stood for God's judgment on the shortcomings and sin which were involved in all the church's efforts—shortcomings and sin which were pitilessly exposed by events in China. Second, the cross reminded the leaders at Willingen that the church in our time is called to share again in the mission of the crucified Christ himself, the mission of suffering.

Missionaries, after all, are not superhuman. They have come

in many sizes, shapes, and temperaments, with widely varying abilities and interests. Like the rest of us, they have made their decisions from mixed motives, frequently unconscious of the real sources of their actions and often obtaining results which were far different from what they had wanted to achieve. Some have felt that they could establish credit with God by the number of souls they "won," so that the persons to whom they preached became mere objects to be manipulated and pressured into "conversion." Works of Christian service even became sometimes just "bait" to draw men within range of evangelization: patients in a mission hospital were a captive audience for these, fortunately few, missionaries. One critic has characterized this distorted concept of evangelism as "a lust for souls instead of a love for souls"; the type is cruelly portrayed in Somerset Maugham's *Rain*.

More widespread than these personal failings were the inadequate understandings of the gospel which brought many to the mission fields. At one extreme, large numbers of missionaries understood salvation very narrowly, as entirely concerned with the rescue of souls from eternal punishment. On the field their preaching often produced a kind of works-righteousness not basically different from the medieval religion against which Luther rebelled. At the other extreme, many others, reacting against this self-centered religion, watered down the gospel or neglected its proclamation altogether in their activities. They tended to identify the Kingdom with a utopian civilization, and they confidently hoped to bring it into existence by education, reorganization of society, and works of benevolence. Oddly enough, both these extremes placed the emphasis on what *man* had to do, rather than on the central news of what *God* had done in Jesus Christ and what he continues to do in the world.

Equally destructive were the inadequate understandings of the church which many missionaries brought with them. A large number came from the smaller and more exclusive sects, and on the mission field they tended to reproduce the same splintery denominationalism that existed at home. There were a few "apostles of discord" who, not content to seek converts to their narrowly conceived versions of Christianity from the non-Christian populations, traveled the globe preaching in established congregations alleging that their pastors were "heretics" and "modernists" and seeking, too often successfully, to create dissident splinter groups. Thus, even though, as we shall see in the next chapter, the modern mission movement has for the most part been a powerful force for the unity of Christians, it has also all too frequently exposed our painful disunity for all the world to see. A leader of the outcastes of India once told V. S. Azariah, the first Indian bishop of the Anglican Church in India, that he could never encourage the outcastes to become Christians, for that would mean their fragmentation into many groups. In Hinduism, he said, they might be oppressed, but at least they were one.

From our perspective today, we can see that the most devastating shortcoming of all was one shared by virtually all the missionaries and by the churches who sent them, although they could hardly ever have been aware of it. That was the involvement of Christian missions in the expansion of Western power and Western culture—in what the majority of the nations of the earth now bitterly call "imperialism" and "colonialism." It was precisely the expansion of western European power which first made missions possible: Carey and his associates went to India with licenses from the British East India Company, and military force blasted China open to Westerners—both to opium traders and to bearers of the gospel. Of course it was natural that missionaries should become the proponents of Western culture, of European ideals and "the American way of life," as well as—and sometimes in the place of—the gospel. They found often primitive societies, humanly destructive conditions of sanitation and education. Rightly they considered it their duty to raise the standard of living, to teach people to read and write, to introduce modern agriculture. But they were hardly aware that in the process they were trying to remake these societies in the images of home. With what must have appeared the utmost arrogance but what was actually blissful naïveté, they referred not only to primitive tribal cultures but even to the ancient and sophisticated civilizations of India and China as "backward" in comparison with their own, scarcely a century-old, American culture. They and the churches which sent them neatly divided the world into Christian and non-Christian lands. A convenient shorthand, a natural way of speaking perhaps, but it revealed an almost fatal flaw in the missionary philosophy which was dominant for a long period. If Christianity was identical with the American or European way of life, then the time was inevitable when Africans and Asians would say, "We must have, not *your* way of life, but our own, and, since the Christian God belongs to *your* way, we must return to our own gods." The way was also paved for the cynical observation that the "Christian" nations behaved surprisingly like some of the "primitive" tribes. If in the third century Roman citizens marveled "how these Christians love one another," the non-Christians of the twentieth century noted with wry humor how these Christians murder one another. As a Christian theologian from India remarked, World War II demonstrated that "Paganism no longer had any geographical frontiers."[4]

One Church in One World

It is a fact that the church today confronts a world in many ways radically different from that so effectively engaged by Zinzendorf, Wesley, Carey, and their successors. Furthermore, some of the changes have been dizzyingly rapid. In the face of the new situation, naturally the patterns of missionary activity which have become familiar during the last two centuries have had to be reexamined. Some of them even have to be junked. Because of this wide-ranging reappraisal, some startled or even secretly pleased voices have been heard asking, "Isn't the day of missions over?" "Haven't missions failed?" Because these are real questions, it has seemed useful in this study to examine quite frankly some of the failings of the modern missionary movement, as well as a few examples of its remarkable achievements. On balance, now, what can we say about missions today? Are we watching the last feeble steps of the church's journey into all the world, or is a vigorous new march beginning?

First of all, this very new situation which has overturned so many of our habitual ways of thinking about missions has to a very large extent been brought about by the achievements of the missionary movement itself. After all, one of the most significant factors calling for a new understanding of the Christian international mission is the existence of churches in almost every nation of the world—most of which did not exist until they were founded by the mission movement. Thus, by its very success, the mission movement destroyed the illusion that faith was geographical. By its accomplishments it has continually made its own language and ideas out-of-date. The division between Christian and non-Christian lands had to give way to discussion of *The Christian Message in a Non-Christian World*,[5] with the awareness that the message might be brought by men from East or West, and that the non-Christian world was to be found in every country and even within the church itself. "Missions" are being rapidly replaced by "younger churches," self-governing and self-supporting, trying to find ways to express the Christian faith in language and institutions which would belong to their own cultures, not to imported models from the West. Instead of "missionaries," many leaders now prefer to speak of "fraternal workers" to emphasize that Christian servants do not enter other countries to organize, command, and direct with a position of superiority being taken for granted, but come as fellow servants of the Christ already at work in that land, submitting to the direction of the indigenous church, and working alongside the Christians of that country in the attempt to discover and follow together new ways of leading men to Christ and living as Christians. The keynote, sounded already at a conference of the International Missionary Council in Whitby, 1947, is "partners in obedience."

Besides the removal of geographical boundaries and the shouldering of responsibility by younger churches, however, there are political factors that have produced a radically different situation for the church today. The upheavals in international relations, the bewilderingly rapid transformation of former colonies into independent nations, the growing sense of jealous nationalism in most of these new nations—do not these developments threaten the very existence of Christian missionary activity? Two things need to be said. First, not even these developments arose entirely independently of the mission of the church. In fact, as we shall see in chapter 18, the Christian mission has played a decisive part in the awakening of colonial peoples to a desire for freedom, more adequate standards of living, and recognition in the world of nations. In this way also, then, the church has helped to create the very challenge to which it must now respond. Second, even those factors which *are* totally beyond the church's control and influence are seen by thoughtful and faithful Christians to lie nevertheless within *God's* control. Maybe it is providential that the church in many places has experienced a renewed interest in Bible study and theology in just the period during which these frightening challenges are hurled at us. For the Christian who is acquainted with God's "mighty acts" as seen by his people of old knows that even the pagan Assyria, the Persian great kings, the Roman procurators could be mere tools in God's hand. As we have seen in Part Two of this book, the People of God at every stage of their pilgrimage have met challenges at least as threatening and uncanny as those we face. But the Bible sees these ominous events always as means which God uses to drive his people *to* their mission, not away from it! Is God not doing the same thing for his church today?

New Patterns of Obedience

One of the characteristics of the mission to which God is driving his church today seems to be flexibility. In a time of rapid social and political change throughout the world, missionary leaders have become aware that the church must be alert and open to an endless variety of brand-new opportunities. In the last few years new opportunities have been met repeatedly by the development of novel, creatively conceived ministries. Naturally some of these have proceeded quietly and unspectacularly; others have been quite dramatic. The significant thing is that in small ways and big ones, in out-of-the-way frontier posts and in "bureaucratic" planning committees, people concerned for the church's mission have been shaking their minds free from all the "normal" things that were taken for granted and striking out in unexplored directions.

As you might expect, some of the most imperative of the new opportunities occur in the newly independent nations of Africa and Asia and in the rapidly developing nations of Latin America. In the Republic of Congo, for example, the vast upheaval of independence brought with it an almost completely new situation for the church and for foreign missionary personnel. First of all, the national churches, long heavily dependent upon the help of missions that founded them, were challenged to match in their life the vigor and zeal for independence which swept through political and social affairs of the nation, while trying to maintain the sense of oneness with Christians around the world which was threatened by the fires of extreme nationalism. On the other hand, the government tended to take a greater hand in social services like education and medical care, formerly the work largely of missionaries. Did this mean that Christians now had less to do? Or should they compete with government in these areas? Or should the increased responsibility by government be welcomed and church resources shifted to new, untouched areas of need?

In a country which did not have a single institution of higher education before independence, colleges and universities were established, and a growing stream of young graduates of these and foreign universities began to flow into the developing structures of business, government, and professions. How should the church minister to these students, who were being catapulted into positions of top leadership in the country? One response was the establishment soon after independence of theological schools, built cooperatively by Congo national churches and the missions of several foreign denominations. Several missionaries shifted from direct evangelistic work to the training of pastors and evangelists. One of them, who had taken off two years to complete a Ph.D. degree, was asked why he went back. Why should Ph.D.'s be needed in a country in which the majority of the population had only a primary education or less? Here is his answer:

> First, it is our conviction that the Protestant Church in the Congo must possess leadership which is capable of speaking to the high school and college graduates, who are yearly growing in number, and of challenging them to dedicate

their lives to Jesus Christ. With education at such a premium here, for the Protestant Church to possess a ministry educated only on the lower levels is to lessen greatly the leavening quality of the Church.

Second, there is a real need for the training of the teaching ministry of the Church. It is a basic goal to have Congolese professors in all of the schools as soon as possible. No outside help can do the job as well. . . . Congo needs her own seminaries staffed by Congolese. . . . Congo needs the Bible translated by her own scholars. She also needs men who can grapple with the problems a resurgent African culture presents to a Church heretofore basically oriented to the West.[6]

The new developments have required also a new and more flexible sense of geography. The freedom to ignore national boundaries—without ignoring the unique needs and concerns of the people within each boundary—the same "thinking in continents" that characterized John R. Mott and Carey and Zinzendorf before him, is coming alive again in today's missionaries. For example, W. H. "Hank" Crane, formerly a Presbyterian missionary to the Congo, was "loaned" by his denomination in 1962 as Africa Secretary for the World Student Christian Federation to work with students throughout the continent of Africa. He began traveling continually to establish fellowship among the scattered new student Christian movements springing up in the rapidly multiplying colleges and universities south of the Sahara, trying to arrange means for pastoral care of students, training of their leaders, regional and continent-wide conferences. He found himself deeply involved in questioning, prayer, and study with students facing terrifying decisions.

Yet a different alteration of the geography of missions brought a missionary couple "home" from the heart of Africa to Washington, D.C. Mr. and Mrs. Tom Cleveland were asked by the Presbyterian Board of World Missions to go to Washington, D.C., as the first missionary couple in residence related to a growing ecumenical ministry to thousands of international students who are coming annually to the American capital as students, government and business interns, and members of diplomatic corps of young nations. A part of their work has been to establish a residence called "The Bridge," which is becoming a center where persons from other countries can be drawn into the life and work of the Christian community in that area.

These examples could be multiplied many times. The mark of the new look in missions is the endless variety of ways in which the Spirit of God is leading churches and the members of churches to respond to the novelties of the age. Never before has such a diversity of skills been called to serve in the Christian ministry to the world. Doctors, nurses, educational specialists, dentists, mechanics, audio-visual and mass-communications experts join with evangelists, pastors, theological teachers, youth workers, specialists in industrial evangelism, ministers to students, anthropologists and linguists, to meet the constantly growing demands. Alongside the basic core of lifetime missionaries, who take upon themselves the discipline of a long-range commitment to life in a different culture, devoting themselves completely to their adopted country, there is a growing place for short-term specialists, who will accept calls from the churches of other countries for a limited number of years to assist in particular undertakings. In addition, a rapidly increasing number of Christian laymen, moving abroad as government and United Nations employees, technical assistants, businessmen, and armed forces personnel, are finding themselves involved in the international mission of the church as they take steps to identify themselves with the national churches in the lands of their work, learning languages and cultural patterns and participating in the difficult but exciting adventure of sharing points of view and common labor with Christians of very different backgrounds.

And You?

If our understanding of the mission of the church has been revolutionized in our time, it is no less true that our concept of what it means to be a member of the church is being renewed and transformed. Above all this renewal is showing up in the dramatic recovery of the Reformation doctrine of the priesthood of all believers. We shall have more to say about this later. Here we merely need to notice that any misunderstanding of the missionary obligation of the church as something which applies only to a class of "professionals" has to go. For too long most of us have regarded missionaries the way the medieval church regarded monks: as people who were more "spiritual" than the rest of us, who had received some kind of mystical and special "call" beyond what every Christian receives, and who would be rewarded for their works which went "above and beyond the call of duty." Luther tried to abolish that nonsense, but it keeps cropping up again. It is time to rid our minds of it. Either the *whole* church— and every local congregation, every campus student movement —is a missionary community, or it is not the church.

A "missionary" is, by definition, someone who is "sent." Jesus Christ (in John 17) prays for all his disciples and for all "those who are to believe in me through their word." He says, "As thou didst send me into the world, so I have sent them into the world." No Christian is left out. There is no one who is called to Jesus Christ who is not sent by him into the world. And, no matter how many iron, bamboo, or dollar-bill curtains or concrete and barbed-wire walls men may have erected across it, there remains only *one* world: the world which God reconciled to himself in the death of his Son. In this world, there is no place that is ultimately "home" for the Christian, but also no place that is "foreign."

One of the striking things we have noticed in this review of the modern mission movement is the extraordinary role played by *students* in the entire development. As we consider the trying tasks which are laid on the Christian community in today's world, can there be any doubt that again a particularly urgent call is being whispered to the Christian students? One world—and every Christian sent to serve it. What does this mean practically —for you and your friends? Does it not mean that your decision of what work you are going to pursue has got to be made in a wide-open international context? You are studying to be a teacher —have you considered the small revolution in human life that could be touched off by a dedicated teacher in a southeast Asian town? You are in engineering—have you thought of the job to be done by engineers in a country like Brazil, and do you see how urgent it is that those engineers care even more for the lives of the human beings they serve than for the precision of calculated stresses and strengths of materials? The result of such thinking is, of course, unpredictable. You may discover that you are being called to serve Jesus Christ in the next continent or in the next county. The distance, after all, is only relatively significant. The important point is that you *are sent,* for to be a Christian means to be on a mission.

17

breaking through
to each other

THE SIN OF SCHISM

Somehow Not Strangers

It was simply a Bible study group, nothing extraordinary about that. In countless college-town churches or campus student centers twenty college students like ourselves might be found, earnestly discussing a verse from the Gospel of John. But this study group was different. Perhaps it was the fact that we had to pause after every statement so that it could be translated from Portuguese to English or vice versa. Perhaps it was the persistent excitement that we, the North Americans, felt at being for the first time in a foreign country, or the uncertainties which all of us, Brazilians and "Nortes," felt about the hard labor and possibly hostile encounters that lay ahead of us as we began our work camp in a slum of Rio de Janeiro's dock district. But, besides all these factors, the thing that gave significance to this conversation of ours was just the fact of who we each were and the fact that we were, nevertheless, meeting. We were all, of course, Christians and Protestants but what an assortment of Protestant Christianities were represented! Methodists, Baptists, Presbyterians, Episcopalians, and Pentecostalists, and a Mennonite! The wide gaps that separated us were already apparent that night as we tried to make sense of that enormous verse, "The Word became flesh." The frictions of work camp life were to make these differences more and more evident in the weeks to come, but nevertheless, there we were, speaking and listening to one another.

274

The Splinters

Such a meeting is remarkable enough to tell about only against the background of the all too familiar fragmentation of Protestant Christianity. A glance at the *Yearbook of American Churches* is enough to reveal how ludicrously we are divided, redivided, and separated from one another. In 1961 at least 227 Protestant church bodies existed in the United States. Besides these there were not only the Roman Catholic Church but also nine Catholic bodies which do not recognize Rome's authority and twenty Eastern churches. The Protestant sects ranged from the Apostolic Overcoming Holy Church of God to the Lumber River Annual Conference of the Holiness Methodist Church. There were twenty-nine different kinds of Baptists alone, including the National Baptist Evangelical Life and Soul Saving Assembly of the U.S.A. and the Two-Seed-In-The-Spirit Predestinarian Baptists. The Presbyterians, though less imaginatively labeled, came in ten different varieties, the Reformed group in five.

From the perspective of history, it is easy enough to see why many of these divisions came into existence. In the explosion in church life that took place under the combined pressures of Reformation and Renaissance, the fragments tended to fall out in patterns of nationalities. After a great deal of bloody fighting to make everybody alike again, weary nations compromised by drawing lines around each political area and announcing that the ruler of each could name its religion: *cuius regio, eius religio* as the Peace of Augsburg put it. This meant that Bavarians would thenceforth be Roman Catholic; Prussians, Danes, and the Scandinavians, Lutherans; the Swiss, Calvinists or Zwinglians, and so on. From earliest times in the pioneer colonies, every one of the established national churches of the Old World was transplanted to America, along with many of the smaller sects, like the Mennonites and the Baptists, which had grown out of the more radical tendencies of the Reformation. When the immigrants poured into the New World "melting pot," forms of religion were the last thing to melt or mix. German and Swedish Lutherans, for example, were not able to get together, despite virtually identical doctrines, for generations after both groups had forgotten their former languages.

To the European divisions, America added a great many more that were homegrown. Perhaps the most important single factor shaping church life, as it shaped all distinctively American life, was the frontier. The revival was invented in response to the vast challenge of the raw western edges of the nation, in the days when scarcely ten per cent of Americans were church members and those were rapidly going astray in the atmosphere of frontier settlements. The revival was highly controversial, and many denominations split over whether it should be used. In general those who used it grew faster than those who did not. Related to the controversy over the right way to approach the frontier were divisions over theology—what has been called the "Great Rebellion against Calvinism."[1] The frontier favored a do-it-yourself kind of religion; the Calvinists' ideas of predestination and grace were hard to swallow for the pioneers who saw themselves creating their own futures with their own hands.

Add to the frontier schisms the divisions created by the Civil War and the new all-Negro denominations that sprang up in its wake, and the picture becomes more complicated. Still later, in the years of turmoil following World War I and especially in the dark years of the Depression, an unbelievable multitude of new sects grew up, most of them offering otherworldly escape or psychological relief to the ignorant, the poor, and the hopeless. The whole process of sect-formation in America was greatly enhanced by the characteristic frontier idea that every man's religion was his own private affair. Anyone who wanted to start a new one, could.[2]

An Attack of Conscience

If our divisions came about so naturally, then where do I get off labeling them with that distasteful word "sin"? What is wrong with each of us simply going his own way, so long as we agree that none of us really has the whole truth? I will ignore the fact that several of our sects would not admit that they do not have the whole truth. I will also pass over the question whether, since the rest of us do *not* have all the truth, we might not possibly get a fuller picture if we got together and pooled our partial views. The problem is much more complicated than that. There are two factors which in our time have made it obvious to anyone who has eyes to see that our continued disunity is both a sin and a luxury we can no longer afford.

First, our developing sense of history has reminded us of the unity which belonged to the church in its beginning and which has tantalized thoughtful Christians throughout the centuries. Divisions already existed when the first New Testament books were written—but those very books attack them as something unthinkable. Paul writes to Corinth, where the Paul-faction, the Apollos-faction, and the Cephas-faction are at one another's throats, while others, who style themselves "the real Christians," look down their noses at all three. Paul's response is incredulous: "Is Christ divided? Was Paul crucified for you?" His letters are always addressed to "*the* church which is at Corinth" or "Rome" or wherever: there can be but one church, for there is but one Christ. Even in the eleventh century the tragicomedy of the pope's excommunication of the patriarchs of the East and their simultaneous excommunication of him was only possible because neither side could conceive of two churches, one Western and one Eastern. The Reformation, which marks the beginning of our modern splintering, was led by men who were passionately interested in the unity of Christians. John Calvin, who remarked once that he would cross ten seas if it would help the cause of unity, labored so diligently to reconcile divergent views among Protestants that he has been called "the counsel for the ecumenical Church." He succeeded in bringing the Swiss factions together in the Consensus of Zurich in 1549; he tried to draw into fruitful dialogue the Lutherans and the Zwinglians, with their widely differing views on the Lord's Supper; he carried out a voluminous correspondence with Germans, Englishmen, Scotsmen, and Poles, urging unity, patience, and mutual understanding and acceptance.[3] It was only the second and third generations of Protestants who became so absorbed in self-defense that they isolated themselves more and more from their brothers.

The second factor which has put the spotlight on the uglier aspects of our disunity has been the modern mission movement. The first Protestant missionaries went out, not to plant outposts of their denominations, but to proclaim the gospel to people who had never heard it. They hardly gave any thought to the kind of church organization these people might form when enough would respond to make that possible. Even later, when more churchly-minded missionaries arrived on the fields and when the organization of new churches had become a necessary step, the rigors of their task forced most of them into some degree of co-operation. Back home in the American small town, the typical scene of four different denominational churches facing each other at the same street crossing could be taken for granted as a sort of cafeteria of religion. But on the mission field that kind of competition would mean a foolish waste of resources. Very early mission boards met together to lay out comity agreements, so that each assumed responsibility for a certain geographical area. It made sense, too, that projects such as Bible translation, language schools, and even theological schools in mission countries should be done jointly instead of separately. But despite these practical cooperative undertakings, the missionary movements inevitably presented to the non-Christian world a bewildering picture of divided and often antagonistic groups, all claiming to offer *the* Christian message. It was the deep pain of this fact, more than the practical considerations, that made the profoundest of the missionary statesmen become as zealous for the reunion of the church as they were for the proclamation of the gospel to those outside it.

IS CHRIST DIVIDED?

The Oikoumene

The more Christians discovered the world and took seriously their mission to it, the more they discovered each other. Count Zinzendorf, who sparked the great missionary endeavors of the Moravians, was equally concerned for the unity of all Christians. In 1741, for example, he spent many months of earnest labor in Pennsylvania in an attempt to get the numerous German-speaking religious groups to unite. William Carey proposed "a general association of all denominations of Christians, from the four quarters of the world," to meet every ten years or so.[4] Carey's best friend thought the idea was just a pleasant dream, but within the century Christian students from all over the world were meeting together in conferences and in the kind of intimate study groups described early in this chapter. The effects of such face-to-face meetings so stirred the imaginations and intellects of a whole generation of Christian leaders that Archbishop Temple of Britain called the resulting movement "the great new fact of our age."

The movement toward recovering the worldwide mission and uncovering the long-broken unity of the church soon reached such proportions that people felt it ought to have a name. The Greeks, of course, were found to have a word for it, a word that had already had a useful history in church language. The word was "ecumenical," which, despite first appearances, is not any harder to pronounce than "economical." In the New Testament, *oikoumenē* means "the inhabited earth." That makes the word appropriate to describe the "ecumenical movement," which, as we have seen, grew out of the church's concern with the whole world and its determination to minister to all its inhabitants. The early church applied the adjective to the great councils which were held in the first four centuries by representatives from the church in every corner of what was then known of the *oikoumenē*. So the word was also appropriate to describe "that spiritual traffic between the Churches which draws them out of their isolation and into a fellowship of conversation, mutual enrichment, common witness and common action."[5]

The Call to Unity

The same sense of being "under orders" that characterized the first generations of Protestant missionaries also has dominated the ecumenical movement. Its leaders have been certain that in our time Christ is commanding all the divisions of his church to listen to one another and to find their way to the historical unity which he established in his reconciling sacrifice. The question which they have raised again and again is "What is the Spirit saying to the churches?" and for answer they have turned together to the Bible as the one common ground where all could meet. Like our small group of work campers in Rio, they found that no matter what cultural and theological differences might separate them, no matter how diverse might be their native languages, when they met in earnest around this book, the living Word still spoke a common command to them. They could not fail to stumble over Christ's prayer to his Father, "that they may all be one." When the World Student Christian Federation chose that as its motto, it was with the determination that the churches must so open their lives to Christ in obedience that that prayer could be fulfilled in their lives.

To this rediscovery of the Bible and this emphasis on obedience, new fuel was added by the revolution in theology which began with Swiss pastor Karl Barth's *Commentary on the Epistle to the Romans* in 1918. To European and American churches which had come more and more to identify Christianity with modern Western civilization, Barth hurled the challenge to recognize the God who was "totally Other." The church was not the church because of its enduring institutions or because of its pleasant reputation in the community or because of its good deeds; the church was the church only when it *listened* to the Word which came from beyond itself, the Word that is "sharper than a two-edged sword." That is the Word that creates the world, makes history, and calls the church into being. Where is the Word to be heard? Not in human philosophy or in the endless playback of our ecclesiastical traditions, but alone in Jesus Christ —there where the Word became flesh. It is this same Jesus Christ who speaks when the written word, the Bible, is studied by the church, the same one who, as the living and contemporary Word, speaks through the mouth of the preacher who uses that Bible to proclaim the gospel to his people.

Barth's "theology of the Word" helped many Christians to see that all of our church institutions and all of our traditional doctrines are "words of men," that they are all infected by our sin and limited by our narrow vision. Above all he helped them to lift their eyes above these to recognize their one Lord. If there is but one Lord, must not those who seek to obey him be somehow united? The various bodies of the Christian church at the beginning of the nineteenth century were like satellites in orbit, each sure that Christ was the center of its movement, but largely oblivious of other bodies which might also think of him as their focus. The mission movement and the ecumenical movement brought the sudden realization that there *were* many others who had an equal right to call him their Lord and Center, and, if these diverse kinds of Christians came closer to the Center, they could not escape coming closer to each other.

The Body of Christ

If the Reformed theologians' concern with the Word can be pictured with a metaphor from physics, Anglican theologians and others were to remind Christians concerned with unity that Paul had described the church with a metaphor from biology. The church, they said, is the body of Christ. Paul's reproachful question to the Corinthians began to burn the consciences of twentieth-century Christians: "Is Christ divided?" Were not all who were baptized, baptized into one body by one Spirit? Did not all who partook of the "one loaf" become "one body"? This meant that the church was the visible manifestation of Christ to a disbelieving world. Could this world, looking at a fragmented church, fail to imagine a divided, schizophrenic Christ? Had not many non-Christians, seeking genuine community in a world already too desperately torn apart, turned away in disappointment from this church?

At the same time, the deepening sense of the church as Christ's body brought to life the conviction that its unity was something already *given*, not just a far-off ideal which it had to build for itself. As Pascal had once said, "We could not have sought thee, had we not found thee," so the divided churches can say, "We could never have begun our quest for unity, if it were not that we already have some unity, no matter how hidden." The task of the church is not to create, but to manifest its unity. Thus when Christians, finding no ground for agreement, painfully aware that they were saying different things with the same words, carrying within their minds old wounds from previous arguments, have nevertheless kept meeting, working, studying, and praying together, they have discovered that they *were* united, that they *could* not separate. That was the meaning of the prophetic slogan chosen by the first Evangelical *Kirchentag,* an all-German conference of Christian laymen, immediately after the end of World War II: "We are *nevertheless* brothers." It is the *nevertheless* of unity, hidden in Christ, that eyes of faith have perceived in the ecumenical movement.

The Spirit and the Churches

It is very important to distinguish between the search for unity which is represented by the ecumenical movement and more superficial types of cooperation. For generations many well-meaning people have urged Christians simply to forget their differences and get together. Why let mere disagreements over theology interfere with the important things? Why quibble over words? Surely a moderate spirit of compromise and charity would enable Christians to lay aside sectarian interests and join together in the main task. Unfortunately no one has been able to show most thoughtful Christians how they could determine just what "the important things" and "the main task" were without resorting to theology. As a result, many of the "undenominational" and "interdenominational" and "religious" movements have managed to win cooperation only by leaving out of their programs everything on which people disagreed, which meant in many cases everything that most Christians thought important. Too often the result was an inoffensive but rather useless lowest-common-denominator religiosity, which gently encouraged everyone to "uphold spiritual values" and work for "moral improvement," whatever these pious phrases might mean.

In contrast, the spirit of the ecumenical movement has been encounter, not compromise. Delegates to ecumenical meetings and study panels have not hidden their differences under their coats, but tried to make them as clear and understandable as possible, to see *why* they were different and what fragment of the whole truth might be embalmed in each of their diverse formulations. The somewhat paradoxical result is that Presbyterians have come away from ecumenical meetings better Presbyterians, and Lutherans as better Lutherans, that is, with a new consciousness of their own peculiar histories and traditions. But this rebirth of confessional traditions was in a brand-new context. No longer were these regarded as denominational possessions to be jealously guarded, but as insights into the gospel, given to our fathers in the faith through their special positions and backgrounds, but now to be shared with the whole people of God.

At the same time, it is clear that if these encounters mean real sharing, the participants will never be the same. The Presbyterian who has joined in the Easter liturgy of the Greek Orthodox Church will never again be able to approach worship in quite the same way. The High Church Anglican who has engaged in Bible study with a Pentecostal from Chile will never again be able to sing the liturgy on Whitsunday with the same understanding of the Spirit. The Russian Orthodox patriarch and the American Baptist layman who have discussed together the Christian's responsibility for world peace will see the world with different eyes. No wonder many have drawn back in fear from such encounters, while those who have participated have spoken with awe of being led by the Spirit. Only the Spirit of God can give to the churches the openness that makes possible genuine speaking and hearing; only the Spirit can lead us, despite our fears and vested interests, into the new tasks and new forms which God has prepared for his people in our time. What is the Spirit saying to the churches? That the church lives by dying to itself.

STUDENTS LEAD THE WAY

One Worldwide Movement

It was students who led in the church's discovery of the world and students who led in the churches' discovery of each other.

It was students, too, who pioneered in finding practical instruments for bringing these discoveries to bear on the life of the church.

The first intercollegiate organization of significance was the YMCA. The idea of community YMCA's was brought to America from England by a letter from an American student at Edinburgh in 1850. The first college "Y" was started at the University of Virginia in 1858. By 1877, a national organization of the intercollegiate YMCA was begun. John R. Mott, the "continent-thinking" young man we met in the last chapter, became one of its leaders ten years later. His first job was organizing the new Student Volunteer Movement, which the "Y" had taken under its wing. At a time when the official church agencies had not yet seen the strategic importance of ministering to the increasingly secular institutions of higher education, the YMCA began a vigorous effort throughout the United States. Many years later, it aroused the churches also to the fact that as Mott put it, ". . . the universities and colleges of the world teach the teachers, preach to the preachers and govern the governors,"[6] and the denominational campus ministries began.

"Thinking in continents," meanwhile, was already a habit of Mott and his friends. The first secretary of the Intercollegiate YMCA, four years before he recruited Mott, had already written:

> This Christian movement amongst students is too mighty in its power for good to be limited to any country or continent. It will not have fulfilled its mission until . . . the students in the old universities of Great Britain and Europe and the students in the new missionary colleges of the Orient and the Dark Continent are united with the students of America in one world-wide movement, whose purpose shall be *Christ for the Students of the World, and the Students of the World for Christ.*[7]

Mott and other leaders of the YMCA and the SVM soon began their travels in Britain and Europe, meeting church and student leaders, speaking in universities, and urging the organization of student Christian movements. By 1895 their dream of "one world-wide movement" became reality.

The scene was a sixteenth-century castle at Vadstena, Sweden, where two hundred and fifty students were meeting to form the Scandinavian Student Christian Movement. Their chairman, thirty-three-year-old Karl Fries, had commandeered the castle, uninhabited for two hundred years, had browbeat the government into permission to use it, borrowed furniture and windows from a contractor who was building a new hospital, and with the help of an electrical engineer who was a "Y" member, rigged up a Rube Goldberg lighting system. Such ingenuity became characteristic of the movement which was born in the castle. At the end of the conference, six men met in the castle's attic to draft the constitution of the World Student Christian Federation. They represented the North American Student Christian Movement (consisting of the YMCA, the Interseminary Movement, and the Student Volunteer Movement of the United States and Canada), the Student Christian Movement in Mission Lands, founded by SVM members who had traveled in the Orient or settled there as missionaries, the Student Christian Movement of Great Britain, the Scandinavian SCM, and the German Student Christian Alliance.

The University and the World

Today the World Student Christian Federation (WSCF) is comprised of national student Christian movements in almost all the countries of the world. The United States' member is the National Student Christian Federation, an association of denominational student movements, the YMCA and YWCA, the Interseminary Movement, and the Commission on World Mission, formerly the SVM. Throughout its history, WSCF has maintained its ingenuity and its role as pioneer. It has continually explored new frontiers between the church and the world. It has helped student Christian movements to get started in countries where the Christian church was a tiny minority. It has "loaned" traveling secretaries to parts of the world where national SCM's were not strong enough to employ their own executives. It has raised millions of dollars for mutual assistance among the SCM's, and it began the worldwide organizations for student relief after World War I and World War II. Through its conferences and those of its member movements, thousands of Christian students have discovered the world, and many have for the first time discovered the church and the church's Lord.

ALL ONE BODY WE?

Getting Organized

Many of the leaders of the World Student Christian Federation later became active in movements to encourage the unity of the churches. These movements have tended to crystallize during the twentieth century in organizations which have brought representatives of the various Christian communions together both for practical cooperation in common tasks and for intensive study of the theological bases of their unity. Three movements have been especially important. The International Missionary Council grew out of the World Missionary Conference at Edinburgh in 1910. As we saw in the last chapter, this organization, through its subsequent conferences and the studies it conducted between them, has brought churchmen and missionaries together from east and west, north and south, to hammer out strategy for the continually new problems arising as the church confronts the world. A second movement, also concerned primarily with the practical side of the church's witness to the world, was called Life and Work. Its pioneer was Archbishop Söderblom of Sweden, whose consuming passion was the obligation of Christians to work for international peace and justice. At a time when these problems had reached crisis proportions, between World War I and World War II, the Life and Work Movement held conferences to wrestle with them which brought together leading Christian laymen and theologians. The third movement was Faith and Order, which held its first conference in Lausanne in 1927. This movement attacked head-on the theological causes for division between the churches. To its work we owe in large measure the transformation of our understanding of what the church is and what it ought to be. By 1938 these three movements had produced the conviction that a unified "World Council of Churches" was needed. In that year the constitution for the World Council was drawn up, but the outbreak of war prevented its foundation. But the war deepened the basis for unity. Not only did it show, in the words of Devadutt already quoted, that "paganism has no geographical boundaries," thus calling churchmen to a new humility, it also demonstrated in many ways the unity which Christians already possessed, which even the inhuman passions of this cruelest of all wars were unable to destroy.

The World Council of Churches was founded in 1948 in Amsterdam. The first assembly is ably described by Bishop G. K. A. Bell, one of the participants:

> It was a thrilling moment, for here at last the hopes and prayers of years were to be fulfilled. Some of the oldest Churches in the world were represented—the Church of Ethiopia and the Orthodox Syrian Church of Malabar, for example; and some of the youngest, like the Presbyterian Church in Korea. Well-known leaders of the principal Churches in the United States and Canada were side by side with leaders of the Lutheran and Reformed Churches in different countries of Europe. Bishops of the Orthodox Church, the Anglican, and Old Catholic Churches, leaders of the Church of Scotland, and of the Evangelical Free Churches in Britain, with their colleagues in every continent, were there. Almost every grade of denomination was to be found: and more striking still, lay men and women and ministers of every colour and race. It was a truly international and inter-racial gathering, ecumenical in the largest sense; and all had come together as belonging to a fellowship of Churches which acknowledge our Lord Jesus Christ as God and Saviour.[8]

The Unfinished Job

Many more pages could be written—and have been—about the movement toward church unity and its concrete results in the last sixty years. Space here is limited, however, and good books on the subject are easily available. It is more important here to ask the question, What is happening on your campus and in your church and your student Christian organization in response to Christ's call to unity and the leadership of his Spirit? Today, even more than when John R. Mott was a student at Cornell, it is true that the college campus is a window to the world. Thousands of students come to our campuses every year from the most distant and different parts of the globe. Among them are men and women who will be diplomats and members of parliament, prime ministers and supreme court justices, teachers and college presidents—as well as ministers and lay leaders of the church—in their nations. What are the Christian students on your campus doing to meet these guests from abroad, really to meet them, to learn to see our alive and ominous world through their eyes? The world is on your campus: have you discovered it?

Moreover, the campus is still the place where experiments in Christian cooperation and unity can take place with far more openness and far fewer collisions with vested interests and ancient prejudices than in hometown churches. At the same time, the campus constitutes one of the primary frontiers of the church's mission today, by virtue of the fact that the boundary between the Christian church and "the non-Christian world" runs straight through the middle of the campus—and squarely through the heart of most of the individuals who work and live there. Yet, in the face of this enormous challenge and thrilling opportunity, is it not true that most of our denominational college work is a timid and halfhearted "outreach by in-snatch," a frantic holding-operation, trying to keep our good Reformed or Presbyterian kids from going over to Wesley, spying on the Newman Club to make sure they don't have better parties than we do, wishing we had a new split-level house like the Episcopalians? Or is it possible that all of us could somehow come to say together and to begin to enact together this affirmation, from the closing service of the World Council of Churches Assembly at New Delhi, 1961:

We confess Jesus Christ, Saviour of men and the light of the
world;
Together we accept his command;
We commit ourselves anew to bear witness to him among
men;
We offer ourselves to serve all men in love,
that love which he alone imparts;
We accept afresh our calling to make visible our unity in
him;
We pray for the gift of the Holy Spirit for our task.[9]

18

breaking into a new age

We've Lost Our World

A rat can be taught many marvelous things. He can run mazes, press levers, choose the door that opens to the food, solve problems, make decisions. He can even, to a certain extent, adapt himself to changes in the way the game is played. Change the markings on the doors, so that the one which should open to the dish of grain stubbornly hurts his head, and after only a few futile tries he will puzzle out the trick his clever tormentor has played on him. But should the scientist, in inquisitive or sadistic mood, jumble all the signals, flash all the stimuli at once, block all the possibilities, then the rat is beaten. He leaps, he runs, he presses, frenziedly he repeats his little repertoire of conditioned responses, he crashes against the door that will not open, but nothing works. His logic shattered, he runs in maddened circles and finally huddles silent in a protective corner. No amount of electric shocks will force him out again; shivering, he resigns, he will not pit his broken brain against this universe, this Skinner box gone mad. Does he suspect, this quivering, white, dying bundle, that the omnipotent Man has made this box? That He is the malevolent Demon who has made havoc of his sensible life? Or does he tell himself that everything is illusion, that there *is* no Man, no meaning, only endless, senseless, all-conquering Box?

A man is much more complex than a rat; even the psychologists who use Skinner boxes have admitted that. Not only is he more adaptable than the rat, more flexible in trying new approaches when his situation changes, but he is qualitatively superior because he has imagination. He can look behind the facts to raise the question "Why?" Nevertheless, he too can be trapped, outwitted by events. There come times when all the answers to his "Why?" contradict each other, when the pressure of new facts rip apart the web of meaning that held his universe together. That was what happened when Alaric smashed "eternal Rome," and when Copernicus quietly announced that the world moved. That is what a Spanish philosopher calls "an historical crisis":

> . . . the world, the system of convictions belonging to a previous generation, gives way to a vital state in which man remains without these convictions, and therefore without a world. Man returns to a state of not knowing what to do, for the reason that he returns to a state of actually not knowing what to think about the world. Therefore the change swells to a crisis and takes on the character of catastrophe. The world change consists of the fact that the world in which man was living has collapsed . . .[1]

Is it true, as Ortega suggests, that we are living through such a crisis, the end of an age? Do we live already in a "post-modern" world? It is certain that ours is a time of extremely rapid and widespread change in various areas of life. None of these changes, taken alone, is completely new. All have grown out of tendencies which can be observed at the end of the Middle Ages. But at what point does the steady accumulation of fissionable material reach critical mass, so that process becomes explosion? When does change become revolution?

It can hardly be denied that the twentieth century has so far been characterized by revolution. Whether we have been or shall be reduced to "not knowing what to think about the world" is revealed when we look at the revolutions that are happening around and within us and try to make sense of them. There are at least two kinds of revolutions. One kind is external. It is made by men wearing beards and carrying rifles or by dedicated dreamers overwhelming the consciences of their opponents with fasts and sit-down strikes or by skilled engineers of political upheaval. The other kind is internal. It happens in the minds and hearts of men, women, and children, and in the mood and manner of the groups they form. The two are interrelated. Together they present us with our crisis.

POLITICAL AND SOCIAL REVOLUTION

The Rich and the Poor

I met the possibility of the first kind of revolution in the summer of 1955, smoldering beneath the deceptively beautiful surface of Rio de Janeiro. With twenty-three other students, from the United States, Brazil, and France, I was engaged in a month-long work camp to help improve the living conditions in a slum and to try to learn something about our world. Straightening to ease the muscles that were not used to the swing of a pick, I had a commanding view of "the most beautiful city in the world." We were standing on the side of one of those strange rounded lumps of hills, green and bare granite, that erupt from Rio's irregular crescent of level land. Beneath us curved the white arcs of sand beaches—Botafogo, Flamengo, Copacabana—gleaming against the deep blue of the bays. Alongside the beaches and crowding together through the valleys were elaborate old buildings dwarfed by towering new ones in contemporary architecture. Immediately in front of us lay the busy docks and warehouses; a luxury liner was discharging its stream of enchanted tourists into the gaiety of this magic city. But longshoremen who unloaded that liner would come home that afternoon to a less attractive scene. Climbing from the cobblestone streets up a steep, narrow dirt path, they would pick their way across crevices and ditches spanned by rotten wooden footbridges, leaving behind the fresh salt smell of the sea for the nauseating stench that lay like a fog on the hill. Here was home: a shack painfully stuck together from odds and ends of brick, tile, splintered wood, and flattened oil drums, held somehow to the rock against all logic and gravity. Garbage and sewage festered in ditches and crevices of rock and seeped constantly down the hill. Water could be had only two days a week, when the two hydrants—on a hill inhabited by four thousand persons—were opened by the property owner, and women and children stood in long lines to fill buckets and oil drums. Children of all ages played on the bare slopes; survival demanded the agility of mountain goats.

The contrast was drawn too clearly for anyone to miss. Down below were the rich, the healthy, the comfortable; up here—significantly, with the rich never out of their sight—were the poor and the desperate. Almost no one was in between. That is the fuel of revolution. What does the dockworker think as he climbs that hill each night? What do his hundreds of less lucky unemployed neighbors think, as they sit the day out and stare at this scene?

All That Glitters

Rich people and poor people, rich nations and poor nations: problems since the world began. Add to this a world shrunk to neighborhood size, add new knowledge of how the others live: show American movies and American magazines to the Indian outcaste or the Sicilian peasant, or bring the Kenya native to work in the house of the British colonial officer, show them the refrigerators and the automobiles and the American dogfood that would satisfy their families for a week. Awaken dreams in minds that slept; breathe possibility into hopeless hearts. Now revolution begins.

The industrial West—Europe and the United States—have taught the poor nations of the world two things. First, science and industrial technology can create goods in an abundance sufficient to give everyone a share. Second, the persons who get a share of this wealth are those who are able to exercise political power.

The revolution which has touched all of these nations boils down to the attempt to grasp these two things: bread and freedom; goods and independence.

The Magic of Independence

In most parts of the world, the improvement of living conditions has had to take a backseat to the transformation of the political scene. The poor peoples of the world have focused their attention on being *free,* by which they mean becoming nations, independent of the colonial powers that have controlled them. In nations already independent, the struggle has also been primarily political, as lower classes of the society have tried to wrest control from the powerful aristocracy, which, in these countries, usually consists of a very few, very rich families. At the same time they strive to become *economically* independent of the older, richer nations. The anticolonialist emotion was summed up by an official of Guinea who said, "We would rather be poor and African than wealthy and French."

Colonialism was a product of the vigorous growth and industrialization of the west European countries in the eighteenth century. When the factory system and the development of savings, or capital, made possible the sudden boom in productivity, new markets and new sources of raw materials had to be found. Both were discovered in the countries which we now call "underdeveloped"—though many, like India and China, were far more developed than Europe in their culture, art, and philosophy. England, France, Holland, and the other European states competed fiercely with one another for these new markets. To secure its own interests, each gradually took control of huge areas of Asia and Africa. The result, in the lands they occupied, was both oppressive and awakening. In India, for example, British rule upset the age-old balance of population and livelihood. Village craftsmen, put out of business by the flood of British factory-made goods, were forced to join the mass of farmers, dividing up the land into tiny plots that could not support a family. Even the very works of compassion by Western missionaries created problems by saving lives. Hospitals and medical training kept babies alive and lengthened life. As a result, population skyrocketed, while improvements in agriculture increased the food supply only very slowly. But at the same time that colonial management was actually increasing the misery of millions, it was introducing to the young leaders of India the techniques of Western science, the ideals of Western democracy, and the skills of Western political organization. Thus Britain taught India to think of herself as a nation, to long for freedom and abundance, and to organize for action, and she became for the Indians the target for their revolt. Similar processes have been repeated many times, usually with less happy results than in India.

The result of the awakening of formerly colonial peoples has been a radical shift in the center of gravity of international political power. The age of dominance by Europe and North America is over. New nations are being created so rapidly that map-makers despair. These new nations find themselves center-stage in the world's attention from the day of their birth, for they are born into the midst of the cold-war struggle. In some ways this attention is of great advantage to them, for the big powers court their favor and frequently compete in supplying the financial and technical assistance they need to organize their industries and schools and to supply the wants of their people. On the other hand, their position subjects them to powerful pulls in the power struggle between East and West, with the constant danger that their countries will become new battlefields. They are robbed of those luxurious years of isolation that the United States had for its development.

Along with independence come, in almost every instance, radical changes in the society of each new nation. Every attempt is made to build industry as rapidly as possible, for industry is seen to be the key to the wealth of the richer nations. Along with industrialization comes the sudden growth of cities. Young men and women pour in from farms and villages, dazzled by the city's bright lights and promise of quick money. Disillusioned almost always, yet they seldom return. They build slums, feed the mobs and gangs of the lost, the lonely, the bitter. Men who were embedded in tribes, castes, or the stable large families of the country, are suddenly individuals: alone, anonymous, and rootless. The family is threatened with destruction. The nation is faced with the overwhelming task of welding together tribes or local groups, frequently hostile to each other, which often do not even have a common language. Throughout the bewildering transformation runs the conflict between the craving for Western things, institutions, and methods, and the passionate desire to hang on to old forms and traditions.

The Christian and the Revolution

Surely the Christian finds much in the revolution that wins his sympathy. To love our neighbor as ourselves must mean to wish for that neighbor the same possibility for a life of dignity, free from the burden of poverty, hunger, and disease, that we take for granted in our affluent society. Indeed, Christian missionaries have played a leading part in awakening and nourishing the desires of many who are now revolutionaries. Of course we want to avoid the fatal identification of the Christian life with the materially abundant life or the free society with the Kingdom of God. But at the same time the abundant life of the gospel is not indifferent to material goods, nor the Kingdom to political freedom. The correction of injustice is one form which Christian love must take in the world. Furthermore, our sympathy for the revolution is strengthened by our own guilty conscience, as Westerners, in the face of it. In the New Testament parable, we are forced to recognize ourselves as the rich man who takes his ease, counting our calories, threatened with heart failure by our own fat, our markets choked by surpluses, while outside our gates all the Lazaruses of the world's nations lie dying. At the Last Day will not our Lord say to us, "I was hungry, and you gave me nothing to eat, thirsty and you gave me nothing to drink, a stranger and you did not invite me in, naked and you did not clothe me, sick and in prison and you did not visit me"?[2]

But there is much in the revolution that frightens, confuses, or dismays us. Above all, there is the terrible cost of political independence which in too many instances has been paid in human life. The drive for freedom has too often associated itself with terrorism and blind hatred, and the accomplishment of freedom has sadly produced new factions, the disruption of organized life, the threat of complete chaos. Furthermore, as Christians we must decry the tendency of new nations to adopt a black-and-white view of the world, in which all ills seem to be caused by the colonialists of the West and all cures to be possible through nationalism. We know that sin does not parcel itself out so neatly. Finally, perhaps we are frightened most of all by the involvement in the revolution of Soviet and Chinese Communism. The Communists have claimed to be the masters of revolution. They provide an ideology which projects a picture of the way history is supposed to work. They provide ready-made identification of "the enemy" which seems to fit the experience of the oppressed groups. They offer the techniques of seizing power proven by fire in Russia, China, North Vietnam, and Cuba. They hold up the promise of a secular version of the Christian's Messianic kingdom, a Utopia on earth. Armed with these formidable weapons, Communists have been able in several instances to take over a national revolution and channel it into the Marxist mold. The dockworkers in Rio, already in 1955, looked mostly to the Communists for hope. The Communists, they said, take us seriously, and they show us a way out. The implications for Christian students are clear. The revolution is not made by Communists. But its leadership will go to those who take it seriously.

THE PERSONAL REVOLUTION

The Decline of Optimism

Men of the Western world, especially Americans, floated into the twentieth century on a cloud of pinkest optimism. In retrospect, the nineteenth had been an enormous Century of Progress. The continents were spanned, the oceans sailed routinely, someone seemed certain to make a flying machine that worked. Already the power of science both to discover and to create were proving so awesome that dreamers could conjure up a day when society, too, could be scientifically organized. Disease, poverty, and ignorance would soon be conquered, eliminating the causes of hostility. Sin would be made as obsolete as buttonhooks by scientific precautions and progressive education. The innate reasonableness of man, freed from superstition and bad environment, would produce a healthy and harmonious world.

After our second dose of total, utterly scientific warfare, the rose glasses are smashed. We have found out that the educated are the most terribly efficient killers: six million Jewish men, women, and children exterminated in the most "advanced" nation of Europe, with the calculating coldness of a chemical experiment. And we learn to live with the knowledge that the weapons are already in the firing pits which can destroy our civilization. We have somehow outsmarted ourselves.

The Elusive Universe

The physical sciences have outdone the dreams of last century's sturdiest optimists. But the result has not been a cozy world in which man the maker could be securely and knowingly at home. Instead, a world unfolds that is permeated with mysteries, that threatens to break our minds with the continual reminder that things are never what they appear to be. Of course certain philosophers had warned that we could never see or touch "things in themselves," but only the "appearances," the pictures that our own minds force on the world to try to make sense of its impressions. But no one reads philosophers, and besides, such an abstract statement is not so disconcerting as to be told that this solid table on which my feet rest is not solid, but mostly empty space, crisscrossed by pulsating fields of electrical energy. Language itself breaks down when someone tries to tell us what these fields really are—notice the obvious frustration of the science reporters in the newspapers, when they try to say exactly *what* the new discovery is that has set the scientists agog. Waves of energy that act like little balls of stuff; little balls of stuff that act like waves of something; little pulses of almost nothing that occasionally act like something. All just models, says the scientist. Just sloppy ways of speaking, in a language that was not designed to describe the things that now we know. It only remains to speak in mathematics, the pure language. I can write an equation for it, says the physicist. But what is *it?* The question has no meaning. We leave his laboratory with the light-headed feeling that we are infinitesimal persons in an infinite universe.

The Hollow Inside

Our "historical crisis" begins when we no longer know what to think about history and politics. It gets deeper when we cannot tell what to think about physical reality. It hits bottom when we no longer know what to think about ourselves. This is terribly frustrating, because we do a great deal of thinking about ourselves. College students always have thought and wondered about themselves. We have had to try to figure out just what we were able to do, where we were going to find our own places in the world. But today our wondering is laden with a peculiar sick uncertainty. Maybe there are not really any "places" in our world; maybe there is really not any world that counts. Moreover, no matter how much our elders may pat us on the head and reassure us that this is just part of growing up, we wonder if anyone ever grows up anymore. We hear too many echoes of our sickness in the tired or raging voices of older and wiser men, men who have climbed the ladder up which we are being pushed, who have bought all the shining and delightful things we want, and now whisper or scream to us that there is nothing up there, nothing at all.

If the changes taking place in Congo and China can be called a social revolution, the same may be said of the quite different changes taking place in the United States and the other wealthy nations. The ingredients of this change are simple, but they have snowballed. First of all, there are more people. Birth rates boom, medicine works wonders; even the automobile cannot kill us off as fast as we reproduce. Second, these people live closer together:

> How're you gonna keep 'em down on the farm
> After they've seen Par-ee?

The growth of American population means growth of the cities. Farms go mechanized; small towns shrink or become suburbs. When the "average American" is not the rugged guy who stands on the front steps he built himself and looks across the fields he cleared and plowed himself, but the fellow who jostles into the apartment house elevator with twenty-five identically dressed strangers, then what goes on inside these men is not the same. No matter that the "average American" in both cases is somewhat mythical; such myths are powerful.

Third, problems of production have been replaced by problems of consumption and organization. The problem in China and India is the same as that of America and Europe until this century: how to raise enough food to feed all the mouths, how to make enough steel to build what has to be built, how to get transportation across those enormous distances. But now the American problem is how to get rid of the surplus, how to persuade people to junk their sixty-five automobile for a sixty-seven model that will fall apart sooner, how to make people want more things, so we can make more things, so the cycle will continue.

The inevitable solution to these new problems has been an increasingly *organized* society. Like tomatoes, people now come in packages. One of the enduring problems in city transportation is that people have not yet been willing to let themselves be shipped like tomatoes—but that stubbornness will go, in time. As a single example of the change, salesmanship has been radically altered. Selling in the old-fashioned way, the jolly Willy Loman opening his sample cases for the neighborhood dry-goods merchants, still has a place—but it is peanuts in the overall picture. The money is made in the "mass market." The package—what's inside doesn't count—the slogan, the TV cartoon, all are engineered to appeal to the unconscious drives of the "average" consumer, whose portrait has been drawn by professional psychologists. A corresponding change has taken place in the organization of business. Increasingly the top jobs are not for people who know how to make things or do things, but for those who can keep the organization running smoothly, keep the human parts happy, spark the harmonious sessions of "group-think," help everybody work for "the team."

Now in this kind of society our dilemma is no longer, "Where can I find a place in this world?" The places are there in plenty, and unless something dreadful befalls the economy there will be personnel men lined up your senior year, waiting to offer you a step on the Up-escalator. No, the dilemma is, "How can I be a human being in that kind of place?" There is the dim sense in the back of our minds that an escalator is only an inclined treadmill.

This is the mood which has forced us back into ourselves, with the awful question, is there anything inside? There is the frightening discovery that has paralyzed two generations: that we do not know who we are; that we do not even know what it means to ask who we are.

This is where we came in. If you have been reading straight

through this book, you have come a complete circle. We asked these questions in the first three chapters. Have we gotten anywhere since then? We have been trying to find out if we had a history, if there was a story of the People of God's Secret which was also our story. The story has been a long one: it started a long time ago and it comes out here, where we are. Not quite, because the story points forward. The People keep marching past us, as if they were going somewhere, as if they were following someone. Shall we climb out of ourselves and go?

THE CHURCH AFTER CHRISTENDOM

The End of Christendom

Ever since the Emperor Constantine, in the fourth century, painted the monogram of Christ on his banner and made Christianity the official religion of the empire, Christianity has belonged in Western society. Even among those who never really participated in its cult, it has been *our* religion. It was something which was just there, taken for granted. Thus America is and always has been, we are assured, "a Christian nation." The great ideals toward which we all aspired, the whole conglomerate of "values" that pulled our common life into an order of sorts, all these were "Christianity." And we, the whole of western Europe and the American transplant and new growth of Europe, we were "Christendom." Now Christendom seems to be ending. Constantine's banner is finally being hauled down.

The first thing we discovered was that Christendom was not very Christian. In itself, this discovery was not new. Constantine himself left much to be desired as a saint. What was new was that in our time the failure was exposed before the eyes of a frankly non-Christian world. If we look for particulars, we can pick World War II and particularly Hiroshima as the events that unmasked "The Christian West." In a famous "letter to the West," President Sukarno of Indonesia has put it bluntly: "You have usurped the powers that stand at the right hand of the Almighty. You have already made certain that the sins of the fathers—your sins—will be avenged on children and children's children. Believe me in this connection, that we in Asia do not regard you as the Savior of civilization or as Pioneer of the future. We see you as agents of death—our death."[3]

The second thing which has slowly become evident in our daily life is that Christianity is unnecessary. Our daily life goes along just as well without God. It is this discovery which we religious people like to call "secularism." Secularism is certainly the prevailing point of view in most of what was formerly Christendom. Of course the most obvious example is to be found in the Marxist governments. Marxist-Leninism, based on the theory that history operates automatically by "dialectical materialism," is atheistic in principle. Its goal is to establish a thoroughly "scientific" society, in which life will be rationally harmonized with the laws of nature and economics. Like Freud, the Marxist wants man to outgrow his need for the "adolescent illusion of the race," religion. Thus Marxism betrays its background in the optimistic and belligerent rationalism of last century. But Marxism is only an extreme fork on the same road that all modern men have been walking. Albert Camus can write simply that man begins the twentieth century with the knowledge that "we are alone" in the universe. In America, unlike France, we do not say things like that. But underneath our official piety the same practical assumption controls most of our lives. To be sure, more of us belong to the churches than ever before in our history, yet what we do in the churches has less and less to do with God and more and more to do with harmonious social outlets for our leisure. We stamp "In God we trust" on all our coins, but the largest slice of those coins is spent for the thing we really trust when the chips are down: those underground silos stored with death, fueled and ready to blast off with a word from the White House's red telephone.

Making Room for God

Faced with the fact that Christendom was over, we have run around feverishly trying to save the system, trying to keep God alive. But the attempts have been either artificial or demonic. The artificial attempts were the things like finding new things to stamp the old slogan on: we trust in God on stamps and dollar bills as well as dimes now. Failure of prisoners of war in Korea to be heroic under torture led to highly organized campaigns to "restore moral values" in American life. In 1962 when a Supreme Court decision forbade New York schoolteachers to read a certain little prayer, one Congressman said the Court had banned God from the schoolroom. But these battles were largely over words. A god who could be got rid of so easily had surely never been there.

More demonic were the several great waves of so-called Christian anti-Communism that swept the country after the Korean war, beginning with the crusade of the late Senator Joseph McCarthy. "Crusade"—a self-description chosen by a number of these movements—was particularly apt. Though their weapons were speeches, radio programs, films, blacklists, and whisper campaigns, rather than swords and lances, these groups sought to save Christian America by making direct war against the Enemy. The medieval crusades had been unable to imagine a better response to the Turks than attack, and when they could not find Turks they vented their frustrations by burning other Christians who happened to be different. So many earnest and extraordinarily passionate souls in our time have looked out on the ominous world of Little Orphan Annie, in which the Bad Guys grow more and more and worse and worse, while the Good Guys are fewer and fewer. Perhaps only Annie and Sandy are left against Them, but they will fight to the end.

Jesus Christ: God for the Godless

Because I believe in Jesus Christ, I cannot put my trust in attempts to shore up old slogans or to kill off the enemies of God. I know what Isaiah said about the gods who had to be defended against their enemies: they are homemade gods; I cannot worship them. God has already spoken the last word about his relationship to the world which he created in goodness and which we have repeatedly spoiled: "Be of good cheer, I have overcome the world." Jesus Christ has overcome the world. Not some other world, not some nice world that once was but now has fallen apart, but our world, the world that crucified the Son of God.

We have talked a lot about crisis. Undoubtedly we are involved in crisis. But we ought to remember that the Bible, too, talks about crisis. Of course the Greek word *krisis* does not mean precisely what we mean by "crisis," so when Jesus says, "Now is the *krisis* of this world," we translate *judgment*. There is exactly the difference between the Christian's understanding of history and that of other observers. Once we see that the world's crisis hides God's judgment within it, the judgment which was exercised once and for all when Jesus Christ absorbed all the hostility the world could muster, then we are liberated from despair.

> Who shall bring any charge against God's elect? It is God who justifies; who is to condemn? Is it Christ Jesus, who died, yes, who was raised from the dead, who is at the right hand of God, who indeed intercedes for us? Who shall separate us from the love of Christ? Shall tribulation, or distress, or persecution, or famine, or nakedness, or peril, or sword? . . . No, in all these things we are more than conquerors through him who loved us. (Rom. 8:33ff.)

Well, you say, that is all very fine for "God's elect," but in our time who is going to be so bold as to put himself in that category? What about the growing numbers of people who, as we have seen, self-consciously identify themselves as "godless"? What about our own increasing suspicion that, in the conduct of our daily affairs, we are "without God in the world"? Here is the real revolution of all times: the revolution of grace. This is the News, this is the one thing by which and for which we exist as Christians: that "while we were yet helpless, at the right time Christ died for the ungodly" (Rom. 5:6). Was it not precisely the prostitutes and the tax collectors, the "ungodly" under the Law, to whom Jesus came? Was it not just the religious elite, the "good people," who whispered behind his back and plotted to get rid of him? Jesus Christ is the God of the godless. "For if while we were enemies we were reconciled to God by the death of his Son, much more, now that we are reconciled, shall we be saved by his life" (Rom. 5:10). But the godless today do not *know* Jesus Christ, do not believe that God comes to them. Then they must be told. That is what the church is for. If they do not hear, then we must make certain that it is not because our fear has made us silent. If they will not listen, then we must listen on their behalf. If they cannot believe, then we must be the more faithful.

Life for the World

If the church is weak in this frightening new world, it is because it has lived for itself. The old bargain struck with Constantine—that we would help the world along insofar as it needed God, if the world would be kind to us—is all off. The world no longer pays us the attention we think we deserve. But this is God's way of reminding us that this was never our true life. The world is not made for the church, but the church for the world. Not for doing the little odd jobs that the world thinks up for religion, but for the *life* of the world, the life that is hidden in Jesus Christ.

The life of Jesus Christ was the life of a servant. He who was very God poured himself out to become man, to live a life of utter obedience to the point of death (Phil. 2:5ff.). This is the life which Christ gives to his church: the life of a servant. "If I then, your Lord and Teacher, have washed your feet, you also ought to wash one another's feet" (John 13:14). It was this command which led the World Presbyterian Alliance, meeting in Brazil in 1960, to declare that the church's mission is to be "the Servant People of the Servant Lord." The same command has led the student Christian movement of eastern Europe to a new depth of understanding of their calling as Christians in Communist-dominated countries. In the face of propaganda for "coexistence," they have adopted for themselves the motto "Pro-existence." One of them writes, "They have learned that they do not have to fear the Communist, because Christ has in mind the freedom of faith even for him . . . but they have to fear the sterility of the Church, the death of the Church at its own hand. They seek no longer to preserve the Church, but to preserve the Gospel. And the Gospel is preserved when it is lived. To live the Gospel, however, means 'Pro-existence,' existence for the world, as Christ exists for the world."[4]

To Live the Gospel

Even this brief look at some of the revolutionary aspects of life in our generation is enough to make us understand why a certain

sense of crisis might burden Christians today. It is understandable
that we might be temporarily at a loss as to what we ought to do,
since we do not quite "know what to think about the world." But
what is incomprehensible is the atmosphere of delicate boredom
which stifles so many of our churches and our church centers on
campus. What is utterly incongruous in this world is the nonchalance with which Christian students trot meekly along, indistinguishable from the campus herd, eyes fixed foggily on nothing
more ultimate than next Friday's date or next Monday's quiz, or
at farthest the senior interview with ABC Corporation that will
catapult us into the suburbs. Of course we can love and enjoy this
world—but only if we first get it through our heads that something radical has happened to it, that "the form of this world is
passing away," that this "good life" as the advertisers like to call it
is not our life. It is by the grace of God that revolution is shaking
our world, so that we can understand that all the things we have
taken for granted are not our life, their preservation not our purpose. Our life is "hid with Christ," our purpose "to live the gospel."

> "Yet once more I will shake not only the earth but also the
> heaven." This phrase, "Yet once more," indicates the removal
> of what is shaken, as of what has been made, in order that
> what cannot be shaken may remain. Therefore let us be
> grateful for receiving a kingdom that cannot be shaken, and
> thus let us offer to God acceptable worship, with reverence
> and awe; for our God is a consuming fire.
>
> (Hebrews 12:26b–29)

PART FIVE

the church
is you

The same Lord who says, "I am the light of the world" (John 8:12) also says, "You are the light of the world" (Matt. 5:14). These strikingly parallel sentences show the astonishing way Jesus Christ has chosen to be present in the world. "I am," "you are"; the tenses are present; the light still "shines in the darkness." The world has not been able to get rid of the one who was crucified. But where is the light? The darkness is obvious enough. If he is alive, why not show everybody that he is really running the show? That is like what was said to him in the wilderness: "If you are the Son of God, throw yourself down . . ."

But God does not twist the arm of the world until it squeals its belief. As Jesus' life, the life he gives to all men, was hidden in his death, so his life today is hidden. He lets his life become visible only in the people whom he calls to live. His light shines through his church.

In *these* people? Through *this* church? Through that boring preacher, these stony people half-listening in their Sunday clothes and their Sunday piety? Through that bothersome classmate, that fussy old lady, that oddball with the strange ideas? Yes, precisely to them he says, "You are the light of the world." This belongs to the "scandal" of the gospel, the "foolishness of

God" (1 Cor. 1:22–25), that he uses such earthen pots to carry his treasure.

Of course the church is always failing. It has to be constantly reminded to stop putting a bushel over the lamp. In a particular place and time its lamp can even become totally dark. In that case, Christ comes and takes the lamp away (Rev. 2:5). But it is Christ who judges these situations, not we. To want to be a Christian outside the church is hopelessly romantic if not sinfully arrogant.

There is no such thing as a solitary Christian. "For by one Spirit we were all baptized into one body" (1 Cor. 12:13). Birth as a Christian is birth into the Christian community, the body of Christ. No member—even an important one—can exist apart from the body. An eye born without a body would be a monstrosity—and useless. "You are the light . . ." The "you" is plural. To "brighten the corner where you are" is impossible unless you receive the light given to the whole body by its Head.

But where is the church? Is that brick thing the church, over on Elm Street? How about Monday morning, when no one is there but the sexton? Maybe it is in the church student center by the campus. Undoubtedly—but sometimes what is going on there is only a rousing good bridge game, just like the one over at the Zeta Upsilon house. Is it the church that is playing in one place and the world in the other? To the church that is scattered and mixed with the world, Jesus speaks the other metaphor: "You are the salt of the earth." The church is both light and salt, the city set on a hill and the scattered leaven.

Jesus called twelve men to be with him, the foundation of the New Israel. These he sent on a mission. He added others to the group, and he adds more in every generation. He sends them stumbling out into the future, not knowing where they are going or what they will encounter, but only that he goes on ahead, that he will meet them on the way and be with them. Some of his meetings are by appointment: "Where two or three are gathered together in my name . . ."; others are unannounced: "Lord, when did we see you hungry . . ."

The church lives in the rhythm of these two kinds of meetings with its Lord. It gathers together to receive its life from him, to hear the word he has to speak to it. It scatters again to live its life, to act and speak his word. We have to ask earnestly how the church is being or not being the church in your college or university and how you are keeping your appointments within the fellowship of Christ's body.

❋   ❋   ❋

19

the city on a hill

The church gathers. God's commandos come straggling in out of the jungle of the world. It is a very strange warfare in which they are engaged, for they are under orders to love their enemies and to bless those who attack them; their weapons are such unorthodox arms as truth, righteousness, the proclamation of peace, faith, salvation, the word of God; only occasionally does their heroism become visible. These unique guerrillas rendezvous at their base camp: they have to be briefed for their next mission.

Where is this base camp? It has to be located not by its street address or by the kind of building that contains it, but by what happens there. So John Calvin says:

> For wherever we find the word of God purely preached and heard, and the sacraments administered according to the institution of Christ, there, it is not to be doubted, is a Church of God; for his promise can never deceive— "where two or three are gathered together in my name, there am I in the midst of them."[1]

The church keeping the first appointment with its Lord is the church at worship, hearing the word and receiving the Sacrament. What is the meaning of this worship? Look what happens on a typical Sunday morning when, perhaps in an utterly routine and therefore blasphemous way, "the word of God" is "preached, and the sacraments administered."

The Call

The people enter and take their places—in silence, if they know what they are doing! This is not the time for small talk, but for awe and waiting, "For yet a little while, and the coming one shall come and shall not tarry." The Lord does not miss

312   GO FROM YOUR FATHER'S HOUSE

his appointments. The minister, who is the prompter in our dialogue with God, enters and says, "Let us worship God." This traditional call to worship means that God is calling his people together in this place. It reminds us that we are not here because we like each other, but because he calls. We do not *choose* our brothers in Christ—we would make a far different selection from the one God makes—but they are *given* to us. The call reminds us, too, that all our mixed motives for coming here—habit, sense of duty, a good ploy for a Sunday date, a place to wear the new hat, business connections, trying to ease our conscience for last night—are only the shell around the real reason. God calls; he has brought us here, even to our surprise. Just in the same way the Hebrews, gathered at Mount Sinai, had come for diverse secular, selfish, and sociological reasons. With some astonishment they had to hear, "You have seen what *I* did to the Egyptians, and how *I* bore you on eagles' wings and brought you to myself." It is God who calls his people—and he is able to use even our mixed motives in the process.

Does he call them "out of the world"? No. The world comes right in through the church door. The world is always in the church and the church is always in the world. It speaks a worldly language—if it keeps a lot of words that the world spoke in the seventeenth century, or even if it says the whole service in the vernacular of the old Italians, that is only a smoke screen. There is no holy language.[2] The church has an organization, like "worldly" groups. It has politics. "I do not pray that thou shouldst take them out of the world, but that thou shouldst keep them from the evil one."

But it is *God* who calls, not the world. However much the world may find itself advantaged by having the church at its beck and call—"a moral force in society"—the flock must learn to listen for the voice of the Good Shepherd (John 10). While we belong *in* the world, we have to be constantly reminded that we do not belong *to* the world (John 17:16).

Who are the ones who gather? "Every one whom the Lord our God calls to him." Often we wonder if he could not be more discriminating, so we correct his call a bit by putting an invisible, sociological filter at the door. ("Those people wouldn't feel at home here.") But the gospel of God's Kingdom is a net flung wide; it pulls in all kinds of strange fish! That is why the Pharisees found Jesus so irritating. If God's Kingdom were really breaking in, in this person's activities, then he ought to be careful of the kind of people he let into his circle. Jesus retorted with parables: fishermen do not sort their fish while the net is in the sea; weeds and wheat look just alike while they are growing. Extortionists and prostitutes will go into the Kingdom ahead of Pharisees and priests.

The very openness of the church is part of its mission. The very fact that it can risk exposing its life to the world's skepticism and disdain, its fellowship to the uncouth and the sinful, this is the fact which marks its real difference from the world. It is holy because its purity does not depend upon itself, but upon him who calls it.

> As His community it is always free from itself. In its deepest and most proper tendency it is not churchly, but worldly— the Church with open doors and great windows, behind which it does better not to close itself in upon itself again by putting in pious stained-glass windows. It is holy in its openness to the street and even to the alley, in its turning to the profanity of all human life—the holiness which, according to Rom. 12:5, does not scorn to rejoice with them that do rejoice and to weep with them that weep.[3]

The Confession

The community confesses its sins, either aloud or silently. This is the only reasonable response to the call of God. It corresponds to Isaiah's "Woe is me! For I am lost . . ." when he "saw the Lord," and includes his standing *with his people* in solidarity with their history of evil: "For I am a man of unclean lips, and I dwell in the midst of a people of unclean lips . . ." Therefore the fact that we may not happen to *feel* particularly sinful—and certainly not "miserable offenders" or people who "most grievously have committed, by thought, word, and deed," "manifold sins"—is beside the point. We confess in the presence of *God,* and not only in the presence of Joe Jones, who, we think, is worse than we are. The question is not: "Are we about as good as most people?" or even, "Have we lived up to our own ideals?" but "Do we live as obedient sons of God or as rebellious sons of Adam?"

In the second place, our confession puts us into solidarity with our brothers—Christian and non-Christian. This is part of our priesthood which we, the Christians, exercise for the world, offering up our confessions and prayers for forgiveness on behalf of those who cannot or will not confess for themselves, but for whom Christ also died, just as he did for us (Luke 23:34; John 2:1–2; 1 Peter 2:4–5, 9–10). For example, I, as a Southerner, confess the sin of racial injustice. It is part of my life, of my history. I have profited by this injustice, even though I may as an individual fight against it. To try to wriggle out of my responsibility as if I lived in some pure tower of goodness and were not mired in my society, would be to take the Pharisee's "out": "Thank God that I am not as other men." This would mean to run away from the cross, where even Jesus laid aside his innocence, and took our sins as his own (2 Cor. 5:21).

By its confession, the church learns to stop pretending. It stands here, not superior to the world, not as "the good people of the community," but *with* the world, as forgiven sinners. It knows that as it gathers at the Lord's table every pharisee in town can snicker, "Look, Jesus receives sinners and eats with them."

Listening

We know a secret. This is the great thing that makes the Christians different from the world: that they know and participate in a secret. The secret is the secret of history, that is, of human existence. We know how the story comes out; we have read the last page, as it were, and we know who wins. Not that we can write a nice explanation of the plot, or tell the world what is going to happen in Berlin or Peking next year! God has not seen fit to show us the pages in between! Nor can we reduce the secret to a handy formula for real living to be pasted on the bathroom mirror. All we can do is *point* to the secret, which is not ours but God's. The center of our gathering together, then, is the act of listening, listening to hear the secret.

The secret is the story, the history of God's people. That is why, in the churches of the Reformed tradition, the Old and New Testaments are read every Sunday. This is our story. *We* are the "wandering Aramaeans" whom God called out of Ur with Abraham; *we* are the grumbling and astonished crowd that Moses dragged out of Egypt to enter God's contract at Sinai; *we* are the "little flock" that Jesus pulled from the fishing nets and tax tables of Galilee; we are the "great multitude . . . from every nation, from all tribes and peoples and tongues" who learned to say "Christ is Lord" instead of "Caesar is Lord." The secret is that the genuinely human life is the life of Jesus Christ. We hear the secret when we listen to the voices of the men who waited for his coming and of those who responded to his presence in the flesh.

Because Jesus Christ is alive, he speaks his word to the church now, today. That is why we have sermons. The sermon (let us hope) is not a collection of the minister's good ideas or scholarly quotations, but the attempt to ask, "What is the Spirit saying to the churches?" It is anchored to the story, the history, but it attempts to tell the story *to us.* Very simply, it tries to explain what the Bible says, but in such a way that we do not hear "mere history," as Luther says, but *our* God speaking to *us.*

Obviously if the minister is the only one in the congregation who studies the Bible, then the church falters in its central responsibility to listen. The sermon is never the responsibility of the minister alone, but of the whole congregation. Our study makes it possible for the sermon to come alive in our hearing; only by the discipline of study can we present ourselves as usable material for the Holy Spirit. Some ministers have dramatized this communal responsibility for the preaching by inviting small groups of laymen to join in weekly Bible study, actually helping the minister to prepare his sermon. In one student Christian group, several students undertook to bring a sermon to the whole group when it gathered for its weekly worship. Each student took his turn preaching but all engaged in the intense study which produced each sermon. Beyond such specialized study, however, all the honest and serious study which the congregation does helps it to open its ears to what Christ is saying to it.

Celebrating the Secret

Some secrets are jealously kept; others lend themselves to being whispered about with embarrassed grins; others are shouted from the housetops. The secret we are talking about is the last kind. Furthermore, this secret cannot just be told; it has to be lived. Living this secret begins by celebrating it. This is the reason that from the very beginning of the church, Christians "shared their meals with unaffected joy" (Acts 2:46, New English Bible). The celebration of the secret is the Lord's Supper.

The Supper is called the Eucharist, "thanksgiving." Joyful thanksgiving is the response of the community to the Good News which has been given to the world. In these very simple acts of breaking and eating ordinary bread, of pouring and drinking ordinary wine, history comes alive. The death of Jesus Christ is symbolically enacted, and we are recalled to our covenanted life with him. "For as often as ye eat this bread, and drink this cup, ye do show the Lord's death till He come." Not only is the past made present, the future is anticipated: "till He come." Here we see that the *end* of history has already come in Christ's death; we live out our lives and work out our mission between the "night in which He was betrayed" after eating and drinking with the nucleus of the church and the day when he will come again, "And men will come from east and west, and from north and south, and sit at table in the kingdom of God" (Luke 13:29). Today, as we eat and drink, the same Lord, the "Beginning and the End," comes and meets us. This is why we "offer our Eucharist," that is, we give thanks.

The Supper is also called "Communion," that is, "fellowship." "Because there is one loaf, we who are many are one body, for we all partake of the same loaf" (1 Cor. 10:17). To understand this remarkable sentence, we have to remember that Paul wrote it to a church that was split into bickering, hostile factions and upset by numbers of self-styled leaders, each of whom wanted to be the whole show. To them he writes, "we who are many are one body." It was obvious that they were "many," and it is obvious that *we* are "many," separated and divided from and against one another. It is *not* obvious that they—or we—are "one body." Of course they could pretend to be one body, put on frozen smiles when they walked into the church, be exaggeratedly polite to the neighbor whose ears are still smoking from what they said behind his back yesterday, offer an all too eager hand to every newcomer. But that is not community, and Paul will have none of it. He has just finished methodically laying out their seemingly hopeless divisions in the plain sunlight for all to see—and then he turns around and says, "We are all one body." "When the morning mists of dreams vanish, then dawns the bright day of Christian fellowship."[4] Therefore Paul does not urge the Corinthians to organize a fellowship committee, but he urges them to pay attention to what happens at the table of the Lord. "We *are* one body"—not because we like one another, but "because there is one loaf." "We are one body"—not because we agree with one another, but "because there is one loaf." Community is something we cannot organize or create; it is something we must *receive,* just as we receive this bread. We have to learn to keep still and receive these brothers whom God gives us—often very undesirable brothers, from our point of view. Because it is Christ's broken body in which we here participate, it is no ideal community we receive, but a community that freely confesses our own brokenness, the superficiality of our fellowship, the self-will that dominates our love. Because God has freely taken on himself our brokenness, here in this Sacrament he freely gives us his wholeness. If we come to this table in quietness and penitence, he will give us of that great love of his, love that was broken for us. For only this love that suffers itself to be broken for the brother, for the neighbor, and for the stranger, can make the broken body whole, and build among us the fellowship that lives in crisis and thrives in adversity.

Learning to Be Priests

The life we have together is sacramental, but not merely

symbolical. If Jew and Greek first were able to break through their mutual hostility to eat and drink the Lord's Supper together, their communion could not be real until they could learn also to eat and drink daily bread together without wincing. This life together which we are given is another part of the church's mission to the world. How the world—that is, all of us—yearns for community, for "togetherness" that does not gloss over loneliness, for unity that does not stifle the individual!

> What life have you if you have not life together?
> There is no life that is not in community.[5]

God creates this fellowship, the church, and keeps it alive as a sign—a weak, distorted sign, much of the time, but a sign that he will not permit to perish altogether—of the life he wills for mankind, the life he creates for mankind in Jesus Christ.

Life in the body of Christ is therefore the life of people who are learning to be priests to each other and to the world. Theirs is the ministry of mutual listening:

> The first service that one owes to others in the fellowship consists in listening to them. Just as love to God begins with listening to His Word, so the beginning of love for the brethren is learning to listen to them. It is God's love for us that He not only gives us His Word but also lends us His ear. So it is His work that we do for our brother when we learn to listen to him.[6]

But mutual listening depends on mutual acceptance. It is not as his judge that I am called to listen to my brother, but as one who has to live always before God as a forgiven sinner. As the forgiveness of God becomes more and more a part of our life, as we are made more and more able to dare to accept this fantastic fact, then we are enabled also to forgive ourselves and each other. Out of mutual acceptance grows mutual concern, for "God has so adjusted the body . . . that the members may have the same care for one another. If one member suffers, all suffer together; if one member is honored, all rejoice together." This mutual concern, which stretches far beyond the gathered congregation but which must begin there, is expressed in the prayers of the worshipers. These prayers are an index of the spiritual health of the group; the congregation that prays only for itself is near death. But if the prayers are not mere words, the mutual concern expressed in prayer quickly takes the form of mutual help, of concrete acts of service to one another. Finally, the priestly life, that is, life for one another, continues to be possible only as the members of the community submit themselves to mutual discipline. The letters of the New Testament are filled with phrases like "I admonish you," "I exhort you," "I beseech you," "I urge you." The freedom which we receive in God's forgiveness gives to each of us the responsibility for the life of the community, the responsibility of exercising discipline, together with the other brothers, and of submitting ourselves to discipline.

Dismissal

The service of worship concludes with a benediction. It *concludes;* the benediction means "farewell." In the older liturgies this was even more emphatic: "You are dismissed; go in peace." For any Christians who are tempted to remain within the sheltering walls of the church, within the warm atmosphere of its fellowship, the benediction has to be understood as a polite boot out the door. When I went to college, I was greeted at Westminster House with the motto, "This is your Church Home away from home." A nice thought, no doubt, but a misunderstanding of the church. The church is not a home (Compare: "Old folks' home," "orphans' home"), but a bivouac, a staging area for God's operations in the world. "Therefore let us go forth to him outside the camp, bearing abuse for him. For here we have no lasting city, but we seek the city which is to come" (Hebrews 13:13f.).

The world has a way of taking its own revenge on the church whenever it tries to withdraw from the world. If you have read Chaucer's descriptions of the Monk, the Friar, and the Pardoner, then you know just how secular the "otherworldly" monasteries became in the Middle Ages. The church today that sees itself as a little island of people saved out of the world goes the same road. It inevitably degenerates until its inner life is a little copy of the world's values. The denominational student group that understands its mission as the snatching of a few souls out of the campus inferno usually ends up a poor man's coeducational fraternity, trying to be as entertaining as the campus social organizations, only if possible without being immoral or spending so much money. The world always laughs up its sleeve at these flimsy little ghettos, and rightly so. The benediction means that the briefing is over; the church goes to the world. It goes to work.

But it goes with a difference. The benediction also means "peace."

> The peace of God, which passeth all understanding, keep your hearts and minds in the knowledge and love of God, and of His Son Jesus Christ our Lord; and the blessing of God Almighty, the Father, the Son, and the Holy Spirit, be upon you, and remain with you always. Amen.

The community goes into the world with the peace of God. The world does not give or understand this peace, and the world cannot take it away. This peace is the freedom to live. More: it is the freedom to live for others. For we, the people of God, scatter from our appointment with him to go and meet him in the completely unexpected byways of this week, where he will suddenly confront us in even the least of these, the brothers he sends into our path.

20

the salt of the earth

Mixing with the World

The function of salt is to season and preserve. Salt kept in the box is useless; it has to penetrate the meat through and through to serve its purpose. Christians kept in the church building are equally useless to the world, no matter how busy they may be or how wonderful the statistical reports they may mimeograph each year. "You are the salt of the earth"; the church has to mix with the world.

The church's penetration of the world involves more than the mere physical presence of its members in the world's jobs, organizations, and affairs. It means openness to the world—an extension of the same openness which they have learned towards each other in the Christian fellowship, an openness which is the gift of God's grace.

First, the church is open to the world's wisdom and the world's questions. It is not afraid or too impatient to listen to the world's own explanations of its problems and its obligations. It recognizes that it does not automatically have the answers to all of the world's problems just because it is Christian, and so it is willing to work with the world and to study with the world to try to understand the problems before it starts handing out pat solutions. A group of students undertook to investigate "the moral implications of atomic bomb testing"—a problem certainly of interest enough both to church and world! Several members of the study group were pretty sure that they knew what "the Christian answer" was from the beginning; they only needed some good, solid evidence to back up their conclusions. The trouble was that the more they studied, the more complicated the "moral implications" seemed. It proved to be ever so much simpler to state what the ideal solution would be than to suggest any sort of solution which appeared actually possible. Moreover, they were somewhat startled to discover that many non-Christian scientists and statesmen not only understood the problem better than they, but were working much harder and more devotedly to find workable solutions. The Christian has to learn to *listen* to the world as well as to speak to it, just as he listens to God and to his Christian brother. Life is lived in dialogue, not in lecturing one another.

Second, Christians are open to persons. A student I knew dropped into our Westminster House one day looking half asleep and begging for coffee. When I made the usual jokes, she replied with a wry grin, "People keep me up all night telling me their problems. My ears are so big, you see!" That is the openness I mean. Every person needs someone with "big ears," someone who has the grace to listen without becoming shocked or angry or envious, simply to listen, to understand, and to try to see the world through the other person's eyes. This, too, belongs to the church's priesthood for the world. We do not have to be in too big a hurry to preach to our neighbors; if we can learn to listen, the time and opportunity to speak will be given to us. Even our fundamental task of telling the Christian News to our neighbors begins with listening to them, as D. T. Niles has so well said:

> We cannot commend the Gospel to our contemporaries unless we can enter into their frustration and their expectation; and then address the Gospel to ourselves as we stand in their situation. If we will listen to Hindus until Hinduism becomes a temptation to us, if we will listen to Communists until we feel the attraction of Communism, if we will listen to Muslims until Islam begins to attract us, then we shall be in a position to get the Gospel across to them. Are we not surprised to read that Jesus was tempted in all points like as we are?[1]

This openness to the world is made possible by the grace of God that liberates us from ourselves and sets us into covenant with him. What shuts up our minds and our ears to the voices of our neighbors is our fear and our presumption. Suppose I find myself in conversation with a student or a professor who turns out to be an agnostic. Immediately I become nervous and afraid—what if I cannot answer his questions? Then I am throwing away an opportunity to "win him to Christ." Even worse, suppose his questioning and his reasoning raise doubts in my own mind. Soon I have become so involved in my own fears that I am not hearing a word he says. How much easier it would be if I would trust that everything did not hinge on *my* answers. How much freer I would be if I could admit that the success of Christ's kingdom did not depend on *my* success. How much more honest I could be if I could recognize that God's acceptance of me depended not on whether I had doubts, but on what Jesus Christ had done! Then I could actually *listen* to this man. Perhaps his very questions would deepen my own faith. Perhaps, together, we would hear the word which comes from beyond us both, in answer to our common doubts.

God's grace sets us free from ourselves, because it undercuts our fear and overcomes our presumption with love. God loves us "while we were yet sinners"; therefore we are set free to love our neighbors.

Loving the World

If the church takes the world seriously, one of its gravest temptations is to despise men and hate the world. Especially if we have high ideals, if we have well-developed ideas of the way men ought to live, if we have some vision of the splendid things of which men are capable, then we are likely to become bitter and cynical over the dark and bloody realities that the newspapers keep throwing in our faces. We are tempted to despise men because they do not live up to our ideals. Perhaps we despise them most of all because they remind us that *we* do not live up to our ideals either. Moreover, the church is tempted to hate the world because the world hates the church— if the church is carrying out its mission:

"If you were of the world, the world would love its own; but because you are not of the world, but I chose you out of

the world, therefore the world hates you. Remember the word that I said to you, 'A servant is not greater than his master.' If they persecuted me, they will persecute you . . ."
(John 15:19–20)

The world will inevitably be against the church, since "these men . . . have turned the world upside down" (Acts 17:6). But the church cannot be against the world, because God loves the world and has given up his Son to reconcile it to himself.

> God sides with the real man and with the real world against all their accusers. . . . In the face of God's becoming man the good man's contemptuous attitude cannot be maintained, any more than can the tyrant's. The despiser of men despises what God has loved. Indeed he despises even the figure of the God who has become man.[2]

The world is good. This is not an idealistic or an optimistic statement, but a statement of faith. The Christian knows that the world is good, because God made it. "And God saw everything that he had made, and behold, it was very good" (Genesis 1:31). This does not mean that the Christian now puts on bright rose-colored glasses and announces that the evil in the world is not really evil, but only an illusion. He knows that the goodness of creation has been perverted by man's rebellion: "Cursed is the ground because of you" (Genesis 3:17). But he also knows that God has not given up on his world, but instead has reconciled it to himself in Jesus Christ (2 Corinthians 5:19). He knows that the hidden reconciliation, now visible only to eyes of faith, will be revealed openly, that the whole world is moving towards the summing up of all things in Christ, when "The creation itself will be set free from its bondage to decay and obtain the glorious liberty of the children of God" (Romans 8:21).

As a result, the Christian is free to enjoy the world even though "the form of this world"—that is, the world in its perversion and its hostility to its Creator—"is passing away." He is free to "serve the present age," even though in Christ "the end of the ages has come." This means that the Christian can and must work for the good of men in this world, even though he knows it will only be a provisional and partial good that he can achieve. And he can do this work shoulder to shoulder with all kinds of co-workers, since he is not working to save himself or to make propaganda for the church, but simply for the good of the world. If he finds atheists or agnostics or Moslems or Buddhists or religiously "neutral" organizations and government agencies working for good, he is free to join with them. If he were not thus free, then the Christian leaven would be withdrawn from the lump, the salt would be kept from the meat, and all might be spoiled. But the Christian must not think of this work as something *ultimate*. He is not working to convert the world, that is, to make the world into the church. Conversion is not his work, but the work of God's Holy Spirit. He cannot "build the Kingdom of God." Nevertheless, his work is good, because the world is good. The world is supposed to be "secular"; as God's creation, it is *world*, and as such it is good. "The purpose of the salt," as D. T. Niles has remarked, "is to keep the fish fish."

Christians Are Different

The salt has to be mixed with the meat, but it also has to remain salt. "If salt has lost its taste, how shall its saltness be restored? It is no longer good for anything except to be thrown out and trodden under foot by men" (Matt. 5:13). The world may seem to like unsalty Christians, Christians who conform to its own standards, but it does not need them. When the church puts all its energies into being like the world and being liked by the world, it becomes insipid. It is no more good, and while the world may not bother to throw it out, it can politely ignore it.

The church goes into the world. Of course, only a few of us are tempted to "hole up" in the church building all week. Most of us go through the formal rhythm of gathering as the church and scattering into our everyday places of work and life. Our problem is not that we do not go from worship to world and back again, but *how* we go. The question is whether we are not after all schizophrenic Christians, who slip into our Sunday ethics and piety just as we slip into our Sunday suits, but as soon as Sunday dinner is over, slip into the more comfortable everyday standards of "what everybody else is doing" and "looking out for number one." The question is, Does the word which we hear and the secret we celebrate when we gather make any *difference* in our scattered lives?

The difference between the Christians and the world does not consist in artifical and arbitrary actions, but in the central quality of life, the free obedience of faith. Very often Christians have distinguished themselves from their neighbors by moralism and pietism which obscures the real difference. The negative moral codes which have sometimes characterized Christian groups, especially those affected by the American frontier, grew out of quite legitimate ethical concerns, but too often they became hardened, stereotyped, and meaningless—deserving the world's ridicule:

> We don't smoke, and we don't chew,
> And we don't go with girls that do:
> Our class won the Bible!

Pietism, too, which may take the form, as one student put it, of "never opening a Coke without saying grace," may point to a genuine life of thanksgiving, "that we may show forth thy praise not only with our lips, but in our lives." When it dries up into external forms, however, it incurs the warning of Jesus, "Beware of practicing your piety before men in order to be seen by them" (Matt. 6:1).

The real difference that marks the church in its function as salt in the world is twofold. First, the church is different because it lives *for the world,* and not for itself. This is a significant difference, for the world can live only for itself. The life of the church for the world shows up in the openness of each Christian for his neighbor, which we have already discussed. But it presses beyond openness to service and self-sacrifice. The lordship of Christ is seen in his kneeling to wash the dirty feet of his Disciples; his kingly throne is the cross. Therefore the reign of the risen Christ takes form in his body, the church, as the church is enabled to empty itself, to take the form of a servant, to give away its life for others.

Second, the church is different because while it lives in and for the world, it does not belong to the world. It is different because it has a King, from whom alone it can take orders. This life under orders in the midst of the world constitutes the uniqueness of this community. This is the way the Christian is called to live his Baptism, in the sense of Romans 6. Baptism means, according to Paul, on the one hand death and the end of slavery to sin, on the other hand the freedom of a new life and submission to a new master: Christ. It corresponds to the Exodus. The Hebrews who had been slaves of the Egyptians were liberated by God, but their liberation set his claim upon them. They were made *his* people, he became their God and King. The life of those who have been redeemed is life under covenant. Calvin describes this life graphically:

> We are not our own: Our own minds and wills do not determine the advice we give and the things we do. We are not our own: Let us not therefore seek what is expedient for us according to the flesh.
>
> We are not our own: Let us therefore forget ourselves as much as possible and everything about our own person. Once again: We belong to the Lord: let us live and die in him.
>
> We belong to the Lord: may his will and his wisdom govern all our actions.
>
> We belong to the Lord: may every part of our life be directed towards him, who is their sole purpose.[3]

The Witness of Invisible Allegiance

It puzzles the world that these Christians, who are living in the midst of the world, involved in all its power structures and loyalties and divisions, report to another chief. It often irritates the world that these Christians, seemingly so silly and weak, suddenly discover such stubborn and exasperatingly hid-

328 GO FROM YOUR FATHER'S HOUSE

den resources of strength when it tries to bend them into its own kind of tools. They insist on singing hymns as one drives them in for the lions. That is why, when the church is really being the church, the *world* often begins the conversation that leads to confrontation with the gospel: Why are you different?

> Always be prepared to make a defense to any one who calls you to account for the hope that is in you, yet do it with gentleness and reverence; and keep your conscience clear, so that, when you are abused, those who revile your good behavior in Christ may be put to shame.
>
> (1 Peter 3:15–16)

The "salty" Christians have to make it clear to the world that they have a King. Sometimes they have to do this quite dramatically. In 1933 the Nazi Party in Germany proclaimed "the necessary solidarity of the Evangelical Church with the National-Socialist State" and appointed a "Reich-Bishop" to make sure that the churches cooperated. Many did cooperate, and the so-called "German-Christians" proclaimed the new gospel of Aryan racial superiority and hero worship. Many other Christians, however, joined together in the "Confessing Church," which took shape at a conference in Barmen in May, 1934. The conference issued the now famous "Barmen Theological Declaration." Here are two of its six theses:

> In view of the destructive errors of the German Christians and the present national church government, we pledge ourselves to the following evangelical truths:
> 1. "I am the way and the truth and the life; no man cometh unto the Father, but by me." (John 14:6)
> "Verily, verily, I say unto you, He that entereth not by the door into the sheepfold, but climbeth up some other way, the same is a thief and a robber. . . . I am the door: by me if any man enter in, he shall be saved." (John 10:1, 9)
> Jesus Christ, as he is testified to us in the Holy Scripture, is the one Word of God, whom we are to hear, whom we are to trust and obey in life and in death.

We repudiate the false teaching that the church can and must recognize yet other happenings and powers, images and truths as divine revelation alongside this one Word of God, as a source of her preaching.

2. "But of him are ye in Christ Jesus, who of God is made unto us wisdom, and righteousness, and sanctification, and redemption." (I Cor. 1:30)

Just as Jesus Christ is the pledge of the forgiveness of all our sins, just so—and with the same earnestness—is he also God's mighty claim on our whole life; in him we encounter a joyous liberation from the godless claims of this world to free and thankful service to his creatures.

We repudiate the false teaching that there are areas of our life in which we belong not to Jesus Christ but another lord, areas in which we do not need justification and sanctification through him.[4]

What this open confession meant in the lives of those who adopted it cannot be told here—how many pastors and laymen helped create an "underground railway" to smuggle Jews out of the country; how thousands of the Confessing Christians were interned in concentration camps or executed. As one of them wrote,

Discipleship means allegiance to the suffering Christ, and it is therefore not at all surprising that Christians should be called upon to suffer. In fact it is a joy and a token of his grace.[5]

Companions on the Way

The way of the "salty" Christian can be a very lonely road. Yet I have tried to make it clear that there is no such thing as a solitary Christian. Even those who seem most alone at the places where they are involved in the world are nevertheless members of the body of Christ. John the Elder, exiled on the island Patmos, nevertheless found himself on Sunday caught up in a vision of the heavenly worship of all the Apostles, martyrs, and angels, and bound to the congregations of Asia Minor for which he had been responsible as bishop (Rev. 1:9–11, etc.). The "scattered" Christian is still sustained by the whole church.

> There is great need to give a tangible sign of this reality of the Church which assists and unites the faithful even in their everyday life. It is obvious that each of us is alone in the place which he occupies and must face his own problems; it would seem possible, however, for a small group, even only two or three . . . to team up in order to build a common fidelity to Christ. What none of them dares undertake alone, dares not even imagine and could not accomplish, might be seen, sized up and effected by them working in harmony. . . .[6]

With a similar thought in mind, three men who were active in a Westminster Fellowship in a Southern university decided to move into the same dormitory, convinced that by quietly working together they could influence the whole atmosphere of the house, while one of them alone, if he had the courage to be different, would only be dismissed as an oddball.

Ingredients of Decision

The difference of the Christian, his "saltiness" by which he lives his mission in the world, comes into sharp focus when he has to make an ethical decision. There are some bases for making decisions that are excluded for the Christian. The way of rugged individualism is not his way; he cannot say, "I do whatever seems right to me"—that is the ethical attitude of those who have no king (Judges 21:25). Neither, however, can his conscience dissolve into the radar of other-directedness: his peers are not his God. Because the Christian lives in an invisible monarchy, his decisions cannot be either inner-directed or other-directed, but must be God-directed. This is not a very comfortable rule, because the Christian does not have any direct wire to heaven. Knowing the will of God is not something automatic; if it were, there would not be any real decisions. Instead, each one has to "test the will of God"—a favorite phrase of Paul.

Decisions are not made in a vacuum, but in the context in which God has put each one of us.

How can you test the will of God? What are some of the ingredients that go into the Christian's deciding? One ingredient must be conscientious Bible study. These pilgrims of God, this community we are marching with, have always been in some sense a People of a Book. As the Westminster Confession puts it, the Bible is "the only infallible rule for faith and practice." But hold on, now! Haven't we seen that the great concern of Paul, Augustine, and Luther was to show that we were free from the Law? Then how can the Bible be an "infallible rule"? Does this mean that I have only to read the Bible and then my decisions will all be right ones? Of course not. Nor does it mean we can use the Bible like the fortune-teller's magic cards, turning up just the verse that solves my problem for the day. No, we go to the Bible with our ethical problems, not because the Bible will make our decisions for us, (in that case what would have become of the freedom God gave us?) but because the Bible is the story of the things God has done for mankind's real life, through his people. The God who did those things is the same God who calls me to obey today. As I study the Bible—and that means living with the story for a long time, not desperately flipping pages tonight because I have to decide something tomorrow—I am helped to understand what God is doing now. What he is doing now may be something quite new. But it will never be inconsistent with what he did in Israel and in Jesus Christ.

Another ingredient of our decision is knowledge of the facts of the case. God calls us to act *in* the world and *for* the world. Therefore we have to know what the world is up to and how it works. Should Christians work for a ban on nuclear testing? The study group mentioned before who tried to answer that question for themselves found that their hardest job was just getting the facts. Alongside their Bibles on the study table they had to have things like the *Bulletin of the Atomic Scientists* and reports of the Atomic Energy Commission and copies of the latest newspapers. And they had to *think*. What are the probable results of action one way or the other? Easy enough to say "in principle" that the Christian is for peace and against war, for life and against death—but which decision is most likely to lead to peace? Which most likely to cause suffering and death? Now the moralist, concerned only with his *own* righteousness, the purity of his conscience, sticks to a mere statement of principles. He does not have to know the facts, because the principles are always valid, and if he sticks to them *he* will be blameless, even if the whole world blows up. But the Christian has been liberated from just this concern for only his own righteousness. In Jesus Christ's obedience and death *God's* righteousness entered the world, and God has given it to us. We do not have to sit around worrying about the spots on our consciences—God has scrubbed them clean! The righteousness that entered the world in Jesus Christ is a continuing, active force that is destined to make mankind anew the way God intended them. This is another way of saying that Jesus Christ is alive and working still and will come at last to judge all men. Now God wants us to get busy on the side of that righteousness, in the footsteps of Jesus Christ.

Some of the other main ingredients in the Christian's decisions can just be mentioned briefly. You can ask yourself how they would help you make up your mind in a concrete instance. The Christian decides within the context of *prayer*. Like Bible study, praying is not magic. It is not a one-shot, direct-wire, dial-an-answer approach to God. Instead, real prayer is a means of putting our whole lives in the presence of God. It is the momentary conversation with God which sets the rest of our times into the framework of dialogue. The God who hears our prayers is the God who perceives all we do, and the God who *answers*—but the answer may not come before you wake up in the morning. The Christian decides, too, within the context of *the Christian community*. It is important that you discover those Christian brothers with whom you can talk and to whom you can listen. It is also important, however, that your decisions be made in the context of the larger community, the whole church in the whole world, including those who do not think the way you do. Finally, the Christian decides within the context of *traditions, moral codes* of his society, and *ethical principles* he can derive from the Bible and from experience. Is this inconsistent, since he has been set free from the Law? No, it is just because he has been set free from the Law as a means of gaining God's favor or his own security that he can receive all these rules as guides and aids in his decisions. Sometimes God may be telling us to break one of these rules in order to obey his will. But other times we will find that one of these rules annoys us only because it cramps our style. In the latter case, may we not be thankful for the Law which God has given to remind us that we are not our own?

The way all these ingredients are woven into the one act of deciding is expressed clearly in this paraphrase of Romans 12: 1–2:

> Therefore, brethren, with eyes wide open to the mercies of God (and that means: constantly remembering the great acts of salvation through which God is redeeming this world and constantly being true to the event of baptism through which you yourselves have begun to play a role in this history of salvation), therefore I beg you to bring up to the altar the totality of your life to be consumed as a living sacrifice. This alone is the service which really does justice to the true nature of both God and yourself.
>
> Now, if you ask me, how can this happen, I tell you three things: (i) Stop being conformed to the spirit of this age, or—to put the same thing in other terms—stop being used as puppets by the powers and principalities of this age, playing their role, while you know perfectly well that they have already been defeated; (ii) let a metamorphosis happen in your life by going back again and again to the radically new faculty of discernment and criteria of judgment which you were given when you joined the people of God; (iii) for only in such a way, in each new time and situation, can you experimentally discern the Will of God and thereby experience that God's Will is good, acceptable, and lets you grow into maturity.[7]

CASE STUDIES OF "SALTINESS"

The following are some very brief accounts of several students like yourself and decisions they had to make. These are not copy-book examples for you to imitate, but only instances in which Christian students had to agonize over the concrete command-ments of God in their own special times and places. Their deci-sions were and are controversial. Whether they were the right decisions, and to what extent they were right, these students had to leave for God to judge and then to act in the certainty of his forgiveness. I pass these stories on to you in the hope that you will find yourself caught up in the process by which they wrestled with the facts and obligations that had hold of them and worked through to some kind of decision.

Like the other parts of this book, these stories are intended to be discussed, if possible, with other students, whether in an organized study group or with only two or three of your friends. If you find yourselves at some points in radical disagreement with the students described here, well and good! If their dilem-mas remind you of some ethical decisions that confront you and other students in your own situation, splendid! The question is not to pass judgment, but to exercise your powers of discernment, your "ethical imagination," as part of the "renewal of your mind," so that you can "test what is the will of God, good, acceptable, and complete."

Who Shall Be Welcome?

The scene is a council retreat of a denominational student group in a Southern university. The council has come to the item on the docket marked "Service." One member rises to speak. She feels, she says, that the group has become ingrown, con-cerned with its own problems, and not with the problems of the university. She feels that they have been avoiding the most ob-vious problem. Two years earlier, the first Negroes have been admitted to the university, as the result of legal action. Now there are approximately thirty Negro students. They have been pas-

sively accepted by the student body: there have been few expressions of hostility toward them, but few expressions of friend-
liness. Certain areas and activities are regarded by the university
administration as "off limits" for the Negroes, although there are
no written rules to this effect. For example, they may eat sandwiches in the snack bar, but if they attempt to eat in the cafeteria
they are called in to be admonished by the Dean of Students.
The council member continues: These Negro students are lonely
and isolated. The church is supposed to minister to the needs of
persons. Doesn't the council think they ought to do something?
She sits down. Some others indicate that they agree completely.
Someone wants to move that the Negro students be invited to
meetings of the organization. Another member objects: There
are already disagreements and personality clashes in the group.
To raise a controversial issue like this might destroy their fellowship. Another person says that some members of the council who
are absent from the retreat would be strongly opposed to inviting
Negroes. They ought to be heard from. Someone else says that
he feels the Negro students are not really in the university to get
an education, but only to break down segregation. Someone else
retorts, "How do you know what they are here for?" The campus
pastor suggests that, in view of the difference of opinion and the
importance of the question, no decision ought to be made until
a council meeting with full attendance. He recommends also
that the council get in touch with some of the Negro students to
hear their own opinions.

Two weeks later the council meets again, with all members
present. Three of the Negro students are there. The council
members have many questions to ask the Negroes. Why did they
come to the university? What do they hope to accomplish? Are
they organized? What does it feel like to be the only Negro in
a classroom of forty students? The questions are answered and
discussed. Several council members note that they have classes
with these students. They seem to have trouble with the same
assignments. Someone observes that this university can get pretty
lonely, no matter what color your skin. The proposal to invite the

Negroes to attend meetings of the group is raised again. One council member says that she agrees that this is the right thing to do, but she also knows that her parents will forbid her ever to come to the meeting again if they are integrated. She does not know how to vote. One of the men reminds the council that a statewide drive is in progress to raise money to build a new student center for them and for groups in other universities. Most of the money will have to come from very conservative people who would be outraged by the proposed action. The president speaks: "The church had to meet in catacombs once," he says, "and it might not hurt this group if it had to meet in a tent." A member of the council who has been silent until now says, "You all think that I am a segregationist. I don't know whether I am or not. I think it's obvious that we will decide the Negroes ought to come, and I think that's right. But I just want to remind you that if you make this decision, you're not making it just for here, in the student center! You can't welcome somebody here and pretend you don't know his name over there on the campus." The group is silent for several minutes. The president asks if the council is ready to make a decision. Slowly, everyone nods. When the motion to issue a special invitation is made again, someone objects. "I don't think we ought to single out any special group to invite to our meetings," he says. "According to our constitution our meetings are open to every student at the university. I think after our discussion our visitors will understand that everyone is welcome here, without our taking any action." The president asks if that is the feeling of the whole group. They all agree.

What would you have said, if you had been a member of that council? Are there any important facts you think were overlooked? What other individuals and groups were involved in the decision or affected by it besides the council members? In what ways? What do you think made the council think that God wanted them to act in the way they did? Can you think of some difficult decisions that members of the group may have had to make later as individuals, as a result of this group decision?

Making Good or Doing Good

Paul MacIntosh was a sophomore when he decided to change his major. Paul's father was a businessman, moderately successful, after a long struggle and several failures. Paul, his only child, was majoring in business administration, since it had always been assumed by his parents that he would enter the business and eventually take over its management when his father retired. It was while his father was driving him back to school at the beginning of his second year that Paul broke the news that he had decided to change to a premedical course. His father was angry at first that Paul had not discussed his decision with him, but then he said that he only wanted what was best for Paul. Medicine was a solidly respected and well-paid profession, and if Paul was willing to put out the hard work that medical school would require, he would back him all the way. Two hours later, when Paul's luggage had been deposited in his room and his father turned to go, he threw his arm around his son's shoulder and told him how proud he was that Paul was going to be a doctor.

A month later Paul wrote a long letter to his father in which he explained that his change of vocation involved something else. His participation in a service project in a west African nation the summer before—with the reluctant approval of his father, who thought the whole thing was a waste of money by a lot of idealistic do-gooders—had deeply impressed him with the terrible lack of adequate medical care in that area. After much thought, he had decided that he wanted to become a medical missionary or fraternal worker.

His father's response to the letter was a forty-five minute long-distance call. "Paul," he said, "I don't know what kind of bleeding-heart dreamers you have been talking to, but I want you to stay away from them and get your feet back on the ground." He went on to explain that his whole life had been spent in hard, exhausting work, for the sole purpose of making sure that his son had a better life. Now, he said, Paul was proposing to throw all that away to go hand out pills to a bunch of savages.

As Paul's decision became known, acquaintances reacted in sharply different ways. His hometown minister called on his parents to tell them how happy he was, and to say that he knew this was the work of the Holy Spirit. He was not warmly received. One of his father's golf partners, however, good-naturedly advised him not to worry. "Paul will snap out of this," he said. "This is just a little adolescent rebellion and idealism. Don't press him too hard, and he'll get over it." One of Paul's professors told him he was being old-fashioned and unrealistic. "The age of the white missionary in formerly colonial countries is over," he warned. "With the new nationalist feelings that animate these countries, you would be viewed with suspicion if not hatred." An old friend of Paul's father, who was also a devoted elder in the church near the campus, came to call on Paul. He reminded him that the Bible says, "Honor thy father and mother." "Have you ever stopped to think," he added, "how much good can be done in this country by a Christian businessman?"

What advice would you have given Paul? How could he be sure he was not merely being dazzled by some heroic and romantic ideals, instead of responding to a real "calling"? If you had to make this kind of decision, how would you go about finding information and guidance?

The Bid

Sara and Lois were best friends in high school, where they shared a number of honors and leadership in several extracurricular activities. It was partly because of their friendship that both decided to go to the state university, although Sara's parents, one of the town's wealthier families, would have preferred that she go to a private girls college. When rush week came, it was of course understood that Sara would take part; Lois, because her family was hard pressed financially even to pay her necessary expenses, said that she could not consider a sorority. Sara, however, when she had accepted one of the several bids which were offered her, kept urging Lois to find some means. Lois, by carefully guarding her expenditures and taking a part-time job, at length saved some money and let Sara persuade her to go out for spring rush. Naturally both girls took for granted that Lois would pledge Sara's sorority.

Lois did not receive a bid. Sara got the news first, because she had waited outside the chapter meeting when the "actives" in her sorority had cast their final votes on all the "rushees." "Lois Jones?" said the rush chairman. "Is she a friend of yours or something? I'm sorry, kid, she didn't make it. She'll probably get a bid from one of the other houses, but she's just not Upsilon material. Did you know that neither one of her parents went to college? No background." Sara fought back the tears until she got to her room. Luckily Lois was not there; she would be on her way already to pick up her bids—if there were any.

It seemed hours later when Lois returned. She managed a smile. "Well," she said, "at least my budget is better off, if my social life isn't."

Sara's face distorted as she tried to answer; with difficulty she said, "Lois, I'm . . . I'm going to give back my pin."

"No! You're not going to do any such thing!"

"Yes I am. Ever since I found out I have been lying here thinking, and I have decided that I do not want to belong to any such group of artificial snobs."

"Look," Lois said. "You and I have both known all along that nobody gets a bid to a fraternity or sorority without being voted on. Some people don't make it. That's life! Every group has to have people who do belong and people who don't belong. There can't be 'ins' without 'outs.' This time it happens I'm one of the 'outs,' that's all."

"I don't care. I think the whole system is rotten, and I'm getting out."

"What good will that do? If you don't like the system, then stay in and change it! You won't change it by getting out."

Is Lois right? Should Sara stay in and try to change the system? Or should she give back her pin, as an open protest? Or would you view the situation differently from both of them?

PICKING UP THE PIECES

Unfortunately, there is no guarantee that the decision the Christian makes will be the right one. No matter how diligently he may study the situation, no matter how prayerfully he may seek the will of God, there are always sides of the question he cannot know and hidden motives of his own he does not or will not recognize. Life has its own current that pushes us along, even when we swim across it. As a result, our good is always mixed with evil. We are forever being surprised by the results of our decisions. The best of intentions often bring evil results, while good acts often arise from bad motives or from unconscious evil. There is no pure act, no pure decision.

What shall the Christian do, then? Retire to the sidelines of life and renounce all action, all decision-making? That is hardly a realistic option. Where is such a sideline to be found? How can a man avoid decisions without being reduced to a mollusk? Is Pilate less responsible because he washes his hands? Not only is withdrawal an unrealistic option, it would be a faithless option. Withdrawal from decision says in effect that I expect to be saved by my own goodness, by how clean my hands are from the mess of life. But is that not the same as denying the Cross of Jesus Christ?

The Christian is free to act boldly, because by his acts he is not saving himself, but only "working out his salvation"—the salvation that he has received as God's gift—although, to be sure, "with fear and trembling." Of course "boldly" does not mean blindly: he is free and obligated to use the brains God has given him. But "boldly" means that he does not have to wait until "all the facts are in," since all the facts are never in. He acts boldly, even though he does not know the results which will come of his acts, because God knows the results. The Christian acts boldly, even though he is only an infinitesimal individual and his actions will be smothered in the vastness of the world, for God does not lose his acts.

For he has made known to us in all wisdom and insight the mystery of his will, according to his purpose which he set forth in Christ, as a plan for the fulness of time, to unite all things in him, things in heaven and things on earth.

(Ephesians 1:9–10)

Hence Christ bids us, "Be of good cheer, I have overcome the world."

The Christian is able to act from day to day in the knowledge of the liberating forgiveness of God. It is in this sense only that Luther's epigram is true: "Sin boldly—and believe in the grace of God more boldly still." That is why the Christian's action in the world sends him back again and again into the visible, worshiping community, to bring the broken pieces of his decisions and actions to the brothers and to God.

acknowledgments and notes

POEM

1. From *A Coney Island of the Mind* by Lawrence Ferlinghetti. (Copyright 1955, © 1958 by Lawrence Ferlinghetti. Reprinted by permission of New Directions, Publishers), p. 72.

CHAPTER 1

1. David Riesman, in collaboration with Nathan Glazer and Reuel Denney, *The Lonely Crowd* (New Haven: Yale University Press, 1950).

2. *Ibid.,* p. 26.

3. Soren Kierkegaard, *The Sickness unto Death,* trans. Walter Lowrie (Princeton: Princeton University Press, 1941), p. 103.

4. Shri Ramakrishna, as quoted in Paul Tournier, *The Meaning of Persons* (New York: Harper & Row, Publishers, Incorporated, 1957), p. 71.

5. Henrik Ibsen, "Peer Gynt" in *Eleven Plays of Henrik Ibsen* (New York: The Modern Library, Random House, 1935), p. 1138.

6. Tournier, *op. cit.,* chapter 7, especially pp. 125–128, very ably describes this process.

CHAPTER 2

1. Their books have been numerous: Riesman, *et al., The Lonely Crowd;* William H. Whyte, Jr., *The Organization Man;* Vance Packard, *The Status Seekers;* C. Wright Mills, *White Collar: American Middle Classes;* Thomas Griffith, *Waist-high Culture,* to name only a few.

2. Philip E. Jacob, *Changing Values in College* (New York: Harper & Row, Publishers, Incorporated, 1957), p. 12.

3. *Ibid.,* p. 4.

4. From "Orpheus Descending" by Tennessee Williams. (Copyright 1955, © 1958 by Tennessee Williams. Reprinted by permission of New Directions, Publishers), p. 47.

5. William H. Whyte, Jr., *The Organization Man* (New York: Simon and Schuster, 1956), p. 287. Reprinted in paperback by Doubleday & Company, Inc.

6. Rose K. Goldsen, *et al., What College Students Think* (Copyright 1960, D. Van Nostrand Company, Inc., Princeton, N.J.), p. 61.

7. *Ibid.,* pp. 64ff., cf. Table 3–1.

CHAPTER 3

1. Paul Claudel, *The City,* trans. John Strong Newberry (New Haven: Yale University Press, 1920), p. 6.

CHAPTER 4

1. See Arnold B. Rhodes, *The Mighty Acts of God* (CLC pupil's book,

344 GO FROM YOUR FATHER'S HOUSE

Year I), chapter 5; Bernhard W. Anderson, *Understanding the Old Testament* (Englewood Cliffs, N.J.: Prentice-Hall, Inc., 1957), pp. 44–50; B. Davie Napier, *Song of the Vineyard* (New York: Harper & Row, Publishers, Incorporated, 1962), pp. 33–42; and B. Davie Napier, *The Book of Exodus*, ed. Balmer H. Kelly, "The Layman's Bible Commentary," Vol. 3 (Richmond: John Knox Press, 1963), or any good introduction to the Old Testament or commentary on Exodus.

2. Martin Buber, *The Prophetic Faith,* trans. Carlyle Witton-Davies (New York: The Macmillan Company, 1949; paperbound edition by Harper & Row, Publishers, Incorporated, 1960), p. 117.

3. Anderson, *op. cit.*, p. 34.

CHAPTER 5

1. See William F. Albright, *From the Stone Age to Christianity* (Garden City: Doubleday & Company, Inc., Anchor Books, 1957), pp. 231–236 for a more detailed description of the Ba'al-myth.

2. Martin Buber, *The Prophetic Faith* is an excellent treatment of the history of the prophetic movement in Israel, especially dealing with its theology.

3. For a discussion of Elijah's and other miracles, see Arnold B. Rhodes, *The Mighty Acts of God* (pupil's book, CLC Year I).

4. See George Adam Smith, *The Book of the Twelve Prophets* (New York: Harper & Row, Publishers, Incorporated, 1928), Vol. I, Ch. III for a good description of the period.

5. For different interpretations, see "The Layman's Bible Commentary," Vol. 14, or any Bible dictionary.

6. Hans Walter Wolff, *Dodekapropheton 1, Hosea,* "Biblischer Kommentar, Altes Testament" (Neukirchen: Verlag der Buchhandlung des Erziehungsvereins, 1961), Vol. XIV/1, p. 14.

CHAPTER 6

1. Cf. George Adam Smith, *The Book of Isaiah* (New York: Harper & Row, Publishers, Incorporated, 1927), Vol. II, Chapter IV.

2. This is the practically unanimous opinion of present-day scholarship. For its basis, see any standard commentary on Isaiah 40—55 or introduction to the Old Testament.

CHAPTER 7

1. Two versions of Cyrus' decree are preserved in the Bible: Ezra 1:2–4 and 6:3–12.

2. Cf. Anderson, *Understanding the Old Testament*, p. 513.

3. 2 Maccabees 4:7ff. The books of Maccabees, which describe the events of this period, are found in *The Apocrypha*. A convenient edition is that published as a supplement to the *Revised Standard Version of the Bible*.

4. 2 Maccabees 5:11–16.

5. 1 Maccabees 1:29ff.; 2 Maccabees 5:24ff.

6. 1 Maccabees 1:41–61. The second book of Maccabees contains many gruesome stories of Antiochus' atrocities.

7. There are a few passages of the apocalyptic type scattered through the late writings of the Old Testament. The New Testament also contains its one apocalypse, that of John, commonly called The Revelation, as well

as apocalyptic passages within other books, e.g., Mark 13. Many other apocalypses were written in the first century b.c. and the first two centuries a.d., and some of these have been preserved until the present time. The most convenient collection of these and other writings of the period is that of R. H. Charles, *The Apocrypha and Pseudepigrapha of the Old Testament* (Oxford: At the Clarendon Press, 1913).

8. Cf. S. R. Driver, *The Book of Daniel*, "The Cambridge Bible for Schools and Colleges" (Cambridge: The University Press, 1900), p. 83.

9. *Ibid.*, p. 84.

10. *Ibid.*, p. 119. Compare Anderson, *Understanding the Old Testament*, p. 525.

11. The Psalms of Solomon comprise an apocryphal work which originated in a Hasidean circle, probably soon after Pompey captured Palestine.

12. The newly discovered scrolls from the Dead Sea region are one of our most useful sources for understanding the kind of expectation that gripped one large group of Jews at the time when Jesus came. Unfortunately a great deal of nonsense has been written about the scrolls and their relation to the New Testament. For a balanced and scholarly, but also very readable study of their nature and meaning, see Frank Moore Cross, Jr., *The Ancient Library of Qumran and Modern Biblical Studies* (Garden City: Doubleday & Company, Inc., Anchor Books, 1958).

CHAPTER 8

1. C. H. Dodd, *The Apostolic Preaching and Its Developments* (New York: Harper & Row, Publishers, Incorporated, 1962), suggests this method of investigation. After you have worked through your own study, you may want to follow it up by reading his essay.

2. For the variety of speculations about the last days, compare pp. 126ff. above.

CHAPTER 9

1. Author's translation.

2. For this illustration as well as for much help in understanding the Letter to the Romans, I am indebted to my teacher Paul Meyer.

3. Rudolf Bultmann, *Theology of the New Testament*, trans. Kendrick Grobel (New York: Charles Scribner's Sons, 1951), I, 272.

4. Martin Luther, "Preface to the Epistle to the Romans," *Works of Martin Luther* (Philadelphia: A. J. Holman Company and The Castle Press, 1932), VI, 452. Used by permission of the Fortress Press.

5. Christian Ethics is the theme of a later study in the CLC, *The Christian Life,* by Waldo Beach.

CHAPTER 10

1. Saint Augustine, *The City of God*, Book XI, trans. Gerald G. Walsh, S.J., and Grace Monahan, O.S.U., "The Fathers of the Church" (New York: Fathers of the Church, Inc., 1952), VII, 219f. Used by permission of The Catholic University of America Press.

2. *Ibid.*, Vol. VII, Book XIV, chapter 3, pp. 350–353.

3. *Ibid.*, Vol. VII, Book XII, chapters 14—15, pp. 267–270.

4. *Ibid.*, Vol. VII, Book XIV, chapter 28, pp. 410f.

5. *Ibid.*, Vol. VII, Book XV, chapter 1, pp. 413–415.

CHAPTER 11

1. Henry Bettenson (ed.), *Documents of the Christian Church* (London: Oxford University Press, 1947), pp. 161–163.

2. A saying of Hugo of St. Victor, quoted by Emile Mâle, *The Gothic Image* (New York: Harper & Row, Publishers, Incorporated, 1958), p. 29. Used by permission of E. P. Dutton & Company, Inc.

3. Quoted from *The Mass of the Roman Rite* by Joseph A. Jungmann, S.J., with permission of the Publishers and Copyright Owners, Benzinger Brothers, Inc., New York, p. 423.

4. Myconius' *History of the Reformation,* as translated in *A Source Book for Mediaeval History,* ed. by Oliver J. Thatcher and Edgar H. McNeal (New York: Charles Scribner's Sons, 1907), pp. 339–340.

CHAPTER 12

1. See Matthew Spinka (ed.), *Advocates of Reform,* "The Library of Christian Classics" (Philadelphia: The Westminster Press, 1953), Vol. XIV, for a brief sketch of the life and work of Wyclif and Hus, together with translations of parts of their major writings.

2. Quoted by Roland H. Bainton, *Here I Stand: A Life of Martin Luther* (New York and Nashville: Abingdon Press, 1950), p. 45.

3. *Ibid.,* p. 65.

4. The tract given here is abridged to fit our space limits. It is translated from the German version (*Weimarer Ausgabe,* VII, 20–38), which was shorter and intended for more popular use than the Latin. Several translations of the Latin version are readily available for anyone who wishes to read the entire tract, including one in inexpensive pamphlet form published by The Muhlenberg Press, Philadelphia.

5. Luther's Latin version is stronger: "I will therefore give myself as a *Christ* to my neighbor, just as Christ offered Himself to me."

CHAPTER 13 (None)

CHAPTER 14

1. Hugh Pope, "Faith," *The Catholic Encyclopedia* (New York: Robert Appleton Company, 1909), V, 753.

2. Christopher Fry, *The Firstborn* (copyright 1952 by Christopher Fry). Used by permission of Oxford University Press, Inc.

3. Horace Leland Friess, *Schleiermacher's Soliloquies* (LaSalle, Illinois: Open Court Publishing Co., 1926), p. 22.

4. Goldsen, *et al., op. cit.,* p. 159.

5. *Ibid.,* p. 178. See Table 8–2, p. 177.

6. From *Revelation and Reason* by Emil Brunner. Tr. Olive Wyon. Copyright 1946, W. L. Jenkins. The Westminster Press. Used by permission, p. 10.

CHAPTER 15

1. There is a difference among scholars as to whether these were Moravians or Anglicans, possibly both. Kenneth Scott Latourette, *A History of Christianity,* p. 1025 supports the idea that they were Anglicans. Edward Langton, *History of the Moravian Church,* p. 104 supports the idea that they were Moravians. A. Skevington Wood, *Christianity Today,* April 26, 1963 calls it a "predominantly Moravian Society meeting."

2. E. H. Harbison, *The Christian Scholar in the Age of the Reformation* (New York: Charles Scribner's Sons, 1956), p. 112.

3. Cf. Karl Barth, *The Word of God and the Word of Man,* trans. Douglas Horton (New York: Harper & Row, Publishers, Incorporated, Harper Torchbooks, 1957), Ch. II.

CHAPTER 16

1. J. E. Hutton, *A History of Moravian Missions* (London: Moravian Publication Office, 1922), p. 13.

2. Kenneth Scott Latourette, *These Sought a Country* (New York: Harper & Row, Publishers, Incorporated, 1950) is a very readable book which tells the story of William Carey in the first chapter.

3. Cf. William Richey Hogg, "Protestant Missions 1864—1914," *The Student World,* magazine of the World Student Christian Federation, LIII (1960), 163.

4. V. E. Devadutt, "From Missions to Younger Churches," *The Student World,* LIII (1960), 213.

5. This was the title of the book by Hendrik Kraemer which served as the basis for preparatory study for the International Missionary Council meeting at Tambaram (Madras) in 1938.

6. From a letter by Dr. and Mrs. Lamar Williamson, Jr., École de Theologie Unie, Luluabourg, December, 1962.

CHAPTER 17

1. From Donald Herbert Yoder, "Christian Unity in Nineteenth Century America," *A History of the Ecumenical Movement,* ed. by Ruth Rouse and Stephen Charles Neill. (Published 1954, The Westminster Press), p. 223. Used by permission.

2. See Yoder, *op. cit.,* pp. 221ff. for a clear summary of the factors which produced the many American sects. For an extensive and illuminating treatment, see H. Richard Niebuhr, *The Social Sources of Denominationalism* (New York: Henry Holt and Company, 1929).

3. Cf. John T. McNeill, "Ecumenical Outlook and Unitive Effort in the Calvinist Reformation," *A History of the Ecumenical Movement,* pp. 49ff.

4. Quoted by Kenneth Scott Latourette, "Ecumenical Bearings of the Missionary Movement and the International Missionary Council," *A History of the Ecumenical Movement,* p. 355, footnote 2.

5. W. A. Visser 't Hooft, *The Meaning of Ecumenical,* "The Burge Memorial Lecture" (London: Student Christian Movement Press Ltd., 1953), p. 28.

6. Ruth Rouse, *The World's Student Christian Federation* (London: Student Christian Movement Press Ltd., 1948), p. 10.

7. Luther D. Wishard, *The Intercollegiate Y.M.C.A. Movement* (1894), as quoted in Ruth Rouse, *ibid.,* p. 53.

8. G. K. A. Bell, *The Kingship of Christ* (Harmondsworth, Middlesex, Baltimore: Penguin Books Ltd., 1954), p. 50.

9. W. A. Visser 't Hooft (ed.), "New Delhi Speaks," A Report from the Third Assembly, World Council of Churches (New York: Association Press, 1962), p. 21.

CHAPTER 18

1. Jose Ortega y Gasset, *Man and Crisis,* trans. Mildred Adams (New York: W. W. Norton & Company, Inc., 1958), p. 86.

2. Matthew 25:42–43, author's translation.

3. Quoted in *Pro-Existenz, Verkündigung und Fürbitte in der DDR,* ed. Elisabeth Adler (Unterwegs-Zeitbuch Nr. 13 [Berlin: Käthe Vogt Verlag, 1960]), p. 94.

4. *Ibid.,* pp. 9f.

CHAPTER 19

1. From *The Institutes of the Christian Religion,* Vol. II, by John Calvin. Tr. John Allen. (Published 1936, The Presbyterian Board of Christian Education), IV, I, ix. Used by permission.

2. Cf. Karl Barth, *Church Dogmatics,* trans. G. W. Bromiley (Edinburgh: T. & T. Clark, 1961), Vol. IV, 3, II, pp. 681–762.

3. *Ibid.,* Vol. IV, 1, p. 725.

4. Dietrich Bonhoeffer, *Life Together,* trans. John W. Doberstein (New York: Harper & Row, Publishers, Incorporated, 1954), pp. 28–29.

5. T. S. Eliot, "Choruses from 'The Rock,'" *The Complete Poems and Plays* (New York: Harcourt, Brace & World, Inc., 1952), p. 101.

6. Bonhoeffer, *Life Together,* p. 97.

CHAPTER 20

1. From *That They May Have Life* by Daniel T. Niles (copyright 1951 by Student Volunteer Movement for Christian Missions. Used by permission of Harper & Row, Publishers, Incorporated), pp. 85–86.

2. Dietrich Bonhoeffer, *Ethics,* ed. Eberhard Bethge, trans. Neville Horton Smith (New York: The Macmillan Company, 1955), pp. 10 and 12.

3. John Calvin, *Institution de la Religion Chrétienne,* edition of 1541, Chap. XVII, as quoted by Jacques de Senarclens, "A Reformed Contribution to a Symposium on Holy Worldliness," *Laity,* No. 5 (June, 1958), p. 24.

4. *Creeds of the Churches,* ed. by John H. Leith (Garden City, N.Y.: Anchor Books, Doubleday & Company, Inc., 1963), pp. 519–520.

5. Dietrich Bonhoeffer, *The Cost of Discipleship,* trans. R. H. Fuller (New York: The Macmillan Company, 1959), pp. 80f.

6. Andre de Robert, "The Role of the Laity in the Life and Ministry of the Church," *Laity,* No. 2 (June, 1956), p. 7.

7. Hans-Ruedi Weber, "Editorial," *Laity,* No. 10 (December, 1960), p. 3.

index

SUBJECTS AND NAMES

STUDY BOOKS FOR ADULTS

1963–64 BASIC ADULT STUDY
        Into Covenant Life   William Bean Kennedy

1964–65 ADULT: BIBLE
        The Mighty Acts of God   Arnold B. Rhodes

        COLLEGE
        Go from Your Father's House   Wayne A. Meeks
        The Way of a Student   W. Taylor Reveley

1965–66 ADULT: CHURCH
        Through the Ages: A History of the
           Christian Church   Ernest Trice Thompson

1966–67 ADULT: CHRISTIAN LIFE
        The Christian Life   Waldo Beach

1967–68 ADULT: BIBLE
        On the Gospel of John   Vernon Kooy
        On Isaiah   Robert H. Bullock
        On Galatians   Bernard J. Mulder
        On Exodus   James Sprunt

1968–69 ADULT: CHURCH
        On Christian Doctrine   Kenneth J. Foreman

1969–70 ADULT: CHRISTIAN LIFE
        On Great Contemporary Issues   Rachel Henderlite

WAYNE A. MEEKS is at the time of writing a graduate student in the field of New Testament in Yale University, where he is a candidate for the Ph. D. degree. He has graduated from the University of Alabama with a B.S. in physics in 1953 and received the B.D. degree at Austin Seminary in 1956; was a student at the University of Tuebingen, Germany in 1956–57; and has been studying at Yale since 1961. As a student, he was active in the Presbyterian Westminster Fellowship; was president of the Westminster Fellowship section of the Assembly's Youth Council 1952–53; is a member of Phi Beta Kappa and Omicron Delta Kappa honor fraternities, and a Fellow of the Society for Religion in Higher Education. He was Presbyterian University Pastor in Memphis, Tennessee, 1957–1961. He married Martha Fowler of Huntsville, Alabama.

MARTHA FOWLER MEEKS, born in Asbury Park, New Jersey, was graduated from the University of Alabama, with the degree of B.A. in Commercial Art, and from the University of New Mexico with the M.A. degree in Painting. She has exhibited work in the Mid-South Painting Exhibition at Memphis, and in the Museum of Contemporary Crafts, New York City. Among other work for magazines and for the University of Texas, she illustrated the *Presbyterian Woman's Workbook* for 1962–1963. Dr. and Mrs. Meeks have three daughters, born 1958, 1960, and 1963.

8030–ANJ